# Neil Young

## LONG MAY YOU RUN
### THE ILLUSTRATED HISTORY

DURCHHOLZ & GRAFF

Voyageur Press

Frontispiece: Circa 1972. *Photo by Gems/Redferns/Getty Images*

Title page: Crosby, Stills, Nash & Young Reunion Tour, Wembley Stadium, London, September 14, 1974. *Photo by Mick Gold/Redferns/Getty Images*

Front cover: Neil Young, Fleadh Festival, Finsbury Park, London, June 16, 2001. © *Richard Skidmore/Retna UK*

Back cover: Neil Young with Crazy Horse, L.A. Sports Arena, Los Angeles, April 26, 1991. © *Robert Matheu*
Bluebird poster. *Artist: Jake Early (jakeearly.com)*
Matchbox. *Courtesy Cyril Kieldsen*

Opposite: Crazy Horse Live in a Rusted Out Garage Tour, Patriot Center, George Mason University, Fairfax, Virginia, September 26, 1986. © *Chester Simpson (Rock-N-RollPhotos.com)*

Contents page: U.S. and Canada Fall Tour, Madison Square Garden, New York, December 15, 2008. *AP Photo/Jason DeCrow*

# For Mary and Shari

First published in 2010 by Voyageur Press, an imprint of MBI Publishing Company, 400 First Avenue North, Suite 300, Minneapolis, MN 55401 USA

Voyageur Press titles are also available at discounts in bulk quantity for industrial or sales-promotional use. For details write to Special Sales Manager at MBI Publishing Company, 400 First Avenue North, Suite 300, Minneapolis, MN 55401 USA.

To find out more about our books, visit us online at www.voyageurpress.com.

Library of Congress Cataloging-in-Publication Data

Durchholz, Daniel.
  Neil Young : long may you run : the illustrated history / Daniel Durchholz and Gary Graff.
    p. cm.
  Includes bibliographical references, discography, filmography, and index.
  ISBN 978-0-7603-3647-2 (plc)
  1.  Young, Neil, 1945– 2.  Young, Neil, 1945---Pictorial works. 3.  Rock musicians—Canada—Biography.  I. Graff, Gary. II. Title.
  ML420.Y75D87 2010
  782.42166092--dc22
  [B]

                                   2009045541

Editors: Danielle Ibister and Dennis Pernu
Designer:  John Barnett / 4 Eyes Design
Design Manager:  Katie Sonmor

Printed in China

# Contents

# Introduction

The crowd is restive and confused—and unhappy—at the Pine Knob Music Theatre north of Detroit on a warm September night in 1983.

The fans came expecting a two-part show from Neil Young. The first went off as planned, with warmly received solo acoustic renditions of favorites such as "Comes a Time," "Heart of Gold," "The Needle and the Damage Done," and "Ohio." But when Young returns to the stage that night, it's not with the Shocking Pinks, the rockabilly-styled group he put together for his latest release, *Everybody's Rockin'*, and with which he has closed shows throughout this tour. Instead he encores with a pair of gentle favorites, "Sugar Mountain" and "I Am a Child."

Goodnight.

House lights up.

Show over.

There are surprised looks—*what the hell?*—and then some boos. Ushers look at each other uncertainly. A few folks up front crane their necks toward the stage wings, as if Young was just kidding and is doing a quick-change into his Shocking Pinks suit. Nobody seems in a hurry to leave, fully knowing that there's supposed to be more to the show.

Backstage there's similar confusion. Pink-suited musicians mill around, shrugging at each other. Larry Byrom, the former Steppenwolf member who's part of the Redwood Boys, the Pinks' adjunct vocal troupe, walks by and asks nobody in particular, "Are we going on?" One reporter grabs Scott Young, Neil's famous sportswriter father, to ask why the Pinks section isn't happening. Another asks tour manager Glen Palmer if he can talk to Neil or if Young will issue some sort of explanation.

"It was the gentlest possible way of giving Neil a chance to explain his cancelation of the Pinks," Scott Young relates in his book *Neil and Me*, "or to say anything else he wanted, even to give an excuse, if he wished, that he wasn't feeling well, or whatever. All of us waited for this answer. 'No, there's really nothing I want to say,' he said. 'Just tell him I hope he enjoyed the concert.'"

On the tour bus, Young told his father and some visitors, "That crowd just didn't deserve the Shocking Pinks! … I guess I'll get criticized, but I just have to follow my instincts."

Neil Young does not explain. He simply does. Over the course of a more than forty-five-year recording career—starting with the Squires and Buffalo Springfield and continuing both on his own and in irregular associations with David Crosby, Stephen Stills, and Graham Nash—Young has followed his muse without question or second-guessing. He'll switch from roaring electric rock to gentle acoustic fare in less time than it takes to put a guitar strap over his shoulder. Projects are launched and either seen through or abandoned as he sees fit—occasionally, as was the case with the short-lived Stills-Young Band, in the midst of a tour.

Collaborators are embraced and moved aside as needed: Crazy Horse, arguably the most popular of all Young's own bands, has suffered through several long periods of inaction. "We're *always* waiting," guitarist Frank "Poncho" Sampedro says with a sigh to PBS's *American Masters*. And CSNY was on ice for sixteen years on record and twenty-six years as a live act.

"He cycles through different entities, one after another, to keep it fresh," Crosby explains to PBS. "He doesn't leave it; he just puts it on hold." Stills, meanwhile, calls his longtime friend "willfully charming, willfully erratic—and willful." And Nash confesses to PBS that "there's a part of me that doesn't like that part of him because I know people get hurt. If you play only a certain amount a year and you're going on a Neil Young tour and the day before it gets canceled, your life is changed desperately, and that makes me uncomfortable. But I have to admire Neil for sticking so true to the muse."

"I'm still trying to do whatever it is that the music makes me do," says Young, who's even been sued for that pursuit, to *American Masters*. "People want to know, 'Why don't you make your most famous record over and over again?' 'Cause it's *death*, that's why. The longer you can go on and do things that people don't like and then occasionally give them something they like just because that's the way it happened, the better off you are. It makes the ones that are more palatable to people more palatable 'cause they feel like they're special and," he adds with a laugh, "because they might have hated the last three or something."

Young has certainly put out music people have liked and hated, but seldom are they indifferent toward it. With a prolific drive and hardnosed work ethic, he's amassed a sweeping body of work that has inspired, confounded, surprised, frustrated, tested, and even downright pissed off his fans and colleagues. For every mainstream hit such as *Harvest* and *Rust Never Sleeps* or critical milepost like *Tonight's the Night*, there are curve balls that range from the impenetrable (*Journey through the Past*, *Arc*) to the unexpected—and therefore initially unwelcome—experiments such as the aforementioned *Everybody's*

*Rockin'*, the electronic excursion *Trans*, the countrified *Old Ways*, and the big band blues of *This Note's for You*. Young's oeuvre is dotted with uninspiring efforts, too, and he's also iced more potential, and promising, projects than some artists release in an entire career—and turned on a dime to rush something out when he wants to comment on the issues of the day.

"My first job is to follow the musical course," he says to PBS. "It's always to the detriment of everything. Relationships, projects—they get derailed. There's gonna be a lot of collateral damage. . . . I'm brutal. I only do it for the music. If the music is saying to do one thing, the people are secondary. You have to do what you have to do. And if you're always like that, people begin to trust that. They realize it's not a personal thing."

That, of course, is what brings those fans and colleagues—and critics—back time and again. Young is nothing if not credible and, most importantly, honest. Even his "failures" have a bravado that lends them potency. He's not right all the time, but he's wrong even less, which keeps everyone on their toes and paying attention. As Stills—who probably has more axes to grind than any of Young's other musical associates—concedes to *American Masters*, "Even though I know there'll be disappointments, I still trust him more than anybody."

*Neil Young: Long May You Run* endeavors to chronicle Young's continually shifting life and career with a critical and analytical eye toward his varying moods and moves. The truth is that no one can explain his intrepid creativity better than Young himself, and he doesn't do that very often—perhaps because *he* doesn't necessarily understand it much, either. Even a work as probing as Jimmy McDonough's *Shakey: Neil Young's Biography*, an authorized work until its subject decided otherwise, raises as many questions as it answers and never pins down the muse that steers Young hither and yon.

But what's certain is that almost no other popular musician—of Young's vintage or before or since—is as fascinating and fun to track. He's on a marathon of unpredictable terrain that seems far from over as of this writing. The story is ongoing, and it's still a great one to tell.

# Dream Comfort Memory

## 1945-1966

Lieutenant Scott Young *(right)* of *HMCS Prince Henry*, Taranto, Italy, October 1944. *Library and Archives Canada/Department of National Defence fonds/PA-188925*

Neil Young, age two, Ontario, August 18, 1948. *© El Scan/Toronto Star/Zuma Press*

**Neil Percival Young** was born November 12, 1945, in Toronto. His father, Scott Young, was a fledgling journalist who would find fame as a sportswriter, newspaper columnist, TV commentator, and writer of fiction. Neil's mother, Edna "Rassy" Ragland, was, as Scott recalls in *Neil and Me*, "a good tennis player and golfer and all around noticeable young woman" when she caught his eye in Winnipeg. They married there on June 18, 1940, and moved to Toronto when Scott secured a job with the Canadian Press news agency. Their first child, Bob, was born April 27, 1942.

Scott Young remembers Neil—"Neiler" in the family parlance—as being smitten with music early on. In his crib, he would "jig to Dixieland even before he could stand up." In 1949, the Youngs moved to Omemee, a small town in north Ontario that Neil would memorialize in his song "Helpless." He led a happy and active existence there, fishing, catching turtles, watching TV, and playing with his train set. "Omemee's a nice little town," Young told Jimmy McDonough, author of *Shakey: Neil Young's Biography.* "Sleepy little place. . . . Life was real basic and simple in that town. Walk to school, walk back. Everybody knew who you were. Everybody knew everybody."

In 1951, Neil fell victim to an outbreak of polio. The dreaded disease, which often killed its victims or left them paralyzed or crippled, left him with no lasting effects beyond fatigue. The family spent half of 1952 in Florida to let Neiler heal in the warmth of the sun.

Two-year-old Neil Young with father Scott, mother Rassy, and older brother Bob in Ontario, August 18, 1948. *© El Scan/Toronto Star/Zuma Press*

The Toronto hospital where Young was born.

TORONTO GENERAL HOSPITAL, TORONTO, CANADA

HOSPITAL FOR SICK CHILDREN, TORONTO, CANADA

The Toronto hospital where Young was treated for polio in 1951.

Looking North on New Smyrna Beach, Fla.
"Florida's Smartest Little City"

To help Young recover from polio, the family retreated to New Smyrna Beach, Florida, in 1952.

The next few years were turbulent, as Scott and Rassy separated and reunited several times. They moved back to Toronto, where Scott wrote a sports column for the *Globe and Mail* and became the intermission host for Canadian TV's most popular show, *Hockey Night in Canada*.

Eleven-year-old Neil thrived, though, earning money by raising chickens and selling eggs. In a school essay about his lucrative hobby, he wrote, "When I finish school, I plan to go to Ontario Agricultural College and perhaps learn to be a scientific farmer."

At the same time, Neil fell in love with rock 'n' roll. His transistor radio, a constant companion under his covers at night, played local station CHUM but also pulled in far-flung stations from around the United States. Rockers

Chuck Berry, Little Richard, Jerry Lee Lewis, and Elvis Presley were among his favorites, along with the country sounds of Johnny Cash, Ferlin Husky, and Marty Robbins. There were no musical instruments around the house until late 1958, when Scott and Rassy bought Neil a plastic ukulele. "He would close the door of his room at the top of the stairs," Scott recalled, "and we would hear *plunk*, pause while he moved his fingers to the next chord, *plunk*, pause while he moved again, *plunk*."

The family fell apart once and for all when Scott went on a long assignment for the *Globe and Mail* and met publicist Astrid Mead. He split from Rassy, taking Bob with him. Scott and Mead would marry in 1961. Neil and his mother, meanwhile, returned to Winnipeg, a painful journey recounted in the first verse of Young's "Don't Be Denied."

# D ddy Went W lki. '
## The Scott Young Story

**HE WOULDN'T BE FAMOUS HIMSELF** until he was in his twenties, but Neil Young grew up in the shadow of notoriety.

His father, Scott Young, was a ubiquitous presence on the Canadian media scene. Starting as a copy boy at the *Winnipeg Free Press*, he spent his life writing for newspapers and magazines, publishing books (more than three dozen, including the memoir *Neil and Me*), and broadcasting on Canadian TV. But as his son's fame grew, "Neil Young's father" became a regular appendage of any reference to him. The elder Young wore it happily, enjoying "the extra credence given my writing by some people, especially those much younger than I am, on the grounds that anyone who was Neil Young's father couldn't be all bad."

Born in Cypress River, Manitoba, and raised in nearby Glenboro, Scott Young, like Neil, left high school prematurely. He began submitting stories to an assortment of publications until he got his job at the *Winnipeg Free Press*, working his way up the ranks to sports editor. He married Edna "Rassy" Ragland in 1940 and a year later moved to Toronto, where he began covering sports for the Canadian Press agency. In 1942, the year his oldest son, Bob, was born, Scott went to England to cover World War II for the CP. Upon his return in 1943, Scott joined the Royal Canadian Navy, serving until the war ended in 1945—the year Neil was born.

Scott moved from the CP to an assistant editor's post at *Maclean's* magazine, later quitting to hang out his freelance shingle, publishing fiction pieces in *Collier's* and the *Saturday Evening Post* and contributing to the fledgling *Sports Illustrated*. His first novel, *The Flood*, was published in 1956. His other credits included the Toronto-based *Globe and Mail*, for which he wrote a column about eleven-year-old Neil's affinity for selling chickens, the *Toronto Telegram*, and a spot hosting *Hockey Night in Canada* on TV that was cut short when some of Scott's blunt commentary ran afoul of the Toronto Maple Leafs' co-owner John Bassett.

Scott and Rassy divorced acrimoniously in 1961, after he moved in with publicist Astrid Mead, who he'd met two years earlier during an assignment in British Columbia. (Scott would break up with his second wife in 1976 and move in with fellow *Globe and Mail* writer Margaret Hogan the following year.) Rassy, who moved with Neil to Winnipeg, never forgave him for splitting up the family; she even refused the flowers he sent to her as she lay dying in October 1990.

Neil Young told *Mojo* that his father "was definitely more musically oriented" than his mother, but biographer Jimmy McDonough described Scott Young as "the more conventional parent, stressing success in school and a career to fall back on." There were, not surprisingly, clashes—with

BOTH: *Little Brown and Company*

his son and with his ex-wife—over Neil's focus on music rather than education. When Neil asked for six hundred dollars to buy an amplifier, claiming his grades were improving, he learned that Scott was in contact with the school and knew that was not the case.

Years later, Neil Young related to *Mojo* that "there was the classic thing that happens in family breakups. . . . the perspective gets changed. The father will always have a negative reaction to what the mother does, particularly if she's being 'soft' on the child. . . . It's a reaction created out of frustration over not being able to really voice an opinion."

Ultimately, however, Scott Young became one of his son's biggest fans, even writing a laudatory and emotional column about hearing Neil play in 1971 at Carnegie Hall. The two built a strong relationship chronicled in *Neil and Me*, which was published in 1984 and updated and reissued in 1997. "He sings in a way that twists my heart," Scott wrote about his son.

The elder Young received the prestigious Elmer Ferguson Memorial Award for his journalism from the Hockey Hall of Fame and was later inducted into the Manitoba Hockey Hall of Fame. Many of his personal papers reside at Trent University in Peterborough, Ontario, where he received an honorary doctorate in 1990. The Scott Young Public School in Omemee, where he lived with Neil and his first family, was named in his honor in 1993. A year later Scott published his autobiography, *A Writer's Life*.

Neil Young's father passed away on June 12, 2005, in Kingston, Ontario, at age eighty-seven following a long battle with Alzheimer's disease.

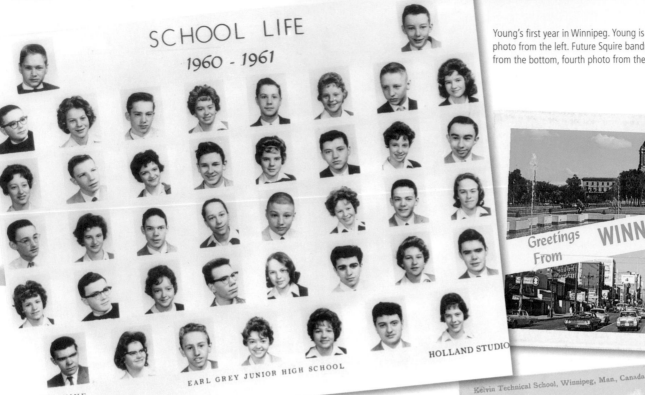

SCHOOL LIFE
1960 - 1961

EARL GREY JUNIOR HIGH SCHOOL

HOLLAND STUDIO

GRADE NINE

Greetings From WINNIPEG MANITOBA CANADA

Kelvin Technical School, Winnipeg, Man., Canada

"If you look at a map of North America, dead center is the town of Winnipeg, Canada," Guess Who/Bachman Turner Overdrive guitarist (and Winnipeg native) Randy Bachman told PBS's *American Masters*. "It's dead center, so it's the middle of everywhere or the middle of nowhere, depending on how you look at it. The nearest city of consequence is three or four hundred miles. So when you're in Winnipeg, you're *in* Winnipeg. . . . The winters are six or seven months long."

Neil's plastic ukulele was succeeded by a baritone uke, a banjo, and finally an acoustic guitar. He formed his first band, the Jades, which performed one gig at the local community center. At Kelvin High School, he was something of a loner, drawn into himself by his family's disintegration. When he was picked on by some bullies, though, he became determined to stand his ground.

"The guy who sat in front of me turned around and hit my books off the desk with his elbow," Young told *Rolling Stone*. "He did this a few times. . . . I went up to the teacher and asked if I could have the dictionary. This was the first time I'd broken the ice and put my hand up to ask for anything since I got to the fucking place. Everybody thought I didn't speak. So I got the dictionary, this big Webster's with little indentations for your thumb for every letter. I took it back to my desk, thumbed through it a little bit. Then I just sort of stood up in my seat, raised it up above my head as far as I could and hit the guy in front of me over the head with it. Knocked him out."

Young's last yearbook photo, Kelvin Technical High School, Winnipeg, 1963. *Courtesy John Einarson*

Young escorted Jacolyne Nentwig to the 1962 Humpty Dumpty Ball, River Heights, Winnipeg. *Courtesy John Einarson*

He was temporarily expelled for his actions, but the word was out on Neil Young. "That's the way I fight," he said. "If you're going to *fight*, you may as well fight to wipe who or whatever it is *out*. Or don't fight at all."

Young took further refuge in music, making friends with a boy named Comrie Smith, who had more rock 'n' roll records than Young as well as a set of bongos. They formed a band, only to realize that they couldn't really play. But there would be other bands. Young was captivated by groups on the local community center circuit—including Chad Allen and the Expressions, which included Randy Bachman and would one day morph into the Guess Who—and obsessed by British outfits such as the Shadows, which featured the echo-laden guitar stylings of Hank B. Marvin. Young practiced feverishly, mostly to the detriment of his studies.

He signed on with a band called the Esquires but was forced to quit by his mother, by then something of a local celebrity as a panelist on the TV quiz show *Twenty Questions*. But Young persisted, forming the Stardusters and then the Classics with another friend, bassist Ken Koblun. With drummer Jack Harper (soon to be replaced by Ken Smythe) and guitarist Allen Bates, Young and Koblun would form the Squires, not to be confused with the similarly named (and at the time, still extant) Esquires.

The Squires' repertoire consisted of old pop tunes and instrumental rock 'n' roll songs that spotlighted Young's guitar. "I always like the primitive in rock 'n' roll," he told *American Masters*. "Link Wray: He's a great player. He was the beginning of grunge way before anybody, you

know. . . . There was quite an influence from the Shadows and the Ventures and the Fireballs from Texas. There were these surf bands that played instrumentals that were really good. We were mostly an instrumental band at first, so we paid a lot of attention to them."

"I think our main influence was definitely the Shadows," Allen Bates recalled. "I think our bass player, Kenny Koblun, lived with an English family in Winnipeg, across from Churchill High School. He received these beautiful British rock 'n' roll records before the rest of Canada did, so we were able to copy them or imitate them and go play at a community club and people would've thought they were ours. Later on, Neil started writing tunes, instrumental tunes that were surely as good as the Shadows. We were only sixteen and we were damn good."

Rassy Ragland Young *(bottom)* on the quiz show *Twenty Questions*. *Courtesy John Einarson*

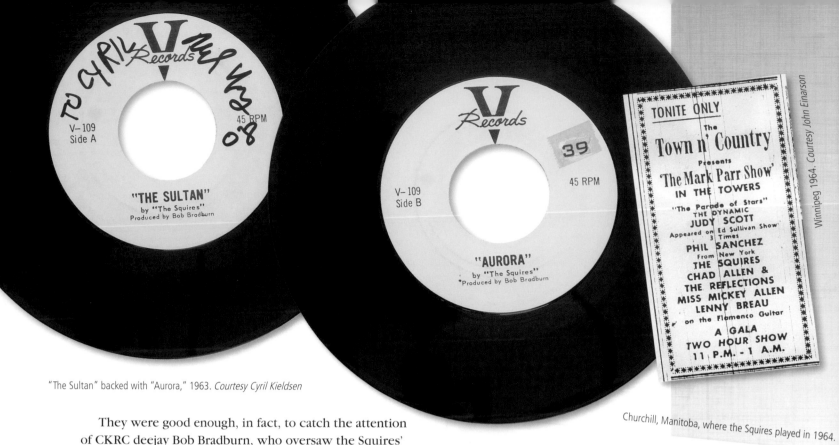

"The Sultan" backed with "Aurora," 1963. *Courtesy Cyril Kieldsen*

Winnipeg 1964. *Courtesy John Einarson*

Churchill, Manitoba, where the Squires played in 1964.

They were good enough, in fact, to catch the attention of CKRC deejay Bob Bradburn, who oversaw the Squires' first recording session. On July 23, 1963, the band recorded two instrumentals, "The Sultan" and "Aurora." Some weeks later, the single appeared on local label V Records.

Caught up by the spirit of Beatlemania, Young attempted to add vocals to the Squires' sonic attack. During a gig, he warbled his way through covers of "It Won't Be Long" and "Money." "After exposing myself in that way, I think I heard the odd cry of 'Boy, don't do that again,'" Young told McDonough. "I don't really remember the reaction, though—I remember more how I felt. I felt great, 'cause I'd *sung*." When the Squires recorded again at CKRC, Young was ready to put his voice on tape as well, singing "I Wonder" and "Ain't It the Truth," though nothing ever came of the tracks.

But even as Young continued to put his rock 'n' roll ambitions into motion, folk music started taking hold of him, too. He hung out at Winnipeg's Fourth Dimension coffee house; discovered records by Bob Dylan, the Kingston Trio, and Ian and Sylvia; and dreamed of ways to combine the elements of folk and rock in his own music.

He also befriended nascent folkie Joan Anderson, who would later gain fame as Joni Mitchell. She was in Winnipeg performing at the Fourth Dimension. "I've known Joni since I was 18," Young told *Rolling Stone*. "I met her in one of the coffeehouses. She was beautiful. That was my first impression. She was real frail and wispy looking. . . . I remember thinking that if you blew hard enough, you could probably knock her over. She could hold up a Martin D18 pretty well, though."

Joni Mitchell. *Photo by Central Press/Getty Images*

Kelvin Technical High School fundraiser, 1964. *Courtesy John Einarson*

He bought a car that could accommodate the band's equipment; it was a 1948 Buick Roadmaster hearse, nicknamed Mortimer Hearseburg. "It had rollers for the coffin in the back, so we just rolled our amps in and out," Young said. "It was like they built it for us."

The Squires pose with Mort before departing Winnipeg, Manitoba, for Fort William, Ontario, April 1965. From left: Ken Koblun, Neil Young, and Bob Clark. *Courtesy Owen Clark*

# Sample and Hold
## Neil Young and the Dylan Dynamic

**NEARLY EVERY MUSICIAN** who has picked up an acoustic guitar and aspired to write songs since 1963 has been influenced in some way by Bob Dylan.

Neil Young is no different.

Young's roots were in rock 'n' roll. He played electric guitar first, in the Squires during the early '60s, then found his way into folk music and, of course, Dylan. "I'd been into Dylan since '63, when I heard his very first album. That left a big impression on me," Young told *Mojo*. The message Young gleaned from listening to Dylan was a profound one—that he could do that too.

"[Dylan] said, 'Listen, I'm not Caruso. I'm not a singer like Caruso. I sing my songs,'" Young said on PBS's *American Masters*. "That made sense to me. So I figured, 'Y'know, I'll just sing, see what happens. I'll keep singing, keep doing this.'" He elaborated for *Shakey* biographer Jimmy McDonough: "I liked Bob's voice when I first heard it. I just said, 'Hey, there's a guy who sounds different doin' this thing, too—I really like this guy. *I* can write songs.'"

But Dylan's influence can be heard even beyond the comfort and confidence with which Young—who would never claim to be Caruso, either—sings his songs. From stinging social commentary, including some of the harshest antiwar treatises of the rock era, to the alternating of gentle acoustic and wildly electric music, Young is clearly a protégé who has long found in Dylan a kindred spirit and fellow iconoclast.

Dylan's unyielding individualism set a course Young would follow throughout his career. Music journalist Dave Marsh noted that Young "is Dylan's greatest disciple, not only because of a shared sound—a wracked voice, an inability to stay in one stylistic space for long—but also because of a shared cunning: Young has mastered Dylan's greatest trick, the art of self-mythology." And Elliott

Students Need Athletics, Culture and Kicks (SNACK) Benefit, Kezar Stadium, San Francisco, March 23, 1975. *Photo by Richard McCaffrey/Michael Ochs Archives/Getty Images*

Roberts, who managed both musicians, once noted that he would ask Young, "What would Bob Dylan do?" when trying to prod a decision out of him.

Young told *Time* magazine:

*If I'd like to be anyone, it's him. And he's a great writer, true to his music and done what he feels is the right thing to do for years and years and years. He's great. He's the one I look to. I'm always interested in what he's doing now, or did last, or did a long time ago that I didn't find out about. The guy has written some of the greatest poetry and put it to music in a way that it touched me, and other people have done that, but not so consistently or as intensely. Like me, he waits around and keeps going, and he knows that he doesn't have the muse all the time, but he knows that it'll come back and it'll visit him and he'll have his moment.*

Young's devotion has its pitfalls, of course. He confessed to McDonough that he's had to be careful to take his Dylan in measured doses. "I think I liked Bob's music so much that at one point I actually had to consciously not listen to it because it affected me so much," he said. "I realized at one point, 'If I listened too much I'd become like him.'"

He's come close. Dylan himself told *Uncut* that Young's 1972 hit "Heart of Gold" cut a bit too close to the bone for him: "I used to hate it when it came on the radio. I always liked Neil Young but it bothered me every time I listened to 'Heart of Gold.' I'd say, 'Shit, that's me. If it sounds like me, it should as well *be* me.'" He had apparently gotten over it by 1997, however, when he name-checked Young in "Highlands," the eighteen-minute-long closing track of his album *Time Out of Mind*: "I'm listening to Neil Young, I gotta turn up the sound."

And in 2008, an unshaven Dylan showed up unannounced at one of Young's childhood homes in Winnipeg, asking the current owner, John Kiernan, to see Young's bedroom and any area where he might have played his guitar.

Young and Dylan have periodically played on the same bills during their careers, mostly benefits. Dylan, by many accounts, sat in on some of the sessions for Young's 1975 album *Zuma*, and Young played three entire shows with Dylan and his band during 1988 in California. At an all-star concert celebrating the thirtieth anniversary of Dylan's recording career in October 1992, at Madison Square Garden in New York City—which Young dubbed Bobfest—Young was the acknowledged best act of the night, cooking through "Just Like Tom Thumb's Blues" and "All Along the Watchtower" while backed by Booker T. & the MGs.

Vacationing at Falcon Lake, seventy-five miles from Winnipeg, Young managed to score the Squires a booking. But when two of his bandmates couldn't make it, Young fired them, later reforming the group with Koblun, drummer Bill Edmonson, and pianist Jeff Wuckert.

"We just kept morphing and changing," Young told *American Masters*. "People would join and we'd go do gigs out of town and they'd quit because they didn't want to leave town. Eventually I got two other guys that wanted to leave town and were ready to take a chance. . . . Some of the guys that I wanted to take I couldn't take because their parents would say, 'You're gonna screw up your life,' and suddenly the thing would derail. Just good musicians who wouldn't step out and take a chance got left behind."

Young's music blossomed, but his studies suffered, and he dropped out of high school. With financial help from his mother, he bought a car that could accommodate the band's equipment; it was a 1948 Buick Roadmaster hearse, nicknamed Mortimer Hearseburg. "It had rollers for the coffin in the back, so we just rolled our amps in and out," Young said. "It was like they built it for us."

The Squires headed east. They landed in Fort William, Ontario, a working-class town that would later join with nearby Port Arthur to form Thunder Bay. There they found work at local clubs and hooked up with deejay Ray Dee (né Delatinsky), who would help guide the next part of the band's career, booking gigs and manning the board for the recording of "I'll Love You Forever." The song is notable both for its use of double-tracking to make Young's singing voice palatable and for its use of overdubbed surf sounds to cover instrumental flubs.

It was in Fort William's Victoria Hotel on or near his nineteenth birthday that Young wrote his coming-of-age classic "Sugar Mountain." But the most important association Young would make in the city was with Stephen Stills, a Texas-born guitarist who had migrated to New York's Greenwich Village and sang in a vocal ensemble called the Au Go Go Singers. A splinter version of the group, the Company Singers, was performing in Fort William. "He was doing exactly what I wanted to do, which was play folk songs on an electric guitar and songs that he'd written himself," Stills told *American Masters*. "Mainly, he was the funniest person I'd met in years. He didn't have another gig until the next weekend, so he stayed in Thunder Bay and we played and he took us to see buffalo. We lived on A&W cheeseburgers and root beer. Very Canadian."

Aware of the fact that Fort William was a dead end, Young wanted to go to England to pursue his musical dreams—or, failing that, Los Angeles. He saw Toronto as a steppingstone, and the band packed into Mort. But the car died in Blind River, Ontario, its transmission splayed out all over the road. (Young would later memorialize the event in his song "Long May You Run.") For all practical purposes, the band was dead, too, as Young left his bandmates to fend for themselves while he hitchhiked the rest of the way to Toronto. He stayed at his father's house until getting his own place in the city's bohemian quarter, Yorkville.

Fort William, Ontario, April 1965. *Courtesy Owen Clark*

The Squires, Fourth Dimension coffee house,
Fort William, Ontario, May 1965.
*Courtesy John Einarson*

I admire him a lot. It sort of freaks me out that he wrote "Sugar Mountain" when he was, what, 17 years old? That's not fair. And he didn't quit then; he challenged himself and challenged his audience to the point of risking losing them. I admire that a lot.

—*Rhett Miller, Old 97's*

Main Street, Blind River, Ontario, Canada   6

*Blind River, Ontario, where Mort—and the Squires—expired.*

Stephen Stills and Neil Young, 1967. The bandmates first met in Fort William, Ontario, in 1963. © *Henry Diltz/Corbis*

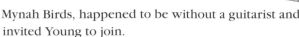

Toronto subway.

Mynah Birds, happened to be without a guitarist and invited Young to join.

The Mynah Birds were fronted by an American, Ricky James Matthews, who would one day gain fame as '80s funkster Rick James. The band was backed financially by John Craig Eaton, scion of the Eaton's Department Store family. Incredibly, the Mynah Birds landed a recording deal with Motown Records. Palmer told Scott Young that the Mynah Birds "were the first white group Motown ever signed." Reminded that Rick James was, in fact, black, Palmer quipped, "He's getting blacker all the time but as far as we knew he was white then."

Young recorded a handful of songs with the Mynah Birds, but the prospective album—and indeed, all of their plans—came crashing down when it was discovered that Matthews was AWOL from the U.S. Navy. He landed in prison.

"Probably 90 per cent of the acts there were better groups than the Mynah Birds," Palmer told Scott Young. "But we were weird, we were really different. We were the only group with a twelve-string guitar on Motown. Playing a country twelve-string with this rock beat. And actually, they kind of liked the sound of it."

Still in possession of the Mynah Birds equipment (which technically belonged to investor John Craig Eaton), Young sold it for money to make a break for California, where he hoped to locate Stills. He bought a 1953 Pontiac hearse that he named Mort Two, loaded up Palmer and some other friends, and took off for Los Angeles, using a circuitous route that would arouse the least suspicion about a bunch of kids with no work permits or money.

Along the way, Young resisted letting anyone else behind the wheel of Mort Two, the better to nurse the hulking but temperamental beast across the country. Fatigued and annoyed at the ragtag bunch, Young ordered everyone out of the car in Ohio, threatening to leave them on the side of the road. He relented and let them back in, driving on to Albuquerque, where he went into convulsions and passed out on the floor for several days.

Young recovered, and the car and some—but not all—of its inhabitants made it to L.A., the others being left behind in Albuquerque. But the picture was far from rosy at that point. Young and Palmer were broke and knew no one. Stills was nowhere in sight. For a few days, they made ends meet selling rides in the hearse. They were about to give up and head north to San Francisco when fate intervened in an L.A. traffic jam.

In Toronto, Young reconnected with Comrie Smith, his friend from Winnipeg, and dove into the local folk scene. With no gigs to be had, though, he got a job in a bookstore stockroom, though it lasted only two weeks. "I got fired for irregularity," he told an audience at the Canterbury House in Ann Arbor, Michigan, in November 1968, "because I couldn't be depended on to be consistent 'cause every once in a while this girl I knew . . . would lay one of these little red pills on me. . . . She said they were diet pills, but they were *really great* diet pills." He continued writing, coming up with "Nowadays Clancy Can't Even Sing," and he and Smith recorded a handful of tunes, including the Jimmy Reed–style blues "Hello Lonely Woman," in Smith's attic.

The Squires—under a new moniker, Four to Go—reunited for one last gig, at a ski resort in Vermont. Once in the States, Young and Ken Koblun decided to head for New York City, where they hoped to find Stephen Stills, who, it turned out, had already left for California. Instead, they met Stills' friend Richie Furay, to whom Young taught his song "Clancy."

Several months later, Young was back in New York, having scored an audition with Elektra Records. Rather than a proper studio setup, Young was given a tape recorder and sent to lay down the tracks in a tape vault. The demos went nowhere. Back in Toronto, a new opportunity popped up when Bruce Palmer, an established figure on the city scene and a fellow Canadian, bumped into Young, who was walking down the street carrying a guitar and an amplifier. Palmer's band, the

BABY WHAT YOU WANT ME TO DO
(J. Reed)
JIMMY REED
VJ 333

# MOTOR CITY  *Neil Young's Motown Flight*

THE "SUGAR MOUNTAIN" MAN AND THE "SUPER FREAK" in the same band—at Motown, no less? Strange but true, and certainly one of the most mythic chapters in Neil Young's career.

The Mynah Birds, led by Buffalo-born Ricky James Matthews (later to become Rick James), had been knocking around Toronto for a while, its frequently changing lineups at times including founding members of Steppenwolf. The group had successfully auditioned for Motown in October 1965 in Detroit, cutting a version of Howard Lemon's "No Greater Love" with producer Harvey Fuqua. But guitarist Tom Morgan felt the label was interested only in Matthews and decided to fly the Mynah Birds' coop.

Not long after that, bassist Bruce Palmer spotted Young—who was working the Toronto folk circuit after bringing his band, the Squires, to the city from Winnipeg—strolling down Yorkville Avenue with an acoustic guitar in his hand and an amplifier perched on his head. Palmer quickly invited him to join the group. Young brought a folk flavor to the groove the Mynah Birds were working in at the time. The group's financial backer, John Craig Eaton, outfitted Young with a Rickenbacker electric guitar and amplifiers, and the twenty-one-year-old was on board, more as a player than a singer by his own description. James told *Rolling Stone* that when Young played his first guitar solo during his first show with the Mynah Birds, "he was so excited he leaped off the stage, the plug came out [of the amplifier] and nobody heard anything."

The Mynah Birds returned to Hitsville U.S.A. in mid-January to cut more tracks with Motown Artist & Repertoire chief William "Mickey" Stevenson and staff producers Mike Valvano and Canadian-born R. Dean Taylor. The band spent four days in Detroit recording four more songs, according to Motown studio records—making for a total of five and not, as some have claimed, an entire album's worth of material.

On January 18, the Mynah Birds cut basic tracks for three of the tunes: "Little Girl Go," co-written by Young and Matthews, and "It's My Time" and "I Got You (In My Soul)," which the frontman wrote with Taylor and Valvano. On January 19 they re-cut "I Got You (In My Soul)," laid down another Young-Matthews co-write, "I'll Wait Forever" (with Taylor and Valvano), and did overdubs on "It's My Time" and "Go On and Cry." Two days later they laid down lead vocals for all four songs.

Drummer Rickman Mason told writer Nick Warburton that during those sessions, the Mynah Birds "never did anything as a band. It was all done in parts, and they put it together. Then everybody would drop in and do songs with us, like Smokey Robinson and Tammi Terrell." On January 26, meanwhile, a session was held for additional "voices"—most likely the Spinners or Motown's in-house vocal group, the Andates—and additional "instrumentation." It's possible that the Mynah Birds were not even present for those sessions.

"It's My Time"/"Go On and Cry" was scheduled to be the Mynah Birds' first single, but fate and financial imprudence intervened. The group's manager,

The Mynah Birds, 1965. From left: Rick Mason, Bruce Palmer, Ricky Matthews, Tom Morgan, and John Taylor. *Courtesy Nick Warburton (nickwarburton.com)*

Morley Shelman, reportedly pocketed the Motown advance without sharing it with the band members; the Mynah Birds fired him, and as revenge, Shelman revealed that Ricky Matthews was AWOL from the U.S. Navy. He had, in fact, fled to Canada after being called up for active duty on the USS *Enterprise*—something even his bandmates were not aware of.

Motown executives convinced Matthews to turn himself in, promising they'd continue to work with him after he served jail time in Brooklyn. But they canceled the single. Young and Matthews made an agreement to work together after the incarceration—"I had gotten really close to the cat," Young told *Rolling Stone*. But the reunion never happened, and Matthews returned to Motown in 1967 with another version of the Mynah Birds before reinventing himself as Rick James. Young and Palmer, meanwhile, sold the equipment Eaton bought for them, purchased a hearse, and drove to Los Angeles, where they became part of Buffalo Springfield.

"It's My Time" and "Go On and Cry" appeared as part of *The Complete Motown Singles* series, while "I'll Wait Forever" and "No Greater Love" remain unmixed in the label's vault. Despite rumors of a fifth song, "Go Girl Go," which some reports call a knockoff of Van Morrison's "Little Girl," there are neither records nor tapes of the track in the Motown vaults.

As a postscript, Young's father, Scott, wrote in *Neil and Me* that investor Eaton later approached him looking for Neil in order to collect on debts he felt the group members owed him, including the equipment they had sold and a line of credit he had opened for them at Eaton's department store. Scott never learned how or if the matter was ever settled, but he did get a note from his son assuring him that "Johnny Eaton didn't lose any money."

# Expecting to Fly

## 1966–1968

Whisky a Go Go, Sunset Strip, West Hollywood, 1966.
*Photo by Ralph Crane/Time & Life Pictures/Getty Images*

**What happened to Young** and Palmer as they abandoned their search for Stephen Stills in L.A. and headed to San Francisco was so improbable that it has become one of rock 'n' roll's favorite tall tales, with embellishments and variations depending on who does the retelling.

But the end of the story is always the same: Suddenly, *there he was*!

Young and Palmer were sitting in the hearse Mort Two, stuck in traffic on Sunset Boulevard. Headed in the other direction were Stills and Richie Furay, Stills having talked his New York friend into flying to Los Angeles by telling him he was doing well and had a band all set to go, which was a bald-faced lie. (Whether or not he mentioned his failed audition for the Monkees is unknown.) Furay glanced into the other lane and remarked on seeing the hearse, having heard about the original Mort from Stills. "All of a sudden we heard this honking and yelling, and it was Stephen," recalled Young. "This was, like, in the middle of traffic, and we're yelling and screaming and just overjoyed to see each other. It was a great moment." And so, one of the most promising young bands of the 1960s was born.

On its face, the Buffalo Springfield seemed capable of taking on the world. (The name was caged from a steamroller parked outside the house of showbiz impresario Barry Friedman, their first manager.) Having added veteran drummer Dewey Martin—who had played with Patsy Cline, Roy Orbison, and more recently, the Dillards—the Springfield ambitiously sought to combine folk, country, and rock 'n' roll with a lineup of three singer/guitarist/songwriters plus a killer rhythm section.

There was much to mine image-wise, as well. Stills, the Texan, wore a suit and cowboy hat; Young favored fringed buckskin jackets, leading many to believe he was an Indian, which the band did not deny; and Furay, the fresh-faced Midwesterner, was the affable man in the middle. At first, Martin and Palmer were the best musicians in the band, and Palmer, who often played with his back to the audience, carried about him an enticingly mysterious aura.

Only a few days after they began rehearsing, the Springfield was on tour, opening a series of shows for the Byrds. On the recommendation of Byrds bassist Chris Hillman, the Springfield scored a six-week residency at the Whisky a Go Go on the Sunset Strip. There, the quintet earned its stripes as a live act, playing five sets a night. "When we were at the high point of our cohesiveness and unity, when we were the original five guys playing every single night at the Whisky a Go Go, we didn't think we had any competition but the Beatles," Furay said.

The band members also got their first taste of the '60s, California style, thanks to established stars fighting to get in to see the Next Big Thing, plus certain extra perks, such as the Whisky's go-go girls who danced in cages while the band played. "It was great! We knew them all," Young recalled for *Mojo*. "We would look up there and say hi to them—they were right there while we were playing, haha. It was an inspiration."

Barry Friedman's early guidance of the group gave way to the management team of Charlie Greene and Brian Stone, a pair of old-school Hollywood hustlers who had guided the careers of Sonny and Cher and Iron Butterfly. Greene and Stone set the Springfield up with everything it needed and got the band incredible bookings—including an opening slot for the Rolling Stones at the Hollywood Bowl—and then a recording contract with Atlantic Records.

But the deal was a usurious one that would haunt the band down the line. Instead of being signed to Atlantic proper, or even its subsidiary imprint Atco, the Springfield was signed to Greene and Stone's York/Pala Records and was leased to Atlantic, giving the managers an inordinately large slice of the pie. In the fine tradition of "can't live with 'em, can't shoot 'em," Palmer told Jimmy McDonough, "They were the sleaziest, most underhanded, backstabbing motherfuckers in the business. They were the best!"

The musical ramifications of the deal were worse. Greene and Stone named themselves producers of the Springfield's debut album, even though it became obvious early on that they were out of their depth. Then, too, they encouraged the sort of competition between Stills and Young that would one day splinter the band. With the first single, Stills' "Go and Say Goodbye," ready to go and Young's "Nowadays Clancy Can't Even Sing" as the B-side, Greene and Stone caved in to the influence of several record distributors intrigued by the latter song and decided to flip the tunes instead. Stills, already self-deluded in the belief that Buffalo Springfield was *his* band, suddenly had stiff competition from his lead guitar player.

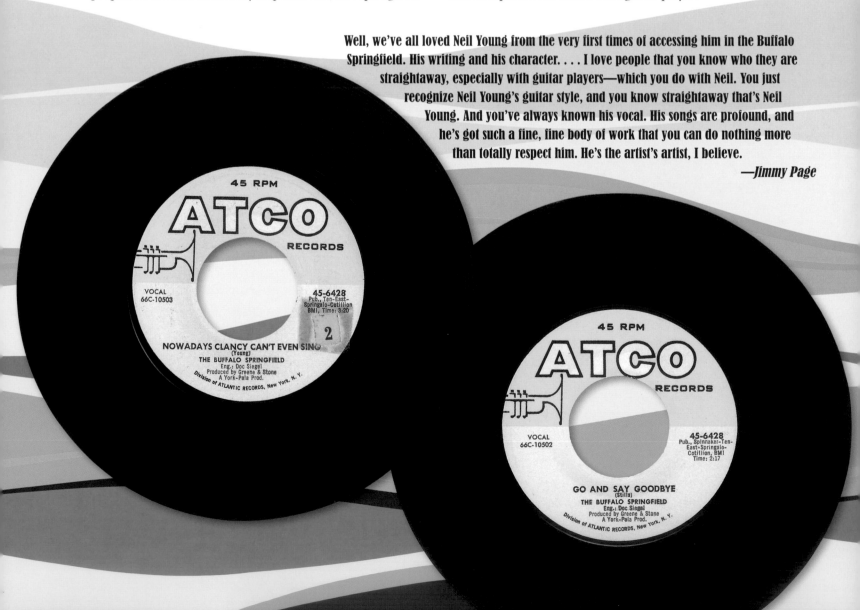

Well, we've all loved Neil Young from the very first times of accessing him in the Buffalo Springfield. His writing and his character. . . . I love people that you know who they are straightaway, especially with guitar players—which you do with Neil. You just recognize Neil Young's guitar style, and you know straightaway that's Neil Young. And you've always known his vocal. His songs are profound, and he's got such a fine, fine body of work that you can do nothing more than totally respect him. He's the artist's artist, I believe.

—*Jimmy Page*

As they continued to record, discontent grew. Stills battled vociferously for his own material. Young fumed over not being allowed to sing "Clancy"; instead, Furay sang it. In fact, no one seemed particularly interested in having Young sing at all. When he prevailed enough to put his own vocals on "Burned" and "Out of My Mind," Furay—whose songs were completely ignored at that point—was pushed to the side. Stills became intoxicated by his sudden association with various stars and sought to be placed in that same firmament as quickly as possible. Young, whose sensibilities were still tuned to the slower pace of Canadian climes, was nonplussed.

Whether it was the same condition that felled him in Albuquerque or a reaction to the stress he found himself under in the studio, Young began having seizures—epileptic fits that left him frightened and disoriented. "We were standing together in a crowd around somebody demonstrating a Vegomatic or some other kind of gadget for chopping vegetables, and when I turned to say something to Neil he wasn't beside me," Bruce Palmer told Scott Young in *Neil and Me*. "Then I saw him on the floor having tremors that led to convulsions. I was scared as hell."

Young's seizures became a semi-regular feature of Buffalo Springfield performances. Confused audience members even wondered if it was a bizarre part of the act. Stills thought it was an act, period. He thought it was a way for his rival to attract attention, garner sympathy,

Buffalo Springfield, 1967. From left: Neil Young, Bruce Palmer (kneeling), Richie Furay, Stephen Stills, and Dewey Martin. *Michael Ochs Archives/Getty Images*

or even pull a few groupies. But the affliction was real. Young underwent several painful medical procedures to try to properly diagnose and relieve his condition.

Living in fear of his next seizure and on the verge of a kind of stardom he didn't want, Young's despair was already being played out in his music. "Burned" is about his inability to keep pace with what's happening all around him. "No time left and I know I'm losin'," he sings. "Out of My Mind" is even more despondent, sounding like the lonely plaint of a superstar musician just past the apex of his career, not at the threshold.

Despite the drama, all of the principals' talents are well represented on *Buffalo Springfield*, which was released in November 1966. Stills' folk-rock tunes, including "Go and Say Goodbye" and "Sit Down I Think I Love You," are well-crafted and his bluesy Southern voice a distinctive feature. Furay's vocals soar, and Young's complex

numbers give the band some much-needed lyrical heft, even if his vocals want for strength and confidence. "The boys gave me some uppers to get my nerve up," Young wrote about "Burned" in the liner notes to *Decade*. "Maybe you can hear that."

What hurt the album more than anything, though, was Greene and Stone's production. Despite the Springfield's strength as a live act, the managers forced each musician to record separately, piecing the parts together. Worse, after the band participated in the mono mix, Greene and Stone quickly converted the album to stereo, resulting in a tinny mix that outrages the group to this day. Young commented that Greene and Stone made them sound like the "All-Insect Orchestra."

Burned, indeed.

Returning from some gigs at the Fillmore in San Francisco, the band found the L.A. scene in chaos. A curfew had been placed on teens along the Sunset Strip, leading to protests, which escalated into riots. At the same time, American involvement in the Vietnam War was intensifying. Using that as his raw material, Stills expanded the topic and came up with the Springfield's first—and only—substantial hit:

> I had had something kicking around in my head. I wanted to write something about the kids that were on the line over in Southeast Asia that didn't have anything to do with the device of this mission, which was unraveling before our eyes. Then we came down to Sunset [Boulevard] from my place on Topanga with a guy—I can't remember his name—and there's a funeral for a bar, one of the favorite spots for high school and UCLA kids to go and dance and listen to music.
>
> [City officials] decided to call out the official riot police because there's three thousand kids sort of standing out in the street; there's no looting, there's no nothing. It's everybody having a hang to close this bar. A whole company of black and white LAPD in full Macedonian battle array in shields and helmets and all that, and they're lined up across the street, and I just went, "Whoa! Why are they doing this?" There was no reason for it. I went back to Topanga, and that other song turned into "For What It's Worth," and it took as long to write as it took me to settle on the changes and write the lyrics down. It all came as a piece, and it took about fifteen minutes.

The rare Buffalo Springfield collage poster commemorating the Sunset Strip riots for which Stephen Stills wrote "For What It's Worth." *Courtesy Robert Ferreira*

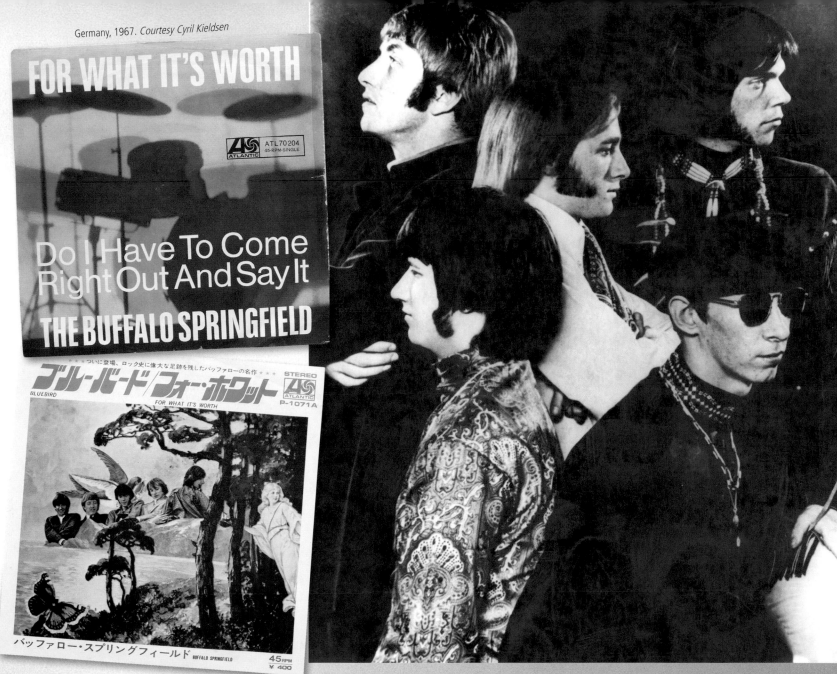

Germany, 1967. *Courtesy Cyril Kieldsen*

FOR WHAT IT'S WORTH

Do I Have To Come Right Out And Say It

THE BUFFALO SPRINGFIELD

ATL 70 204
45-RPM-SINGLE
ATLANTIC

★★★ ついに登場、ロック史に偉大な足跡を残したバッファローの名作 ★★★

STEREO
ATLANTIC
P-1071A

ブルー・バード／フォー・ホワット
BLUEBIRD
FOR WHAT IT'S WORTH

バッファロー・スプリングフィールド BUFFALO SPRINGFIELD

45RPM
¥ 400

Japan, 1967. *Courtesy Cyril Kieldsen*

Buffalo Springfield, 1967. *Redferns/Getty Images*

Recorded live in the studio, without Greene or Stone present and with Young's pinging harmonics blending with Stills' and Furay's steady but urgent picking, the Springfield's magic was finally captured on tape. It was on the radio only days after being recorded, and Atlantic decided to pull the album back and insert the song as the lead track.

But it was one step forward, two steps back: Bruce Palmer, who spent much of his time since arriving in Los Angeles in a drug haze, was busted repeatedly—twice in a single day, even. He spent time in jail and was deported to Canada. The band employed a number of substitutes, including Young's Canadian sidekick Ken Koblun, and Palmer would occasionally sneak back over

the border and rejoin the group. But with the loss of its "guru," as Atlantic chief Ahmet Ertegun called Palmer, and one-half of its rhythmic core, the Springfield was never really the same.

Thus began the parade of attrition. Greene and Stone were the next to go, the band buying out their contracts for an exorbitant fee. Young was outraged at the cost but in time was able to take the long view. "I saw eventually that they had done things the way they were done in Hollywood back then," he told Scott Young. "If we had made it a lot bigger, they would have been heroes—same as they did [for] Sonny and Cher, which worked." Or as he commented to Jimmy McDonough, "They were jive. . . . That didn't mean that they didn't have soul."

Buffalo Springfield taping "Go and Say Goodbye" on NBC's *Go!!!*, Burbank, California, March 5, 1967. Jim Fielder had stepped in after Bruce Palmer's deportation to Canada on drug charges. Fielder also played with Tim Buckley, Mothers of Invention, and Blood, Sweat & Tears.
*Charlie Gillett Collection/Redferns/Getty Images*

*Stampede*, 1967.

turned into an asset. It's only one song, true; but it proved that Young's music could keep pace with other trendsetters of the time such as Brian Wilson, who'd created the complex *Pet Sounds*, and the Beatles, whose *Sgt. Pepper's Lonely Hearts Club Band* was freshly released.

Suddenly Young was back in the Springfield, bringing his new sound with him as the band assembled its next album, *Buffalo Springfield Again*. But his ambitions ran amok on another heavily arranged song, "Broken Arrow." Like "Expecting," it was ornate and expansive, but this time to a fault. Sound snippets in the song varied from a piss-take on his own "Mr. Soul" (whose original version led off the album) to a stadium organ playing "Take Me Out to the Ballgame" to a jazzy combo and the sound of a heartbeat. It was hard to know what the sonic mishmash was meant to signify.

Young may have been getting his creative jollies with such stuff, but "Mr. Soul" was likely more indicative of where his head truly was. Much like the songs from the Springfield's debut, "Mr. Soul" suggests that Young's work was still razor-sharp, especially when it was coming from a very unhappy place. The song muses once again on fame and includes an aside critical of his own performing abilities: "Stick around while the clown who is sick does the trick of disaster."

The album, released in the fall of 1967, revealed that Stills had upped his game as well. "Rock & Roll Woman" and "Bluebird" are songs that endured beyond the Springfield's demise. And Furay finally got in on the action.

Young himself made his departure from the group on the eve of what should have been its ticket to superstardom. The Springfield was booked on Johnny Carson's *Tonight Show*, at the time one of the primary television showcases for talent. Young was vehemently opposed to doing the show. "I thought it was belittling what the Buffalo Springfield was doing," he told *Mojo*. "That audience wouldn't have understood us. We'd have been just a fuckin' curiosity to them."

So he bailed.

Young's departure also left the band shorthanded for the Monterey International Pop Festival. Guitarist Doug Hastings was hired as Young's replacement in the band, and Stills' friend David Crosby sat in for the performance, which turned out to be so lackluster that it was not included in D.A. Pennebaker's documentary film of the fest.

On his own, Young began working with producer Jack Nitzsche, a dark prince of the L.A. recording scene. Nitzsche co-wrote the hit "Needles and Pins" with Sonny Bono and was an integral part of Phil Spector's "Wall of Sound," arranging and orchestrating songs such as the Crystals' "He's a Rebel" and Ike and Tina Turner's monumental "River Deep, Mountain High." Nitzsche was one of the few authoritative figures supportive of Young's vocal abilities. In time, he became a trusted source who could deliver Young his unvarnished opinion without fear of reprisal.

With Nitzsche, Young spent weeks crafting his most ambitious work to date, "Expecting to Fly." A lush, stately production with shifting rhythms and roiling emotions, the song marks the first time, on tape, that the singer's fragile voice is

"Bluebird" backed with "Mr. Soul," France, 1967. *Courtesy Cyril Kieldsen*

# I Believe in You
## The Elliot Roberts Story

**ELLIOT ROBERTS AND NEIL YOUNG** are a match made in heaven—even if it started in a hellacious fashion.

Young actually fired Roberts on one of the first days of their association, during a Buffalo Springfield tour in 1967. Roberts had been introduced to Young by his first client, Joni Mitchell, and was even living in the guesthouse at Young's Laurel Canyon home while making a bid to manage the Springfield. Joining the band for a road date, Roberts spent a half-hour smacking golf balls at a driving range next to the hotel—while, unbeknownst to Roberts, Young wasn't feeling well and was looking for the would-be manager to find him a doctor. Roberts was instantly persona non grata.

But when Young left the Springfield shortly thereafter, he knocked on Roberts' door, asking him to be his manager and beginning an association that's been constant throughout Young's career. "How did I know Elliot was the one? It was obvious. He was a lotta fun. Just like that," Young told biographer Jimmy McDonough. "As long as I give Elliot good direction, he does what he has to do to protect me. . . . Elliot's got soul."

For his part, Roberts told McDonough the key to his longevity with Young is recognizing who's the artist and what the manager has to do to best serve him: "I couldn't write all those great fuckin' albums for Neil, or have the pain that he has so he could get those emotions out. I can protect him, I can showcase him, I can make sure when it's special, everyone knows." Within that relationship, Roberts has been called upon to be "a tough negotiator" (a gross understatement, according to many of those who have been on the other side of the table) as well as an apologist. He is frequently put in the position of doing damage control when Young suddenly veers from one already-in-motion project to another.

He apparently has the temperament for it, though. "He has no rules," onetime business associate John Hartmann told Q. "Whatever it takes, Elliot will do."

Roberts was born Elliot Rabinowitz on February 22, 1943, in the Bronx. He was a jock, playing basketball and running track, as well as a member of the Fordham Daggers teen gang. He attended Bradley University briefly on a hoops scholarship, then returned to New York to work as a page at NBC before getting a job in the mail room of the William Morris Agency. There he was mentored by an upwardly mobile David Geffen before taking over a roster of comedians and singer Buffy Sainte-Marie. It was Sainte-Marie who gave Roberts a tape of a fledgling Joni Mitchell.

Mitchell, who Roberts managed until 1985, was his entrée to Los Angeles, where he netted her a deal at Warner Bros. Records. Through her he met David Crosby (who was briefly her boyfriend), Graham Nash, Stephen Stills, and other principals in the burgeoning southern California singer-songwriter scene. His company was called Lookout Management; in 1970, he joined forces with his old friend and it became the Geffen-Roberts Company. They handled Mitchell, Young, CSNY, the Eagles, and Jackson Browne, among others. In 1972, Roberts and Geffen started Asylum Records, a successful label—though not without some questioning about conflicts of interest. They eventually sold Asylum to Warner Bros. for $7 million.

After Asylum, however, Roberts decided that management was his preferred profession, and over the years, Lookout's clients have included Devo, Talking Heads, Tracy Chapman, Yes, Morrissey, Spiritualized, and Devendra Banhart. He has executive produced Young's film projects, usually as Elliot Rabinowitz, and in 1995, he and Young launched Vapor Records, whose roster includes Tegan & Sara, Jonathan Richman, Catatonia, Everest, Vic Chesnutt, Young's wife, Pegi, and his longtime sideman Ben Keith.

Ever since the Buffalo Springfield, "Broken Arrow"—I think that's the one that did it for me, that just put him at the top of my list as one of my favorites. And to have him and Stephen Stills in the same band, 'cause I love both of them, was incredible. But Neil is just an amazing performer as well as, obviously, the amazing songs he's written. I'm a big fan.

—*Peter Frampton*

He contributed "A Child's Claim to Fame"—which some consider a shot at Young—plus "Sad Memory" and "Good Time Boy." The sound quality of the album, which was self-produced (aside from Nitzsche's guidance of Young), is a marked improvement over *Buffalo Springfield*, although still not indicative of the band's magical live sound, which was never properly captured on tape.

Jim Messina, who later gained fame with Poco and Loggins & Messina, was Bruce Palmer's last replacement in the band, after the bassist was busted and shipped off to Canada one last time. Messina rallied the Springfield for what became its final album, *Last Time Around*, but the results were little more than a collection of solo tracks. Young vowed to leave the band after its touring commitments were fulfilled, a promise he kept. His chief contributions to the disc are "On the Way Home," which is sung by Furay, and "I Am a Child," on which the rest of the band doesn't appear at all.

Buffalo Springfield, Santa Monica Civic Auditorium, Santa Monica, California, December 9, 1967. © Nurit Wilde (WildeImages.com)

CARNABY PRODUCTIONS presents BUFFALO SPRINGFIELD IN CONCERT Liberty Hall

BUFFALO SPRINGFIELD · DICK GREGORY · BLUE CHEER · BROWNIE MC GHEE & SONNY TERRY · THE COLLECTORS · UNITED STATES OF AMERICA

KPFK presents SOUND '68

· FIRESIGN THEATRE

santa monica civic aud.      tickets: music city
                                      all mutual agencies
sat. dec. 9                           kpfk

8:30 pm                               santa monica civic box office

PRESENTED BY: CONCERTS INC.

ELECTRIC CARNIVAL

★ BUFFALO ★★
SPRINGFIELD
COUNTRY JOE & FISH
CANNED HEAT
H.P. LOVECRAFT
SUNDAY MAY 5 4 PM
LONG BEACH SPORTS ARENA
SPECIAL GUEST SMOKESTACK LIGHTNIN'

Germany, 1968. Courtesy Cyril Kjeldsen

Atl. 70 282
45-RPM-SINGLE
UN~MUNDO
MERRY~GO~ROUND
THE BUFFALO
SPRINGFIELD

SOMETHIN' ELSE

FRI. & SAT. (MAY 23 & 24) FROM 8 P.M. TIL 2 A.M.
"SOMETHIN' ELSE"
FEATURING
DEEP PURPLE
(APPEARING 10 P.M. & 12:30 A.M.)
NEIL YOUNG
(FORMERLY OF THE BUFFALO SPRINGFIELD)
CRAZY ELEPHANT
BILL DEAL & THE RHONDELLS
COMING FRI. & SAT. (MAY 30 & 31)
JAMES COTTON BLUES BAND · BLACK PEARL
RUBY & THE ROMANTICS · CRAIG HUNDLEY TRIO
HOST: HAL JACKSON·GUEST M.C. CHUCK BROWNING, WMCA
LIGHTS BY PABLO·CONTINUOUS DANCING
ADMISSION $3.50
TICKETS AVAILABLE NOW AT MADISON SQUARE GARDEN CENTER
BOX OFFICE OR ON NIGHT OF PERF. AT THE FELT FORUM
4 TOP ROCK ATTRACTIONS EVERY FRI. AND SAT. NIGHT
THE FELT FORUM MADISON SQUARE GARDEN CENTER
8TH AVE. BETWEEN 31 ST. & 33RD ST.

Young told *Rolling Stone*:

*It wasn't me scheming on a solo career, it wasn't anything but my nerves. Everything started to go too fucking fast. I can tell that now. I was going crazy, you know, joining and quitting and joining again. I began to feel like I didn't have to answer or obey anyone. I needed more space. That was a big problem in my head. So I'd quit, then I'd come back 'cause it sounded so good. It was a constant problem. I just wasn't mature enough to deal with it. I was very young. We were getting the shaft from every angle and it seemed like we were trying to make it so bad and were getting nowhere.*

Stills concurred with Young:

*The most important thing to remember is that when Bruce [Palmer] was there . . . Bruce kept getting in trouble and getting bounced out of the country. Our soul kept getting ripped away from us. But when we played—the original, with Bruce on the bass—we just fuckin' baked . . . and as I got better on the lead guitar, we started getting our conversations going, me and Neil. We were trouble on the hoof, man. We really cooked.*

*We were of the age where you can very easily get the diva syndrome before you've sold any records or anything and all that stuff, and there was a little of that. And it was so laden with talent, this bunch, that we just hit the track going too fast that we went into the wall with no skid marks. It was just. . . . We spun out. But we spun out because we didn't realize how hot the car was.*

# UNKNOWN LEGENDS
## *Neil Young's Primary Studio Collaborators*

## DAVID BRIGGS

**DAVID BRIGGS' MANTRA WAS**, "When you make rock and roll, the more you think, the more you stink."

Is it any wonder he was such an integral part of Neil Young's creative world?

From 1968, when Briggs picked up a hitchhiking Young in Malibu, until his death from lung cancer on November 26, 1995, at the age of fifty-one, Briggs was a constant in Young's work and in his life. He worked on eighteen albums with Young, starting with his self-titled solo debut and continuing through 1994's *Sleeps with Angels*. In the film *Year of the Horse*, Scott Young noted that, to Neil, David Briggs "was like a big brother in helping steer him in ways that Neil was probably willing to go, but he hadn't thought of yet." Crazy Horse guitarist Frank "Poncho" Sampedro said the group considered Briggs "more the fifth member of Crazy Horse than anybody could ever be."

Young himself once told British interviewer Nick Kent that "I always listened to what [Briggs] had to say and took note of it." In *Year of the Horse*, he said that Briggs "was a really close friend and in some ways my best friend. . . . Luckily he was with us long enough we learned from him. And really, he's a guy who taught us more about ourselves at the same time as he was learning it. He just kept things coming back and kept me moving along."

Briggs was no mere yes man, either. Young laughingly recalled to Kent that Briggs was quick to take him to task after what most considered a stellar performance at the Bob Dylan thirtieth anniversary concert in 1992 at New York City's Madison Square Garden. "He told me what was wrong with my performance at Bob-Aid. Everyone else was telling me how great it was. . . . His opinion was, 'Yeah, it was great, OK. It was great, *but* forget about that because what was wrong was . . . this, this and this. . . . No one'll probably notice, but. . . . '"

Briggs was born in Douglas, Wyoming, and ran away from home when he was fifteen, hitchhiking to Los Angeles. He ultimately landed a job as a staff producer at Tetragrammaton Records, a label owned by Bill Cosby, where Briggs first worked with comedian Murray Roman. Young was hardly Briggs' only rock association, however; his credits also include Spirit's landmark *The Twelve Dreams of Sardonicus* as well as albums by Alice Cooper, Steve Young, Nick Cave and the Bad Seeds, Royal Trux, and 13 Engines. His wife, Bettina Linnenberg, often worked alongside Briggs as his production coordinator.

Briggs was also a mentor to a young Nils Lofgren and his band, Grin, which had moved from the East Coast to Los Angeles at the behest of Briggs and Young. Lofgren said:

*David really took us under [his] wing and taught us so much, not just about recording but about writing songs and performing and just making music—and life. He let you know when something wasn't right but always knew how to fix it and make sure you knew how to fix it next time. It was like being in a master class on music every time you were with him, and I really treasured that.*

Briggs also played the role of Dr. Decibel in the theatrical *Rust Never Sleeps* show. And he worked on some material that posthumously surfaced on *Year of the Horse* and on the 2009 *Archives Vol. 1* set.

## JACK NITZSCHE

**JACK NITZSCHE WAS ALREADY** a known and proven commodity when he first worked with Neil Young in 1967.

The Chicago-born, Michigan-raised Nitzsche moved to Hollywood in the mid-'50s to attend Westlake College of Music. He got a job first as a copyist and then as a writer and arranger at the Specialty, Capitol, and Original Sound labels. Phil Spector hired him as one of his in-house arrangers, and his résumé grew to include the Rolling Stones, Marianne

Faithfull, Bobby Darin, Tim Buckley, the Monkees, Frankie Laine, and Doris Day, as well as some film scoring. Nitzsche and Sonny Bono also co-wrote the Jackie DeShannon hit "Needles and Pins."

Nitzsche's association with Young began when they worked together on "Expecting to Fly," an epic that they spent a month recording while Young was out of Buffalo Springfield in 1967 but that wound up on *Buffalo Springfield Again* after he rejoined the band. Young has long considered it "probably one of the best records I ever made." The Springfield had, in fact, considered Nitzsche to produce its first album until managers Charlie Greene and Brian Stone talked the group into using them instead. Meticulously arranged and lushly orchestrated, "Expecting to Fly" was a decided product of the Summer of Love that took the Springfield's sound in an entirely different direction.

When the Springfield split for good, Young retained Nitzsche to co-produce the *Neil Young* album. Nitzsche also made contributions to *After the Gold Rush*, *Harvest*, *Time Fades Away*, and *Tonight's the Night*, and he toured with Young as part of the Stray Gators. He also co-produced and played as part of the band on Crazy Horse's 1971 self-titled debut and the following year's *At Crooked Lake*. Nitzsche and Young had a falling out when the former made some scathing interview comments in 1974—not to mention his subsequently taking up with Young's ex-girlfriend Carrie Snodgress—but Nitzsche returned to the fold later on to help out with *Life* in 1987 and *Harvest Moon* in 1992.

Nitzsche had acknowledged battles with depression and substance abuse. "Jack was pretty steady. Really. He was just fucked up all the time," Young told McDonough. And yet he also produced Graham Parker's celebrated *Squeezing Out Sparks*, mentored and championed Willy DeVille, won an Academy Award for co-writing "Up Where We Belong" from 1982's *An Officer and a Gentleman* (with Buffy Sainte-Marie, whom he married in 1983); and worked on film scores for *Performance*, *The Exorcist*, *One Flew over the Cuckoo's Nest*, and *Stand by Me*.

Nitzsche died on August 5, 2000, after suffering a heart attack in Hollywood at the age of sixty-three.

## NIKO BOLAS

**BEFORE HE BECAME A PRODUCER** and engineer, Niko Bolas ran a racing pit crew team and a Suzuki motorcycle dealership in New York—an appropriate enough background for someone who has dealt with high-octane vehicles in the music world, too.

Since he helped build Record One Studios in Los Angeles during the mid-'70s, he's worked with the likes of Sting, Keith Richards, Warren Zevon, Melissa Etheridge, John Mayer, Billy Joel, and Don Henley, as well as film luminaries such as Martin Scorsese and Pixar Animation Studios. But Neil Young has been Bolas' most frequent client, with production and/or engineering credits on eleven Young albums since *Landing on Water* in 1986 and one Crosby, Stills, Nash & Young album: *American Dream*.

In a testimonial on Bolas' website, Young announces, via a word balloon on a photo of him and Bolas, that "Niko's great. He'll try anything." And Young, apparently, will listen to anything; his half-sister and sometimes backing vocalist Astrid Young told biographer Jimmy McDonough, "If Niko has an idea about something, he's not scared to tell Neil. A lotta people tiptoe around Neil, 'cause he's really intense and can be volatile, but Niko has no fear. Neil once said that Niko is God."

Bolas—who co-produces with Young as the "Volume Dealers"—told McDonough that he did not come into Young's orbit as a fan but rather as a gun for hire. He had already established a rep for capturing up-front, in-your-face vocal recordings while working with Danny Kortchmar on *Landing on Water* after their success on Don Henley's *Building the Perfect Beast*. "It was just another gig to me," Bolas explained, "so I met Neil on a brand-new level."

Young has kept Bolas busy but not so much so that he can't work with other artists or try other endeavors. Among the latter have been Fakespace Music, which created virtual reality music experiences; the Internet radio receiver Sonicbox; and the Just Great Entertainment music marketing company. He remains primarily a producer and engineer, however, and has a home base in Nashville's Blackbird Studio.

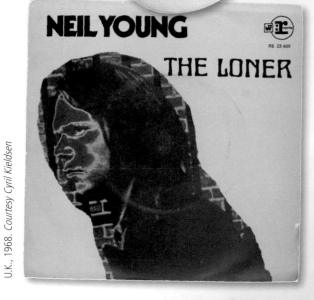

U.K., 1968. Courtesy Cyril Kieldsen

California, 1969.

DOUG WESTON'S
*Troubadour*
CR. 6-6168
9081 SANTA MONICA BLVD., L.A.
• DINNER
• COCKTAILS
• HOOT ON MONDAYS
• NO AGE LIMIT

THRU JUNE 22
**NEIL YOUNG**
AND
**CAMP HILLTOP**
COMING JUNE 24
POCO

**Unshackled from Buffalo Springfield,**
Young sought to distance himself from the hectic Hollywood
music scene he'd helped expand. He signed a solo deal with
Warner/Reprise Records and used the advance money to
buy a house in Topanga Canyon, a bucolic artist enclave
and hippie hangout just outside Los Angeles. He also met
and married Susan Acevedo, an earthy, no-nonsense woman
eight years his senior who ran a local diner called the
Canyon Kitchen.

As much as it was his intention to "get out to the sticks
and just relax," as he told *Rolling Stone,* Young quickly
began work on his first solo album. Jack Nitzsche, whose
production and arranging skills served Young so well near
the end of the Springfield era, helped him painstakingly
create the lush, layered soundscapes of "The Old Laughing
Lady" and "I've Loved Her So Long."

Another long-term collaborator soon entered the mix:
producer David Briggs, who first met Young in 1968 when he
saw the scraggly guitarist hitchhiking on the side of the road
and offered him a ride. A wildman denizen of Topanga and
staff producer for Bill Cosby's Tetragrammatron label, Briggs
had his own ideas about how to produce rock 'n' roll records.
But the loose, spontaneous style he would develop with
Young as years progressed is not in evidence on *Neil Young.*
Instead, the basic tracks—featuring Springfield bassist Jim
Messina and George Grantham, the drummer from Messina's
new band, Poco—were recorded in standard fashion in
several L.A. studios, with strings, keyboards, and Young's
vocals added later.

**RIVERBOAT**
COFFEE HOUSE
134 YORKVILLE AVE. 922-6216
EVERY NIGHT
(EXCEPT MONDAY)
8 p.m. - 3 a.m.

The Riverboat re-opens Jan. 6 with an important new composer
and folksinger that everyone is talking about . . .

**Maurey Haydn**

JAN.
14—26
**BUDDY GUY**
CHICAGO BLUES BAND
Brilliant guitarist, outstanding blues vocalist

JAN. 28—FEB. 2
**MIKE SEEGER**

FEB.
4—9
**NEIL YOUNG**
former lead guitarist, singer, composer with
THE BUFFALO SPRINGFIELD

FEB. 11—16
**DOC WATSON**

FEB. 18—23
**JOHN HAMMOND**
His voice is a supple multi-coloured instrument capturing the
tension, rhythmic drive and emotional anguish of the deep blues...
Robert Sheldon, New York Times

**SPIDER JOHN KOERNER**
FEB. 25 — MARCH 2

**JERRY JEFF WALKER**
MARCH 4 — 9
Hit single and album Mr. BOJANGLES

**Lenny Breau**
master guitarist jams the Riverboat every time.
MARCH 11 — 16

THE RIVERBOAT presents at MASSEY HALL
**GORDON LIGHTFOOT** MARCH 29, 30, 31

Toronto, Ontario, 1969. Courtesy John Einarson

Broken Arrow Ranch, Redwood City, California, June 1, 1971. © Henry Diltz/Corbis

Young would come to characterize his solo debut as "overdub city."

Each side of the LP begins tentatively, with an instrumental track: side one with "The Emperor of Wyoming," a polite, Western-inflected number, and side two with Nitzsche's moody composition "String Quartet from Whiskey Boot Hill." Some classic numbers emerge along the way, however, including "The Loner"—a bit of self-mythologizing on Young's part, perhaps, as it concerns a menacing (but emotionally vulnerable) figure who is "the unforeseen danger, the keeper of the keys to the locks." "The Old Laughing Lady" is given both grandeur and grit by Nitzsche's use of strings complemented by the middle section's haunting tribal chant, courtesy of a chorus of female singers that included Merry Clayton and Nitzsche's wife, Gracia. Perhaps Briggs' most substantial contribution to the proceedings is Young's electric guitar tone on "The Loner" and "I've Been Waiting for You." It's fat, frenzied, and fuzzed out—a hint of the souped-up sonics to come.

When the album was released, it made minimal impact, hampered in part by a cover that didn't include Young's name. There was only a painting—and a slightly creepy one at that—of Young's visage, with hills and a fiery sunset in the background, plus upside-down skyscrapers surreally reflected in his clothes. It was painted by Topanga artist Ronald Diehl, a friend of Acevedo's.

More significantly, the sound of the music was off, too, since it had been run through an experimental mastering process without Young's consent. A second pressing of the disc eliminated the sonic flaws and included Young's name on the cover. Still, Young himself took responsibility for the album's overly cautious approach. "If I had left it alone at an earlier stage, it would have been better," he told Jimmy McDonough. "Like a lot of that Buffalo Springfield stuff—I went on working and fucked it up. I don't do that anymore. Thank God I got that out of my system at an early age."

Soon enough, Young would find the band he needed to create music that was ragged, yes, but undeniably right. In fact, he'd found it already.

Sometime in the hazy days of the Springfield's rise to fame, Young met the Rockets and jammed at the group's Laurel Canyon "headquarters." Danny Whitten, Billy Talbot, and Ralph Molina had relocated to California from the East and formed the vocal group Danny and the Memories. They recorded a single that went nowhere before moving to San Francisco and picking up instruments—guitar, bass, and drums, respectively. They recorded another single, this time as the psychedelic Psyrcle, but failed to break through once again. Back in L.A., they joined with violinist Bobby Notkoff and guitarist Leon Whitsell—later adding his brother George, another guitarist—and formed the Rockets.

Young heard the band's 1968 self-titled debut album and agreed to sit in when the Rockets played the Whisky. For the occasion, he broke out his new guitar—a sonically unwieldy 1953 Gibson Les Paul that had previously belonged to Jim Messina. It had been daubed with black paint and christened Old Black. Matched with a vintage Fender Deluxe amplifier, the guitar would inspire Young to create some of the most exciting electric music of his career. And so would the Rockets. "They were real primitive, but they had a lot of soul," he told PBS's *American Masters*.

# INTO THE BLACK *Neil Young's Favorite Guitar*

**JIM MESSINA, NEIL YOUNG'S BANDMATE** in Buffalo Springfield, owned a black-painted 1953 Gibson Les Paul Goldtop that he found, in the words of Young biographer Jimmy McDonough, "uncontrollable"—and therefore perfect for Young. "I liked the way it looked, but it was just terrible," Messina, who traded the guitar to Young for one of his Gretsch models, told McDonough. "It sounded like hell. Neil loved it."

He still does.

Old Black, as the instrument came to be known, has been Young's primary electric guitar since he played it on an album by Elyse Weinberg, a musical colleague from Toronto. He then unleashed it on his self-titled solo debut and, to better effect, on its successor, *Everybody Knows This Is Nowhere*. It's the guitar with which he gets the "big, distorted mess" of a sound he favors, especially when playing with Crazy Horse. Young has noted, though, that "occasionally other things come out of it, a lot of clear things" as well.

Old Black has a well-worn exterior and a strip of exposed wood along the backside. Like the rest of Young's instrumental arsenal, it has been highly customized. A sensitive, semi-humbucking Firebird pickup was installed in the bridge position circa 1973, with the original P-90 neck pickup covered by a metal P-90 cover that's more common to Gibson ES-330 models. A small toggle switch that sits between the guitar's volume and tone knobs allows Young to bypass the usual capacitors and potentiometers and instead send the signal directly to his amplifier—or, more accurately, to the Whizzer, a self-invented device that controls the flow of sound to Young's assortment of amps.

Old Black also has a wealth of metal hardware, including Schaller M-6 tuning keys, a metal truss rod plate, a more secure set of knobs for the guitar strap, an aluminum pick guard on the front, and an aluminum access plate on the back that allows Young—or his longtime guitar tech Larry Cragg—to adjust the guitar's intonation. Young also uses a Bigsby V-7 vibrato "whammy bar" tailpiece, an old-fashioned accessory that he considers more flexible and "expressive" than more contemporary models.

Young almost always lays Old Black across his shoulder with a strap—made by Souldier and later attached to a wider Levi's fabric—with embroidered images of peace symbols and doves.

Gibson's custom department made a small number of Old Black reissues for Yamano Music, the company's distributor in Japan, circa 2003. They all quickly sold and have since demanded five-figure (or higher) prices on the collector's market.

*Neil Young* and
*Everybody Knows This Is Nowhere*
compilation double LP.

After inviting Whitten, Talbot, and Molina to jam at his house in Topanga, Young sensed the moment was there to be captured and booked studio time immediately. As a consequence, the Rockets were history. The new band was called Crazy Horse.

"I think I went in there and I asked those three guys to play with me as Crazy Horse," Young recalled in the film *Year of the Horse*. "And I thought the Rockets could go on, too. But the truth is, I probably did steal them away from the other band, which was a good band. But only because what we did, we went somewhere. What they were doing, it didn't go anywhere at that time, so this thing moved, this thing took off, and the other thing didn't. But the other thing could have gone on, I

guess. That's the hardest part, is the guilt of the trail of destruction that I've left behind me."

Wherever the Rockets might have gone, it seems unlikely that the band could have reached, on its own, the heights to which Young took Crazy Horse on *Everybody Knows This Is Nowhere*. Recorded quickly with the band playing live and loud in the studio (although the vocals were still overdubbed), it's the antithesis of Young's debut album. Among the songs are several of his most enduring classics: "Cinnamon Girl," "Cowgirl in the Sand," and "Down by the River," all of which were written in a single day while Young was sick with the flu and a high fever. In the liner notes to *Decade*, Young said he wrote "Cinnamon Girl" "for a city girl on a peeling pavement

CSNY with drummer Dallas Taylor and bassist Greg Reeves, July 14, 1969. © *Henry Diltz/Corbis*

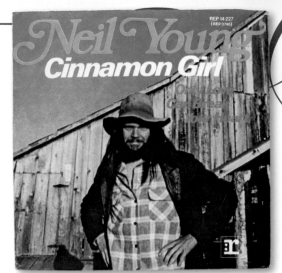

coming at me, thru Phil Ochs' eyes playing finger cymbals. It was hard to explain to my wife."

No doubt.

The title track reflects Young's desire to escape the empty hustle of the L.A. scene, while two songs, "Round & Round" and "Running Dry," pay their respects to two bands—the Springfield and the Rockets, respectively—that died in part because of his actions.

"River" and "Cowgirl," the album's true showcase numbers, unwind into extended jams, allowing Young to fly high and far on Old Black, safe in the knowledge that he is tethered to the earth by the Horse's leaden, locked-in groove. And it's not just his playing that's improved here. Bolstered by the vocal harmonies of the Horse, he sings with heretofore unheard confidence. "There's a chemistry when I play with [Crazy Horse] that frees me to go places I don't go with anybody else," Young told *American Masters*. "It's just a matter of choosing the ride."

With the Horse in full gallop, Young's next move proved nothing short of astonishing. He set the band aside and agreed to work again with his chief Springfield antagonist, Stephen Stills. This time, though, it would be in the context of the most popular band in the land: the newly constituted Crosby, Stills & Nash.

In the wake of the Springfield's demise, Stills had taken up with former Byrd David Crosby, who had been cast out of that band over creative and personal differences, and Graham Nash of the Hollies, who felt the staid English group was holding him back creatively. Brought together by Crosby's then-girlfriend Joni Mitchell and musical matchmaker Mama Cass Elliot (although that tale, like Young and Stills' cute meet on Sunset Boulevard, has its own variations), the trio instantly recognized its potential and joined forces. Their album *Crosby, Stills & Nash* was a smash hit out of the gate. But the idea of touring presented a problem: Stills had played most of the

## With the Horse in full gallop, Young's next move proved nothing short of astonishing. He set the band aside and agreed to work again with his chief Springfield antagonist, Stephen Stills.

instruments in the recording studio; in concert, they'd need a band.

Despite their fractious past, Stills wanted Neil Young for the job. As offered, it was something less than a full partnership. Young rejected that proposal and had manager Elliot Roberts inform CSN that if he were to join, they'd have to add a Y to the group name.

Choosing to remember the good times, Young claimed that reuniting with Stills was a major factor in his decision to join the group. But he also acknowledged that the job put him in the catbird seat: There was much to gain and little to lose in joining a group already on top. Young told *Rolling Stone*:

> I knew it would be fun. I didn't have to be out front. I could lay back. It didn't have to be me all the time. They were a big group and it was easy for me. I could still work double time with Crazy Horse. With CSNY, I was basically just an instrumentalist that sang a couple of songs with them. It was easy. And the music was great. CSNY, I think, has always been a lot bigger thing to everybody else than it is to us. People always refer to me as Neil Young of CSNY, right? It's not my main trip. It's something that I do every once in a while. I've constantly been working on my own trip all along.

His refusal to commit 100 percent to the band gave Young an inordinate amount of power, and he had no misgivings about wielding it. At the freshly minted supergroup's second gig, the Woodstock Music and Art Fair in Bethel, New York, Young refused to allow filmmakers to document his portion of the performance. As a result, only CSN are seen in the resulting movie. Young told *Mojo*:

> *I didn't allow myself to be filmed because I didn't want [the cameramen] on the stage. Because we were playing music. I thought, if they were going to film they'd have to stay off the stage—get away, don't be in my way, I don't want to see your cameras, I don't want to see you. I'm still very much the same way. I really didn't see what television and films had to do with making music. To me it was a distraction—because music is something that you listen to, not that you look at. You're there, you're playing and you're trying to get lost in the music, and there's this dickhead with a camera right in your face. So the only way to make sure that that wouldn't happen is tell them that I wouldn't be in the film, so there was no sense in filming me—avoid me, stay away from my area. And it worked.*

Artist: Peter Pontiac
(www.peterpontiac.com)

As the band's popularity grew, so did the quartet's individual egos. As vocalists, CSN (and sometimes Y) were capable of tight and gorgeous harmonies. As instrumentalists, Stills and Young's guitar duels—whether born of camaraderie or competition—became the stuff of legend. But inevitably, it all went to their heads, as did, in the case of Crosby and Stills in particular, copious amounts of cocaine and other drugs. "The reaction to CSNY was ridiculous," Young told *American Masters*. "It was so over the top, and then we all became distracted by that. We were just showy. And it was because we had no idea what we were doing. It's not because there was anything wrong with anybody in the band. It's just that what we were confronted with . . . changed us. The crowd, the adulation, the roaring sound. It changed us."

The group also angered Young by signing on for glitzy showbiz gigs, such as two appearances on TV's *This Is Tom Jones*. Young, after all, once left Buffalo Springfield temporarily because he didn't want to appear on the far more legit *Tonight Show*. On the second *Jones* show, the ultraswanky host even joined the band to sing, "Long Time Gone." Neil reluctantly showed up for the TV appearances.

Through all the ego trips, arguments, and temporary breakups—as well as more serious matters, such as the death of Crosby's girlfriend, Christine Hinton, in an auto accident—the band did manage to record the album *Déjà Vu*. Predictably, it was a torturous experience. "I remember one session towards the end of the *Déjà Vu* record where

CSNY, Woodstock Music & Art Fair, Yasgur's Farm, White Lake, New York, August 17, 1969. *Photo by Barry Z Levine/Getty Images*

we were arguing," Nash told *American Masters*. "There were too many drugs involved. Stephen was staying up all night trying to write and trying to create. And there was one point towards the end there where I started crying and I said . . . that we're blowing this."

"Young guys, big egos," Crosby concurred. "Lots of money. Very easy, very unstable, very easy for us to come unglued at any point. 'Well, I don't need that sonofabitch.' . . . In my case, hard drugs were damaging me enormously at that point and made it difficult for me to do a good job or be a good brother to my brothers."

As for Young, he remained reticent throughout the sessions, hoarding songs for his future solo releases. He also chafed at the method of recording, which emphasized overdubbed perfection over the live, on-the-fly method he now preferred. Young told *Rolling Stone*:

*The band sessions on that record were "Helpless," "Woodstock" and "Almost Cut My Hair." That was Crosby, Stills, Nash & Young. All the other ones were combinations, records that were more done by one person using the other people. "Woodstock" was a great record at first. It was a great live record, man. Everyone played and sang at once, Stephen sang the shit out of it. The track was magic. Then, later on, they were in the studio for a long time and started nitpicking. Sure enough, Stephen erased the vocal and put another one on that wasn't nearly as incredible. They did a lot of things over again that I thought were more raw and vital sounding. But that's all personal taste. I'm only saying that because it might be interesting to some people how we put that album together. I'm happy with every one of the things I've recorded with them. They turned out really fine. I certainly don't hold any grudges.*

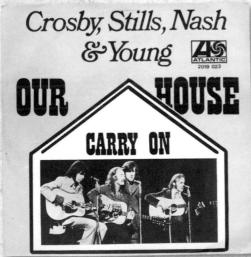

U.K., 1970.

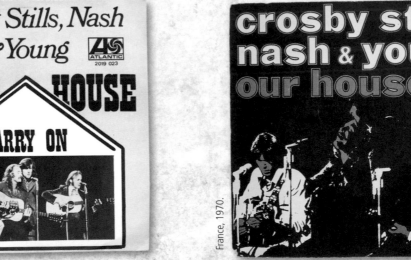

France, 1970.

Germany, 1970.

Japan, 1970.

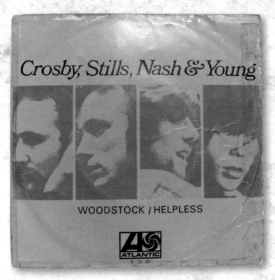

Portugal, 1970.

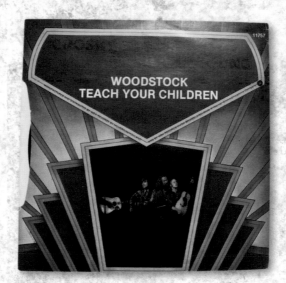

The Netherlands, 1970.

Spain, 1970.

Germany, 1970.

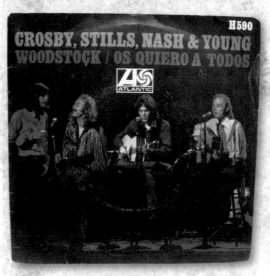

Spain, 1970.

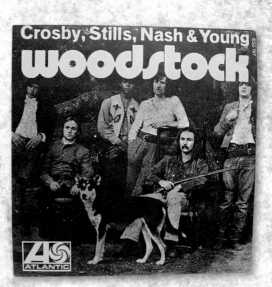

Backed with "Helpless," France, 1970.

Japan, 1970.

The Netherlands, 1970.

Japan, 1970.

Young's contributions were the exquisite "Helpless," his loving tribute to Omemee, the "town in North Ontario" where he most enjoyed growing up; and "Country Girl (I Think You're Pretty)"—a suite of songs that, despite Young's claims of satisfaction, suffered a bad case of "overdub city."

Divisiveness often threatened to swallow CSNY whole, but Young tried to separate the creative friction from outright hostility. "Everyone always concentrates on this whole thing that we fight all the time among each other," he told *Rolling Stone*. "That's a load of shit. They don't know what the fuck they're talking about. It's all rumors. When the four of us are together it's real intense. When you're dealing with any four totally different people who all have ideas on how to do one thing, it gets steamy. And we love it, man. We're having a great time."

Young shuttled back and forth between CSNY and Crazy Horse, recording a batch of songs intended for his next album, *After the Gold Rush*. The title and the inspiration for some of the songs was a script written by actor and Topanga resident Dean Stockwell. Young told *Mojo*:

> It was all about the day of the great earthquake in Topanga Canyon when a great wave of water flooded the place. It was a pretty "off-the-wall" concept, they tried to get some money from Universal Pictures. But that fell through because it was too much of an art project. I think, had it been made it would stand as a contemporary to Easy Rider and it would have had a similar effect. The script itself was full of imagery, "change." . . . It was very unique actually. I really wish that movie had been made, because it could have really defined an important moment in the culture.

On tour, the Horse was joined by Jack Nitzsche on piano and played some torrid concerts, including two in New York that would eventually see the light of day as *Live at the Fillmore East March 6 & 7, 1970.* The shows represent the original Crazy Horse at its creative peak.

But it was short-lived. Danny Whitten had begun using heroin, and his ability to play—and indeed, to even *maintain*—atrophied quickly. When Whitten nodded off onstage, Young became resolved; as soon as the tour ended, he fired the band.

After scrapping most of the earlier sessions with Crazy Horse, Young began the *Gold Rush* album again, this time recording in the basement of his house in Topanga. Along for the ride this time were Ralph Molina, CSNY bassist Greg Reeves, and Nils Lofgren, a seventeen-year-old guitarist from Washington, D.C., whom Young had taken under his wing. The songs were cut live, including the

*(continued on page 62)*

London, January 1970. *Photo by Dick Barnatt/Redferns/Getty Images*

SIGHT & SOUND PRODUCTIONS presents

★ IN CONCERT ★
**NEIL YOUNG**
and
**CRAZY HORSE**
SAT. MARCH 28
SANTA MONICA CIVIC AUDITORIUM
TICKETS: $5.50, 4.50, 3.50

On sale at Civic Aud. Box Office, All Mutual Ticket Agencies, Music
City Stores, Sight & Sound Stores. Mail Orders to Civic Aud.

PRODUCED IN CONJUNCTION WITH KRLA

*California, 1970.*

With Crazy Horse, California, March 1970. © Robert Altman/Retna Ltd.

*New York, 1970.*

BILL GRAHAM PRESENTS IN NEW YORK

Tuesday Nights
at 8 PM
3 New Groups
1 New Light Show
$1.50 at the Door

FRIDAY & SATURDAY, FEBRUARY 20 & 21
**SAVOY BROWN**
**KINKS**
Keith Relf's
**RENAISSANCE**

SUNDAY, FEB. 22—7:30 PM ONLY
**RAVI SHANKAR**
Sitar
W/ZAKIR QUERESHI
(Son of Alla Rakha)
Tabla
ONLY USA APPEARANCE
Produced in association with Jay K. Hoffman

BY POPULAR DEMAND
THURSDAY, FEBRUARY 26
**TEN YEARS AFTER**
**ZEPHYR**
EXTRA ADDED ATTRACTION:
**JOHN HAMMOND**

FRIDAY & SATURDAY, FEBRUARY 27 & 28
**TEN YEARS AFTER**
**DOUG KERSHAW**
**ZEPHYR**

FRIDAY & SATURDAY, MARCH 6 & 7
**NEIL YOUNG**
and
**CRAZY HORSE**
**STEVE MILLER**
**BLUES BAND**
EXTRA ADDED ATTRACTION:
**MILES DAVIS**
QUINTET

FRIDAY & SATURDAY, MARCH 13 & 14
**JOHN MAYALL**
w/Duster Bennett
**B.B. KING**
**TAJ MAHAL**

SUNDAY, MARCH 15—8:30 PM ONLY
**JOHN MAYALL**
w/Duster Bennett
**TAJ MAHAL**

FRIDAY & SATURDAY, MARCH 20 & 21
**MOODY BLUES**
**LEE MICHAELS**
**ARGENT**

FRIDAY & SATURDAY, MARCH 27 & 28
**JOE COCKER**
AND
THE **GREASE BAND**
**BRIAN AUGER & THE TRINITY**
**STONE THE CROWS**

FRIDAY & SATURDAY, APRIL 3 & 4
**QUICKSILVER**
MESSENGER SERVICE

SUNDAY, APRIL 5—8:00 PM
**TOM PAXTON**
ONLY NEW YORK APPEARANCE
Produced in association with Jay K. Hoffman

THURSDAY, APRIL 9—8:30 PM
J. K. Hoffman presents
**PINK FLOYD**
ONLY NEW YORK APPEARANCE

FRI., SAT. & SUN., APRIL 10, 11 & 12
**SANTANA**
**BEAUTIFUL DAY**
AND AT EVERY SHOW
**JOSHUA LIGHT SHOW**

**FILLMORE**
**EAST**
SECOND AVENUE AT SIXTH STREET

PROGRAM SUBJECT TO CHANGE

53

2 SHOWS NIGHTLY-8 & 11:30. ALL SEATS RESERVED: $3.50,
4.50, 5.50. BOX OFFICE OPEN MON.-THURS.: NOON TO 9
P. M./FRI.-SAT.: NOON-MIDNIGHT/INFO:(212) 777-5260
MAIL ORDERS: CHECK OR MONEY ORDER PAYABLE

# Four Strong Winds

## CSNY Then, Now & Forever

David Crosby, Stephen Stills, and Graham Nash were happy enough after recording the first *Crosby, Stills & Nash* album, released *May 1969*. But as the group prepared to perform live, it was clear that another musician was needed to deliver a fuller sound and to free up Stills—who had been dubbed Captain Manyhands for his prodigious work on the album—on the stage. "Stephen was the only lead guitar player," Nash recalled. "He needed someone to play off, and it wasn't me and David. We're fine musicians, but we're rhythm guitar players. He needed another solo axe to play off, to converse with. He needed sparking by someone else who he could say, 'Well, fuck you, listen to *this*' and drive each other to new heights. And he had just spent the previous six years playing against Neil in the Springfield."

CSN first considered inviting Mark Naftalin of the Paul Butterfield Blues Band and Steve Winwood, late of Traffic and at the time headed into Blind Faith. Atlantic Records chief Ahmet Ertegun suggested Young to Stills, who initially rejected the idea, still smarting from Young's decision to bail on Buffalo Springfield just before its appearance on NBC's *Tonight Show*. Stills eventually changed his mind, but Crosby and Nash had to be convinced. "I wanted to find out who this was," said Nash, who met with Young over breakfast at a diner on Bleeker Street in Greenwich Village in the spring of *1969*. "I had great respect for him as a writer and musician. But I didn't know who he was. After that breakfast, I'd have given him my firstborn. . . . He had such an incredible outlook on music, an incredible outlook in life. He was funny as fuck. And he picked up the check—not necessarily in that order."

Buffalo Springfield cohort Bruce Palmer was CSNY's bassist briefly in the spring of *1969*. After reported ego clashes, he was replaced by Motown session man Greg Reeves, who played on the Temptations' Grammy Award–winning "Cloud Nine" and was recommended by Young's former Mynah Birds bandmate Rick James.

CSNY's second concert was in the wee hours of *August 17, 1969*, at the Woodstock Music and Art Fair—where Young was the only musician to refuse the film crew permission to shoot him. "I was there, but I wasn't really into it," Young later explained. Crosby remembered the night as "kind of nerve-wracking for us. It was only our second show.

Everybody we knew or cared about in the music industry was there. They were heroes to us—The Band and Hendrix and the Who. . . . They were all standing behind us in a circle, like, 'OK, you're the new kids on the block. Show us.'" Bob Weir of the Grateful Dead remembered that the quartet's potential spoke louder than its actual performance. "I was a little disappointed," he said. "They were new to the stage, at that point still mostly a studio band, and they weren't as tight as they got to be in the years since."

CSNY also performed at the Altamont festival in *December 1969* but avoided the controversies of other bands that played at the violence-plagued event.

Young was only a part-time presence in the studio while recording *1970's Déjà Vu*, the quartet's debut album. He recorded the basic tracks for "Helpless," which he'd also tried out with Crazy Horse, and the "Country Girl" suite on his own and simply had his partners add their vocals to the tapes—although he did perform Crosby's "Almost Cut My Hair" and the Joni Mitchell cover "Woodstock" live in the studio.

Despite his reputation as a rocker and his fierce electric guitar duels with Stills, Young's contributions to CSNY over the years have been, on balance, surprisingly mellow. "You have a point there when relating it to *Déjà Vu*, *American Dream*, and *Looking Forward*," Young acknowledged. A notable exception is the fierce "Ohio," which protested the shooting of four students during a demonstration on *May 4, 1970*, at Kent State University in Ohio. Young wrote the song immediately upon hearing the news, and the group recorded it less than two weeks later. It was out the following month, peaking at No. 14 on the *Billboard* charts. "It's very personal with Neil," Crosby explained to PBS's *American Masters*. "He's not very political in the sense of politics. He doesn't like 'em. . . . But if you show him a picture of that girl kneeling over that kid in a pool of blood at Kent State, then he writes 'Ohio.' . . . He was pissed. And sad."

Crosby, Stills, and Nash all contributed backing vocals on Young's smash *1972* album *Harvest*. CSNY considered touring again that year, but it never materialized.

- CSNY did some recording in Hawaii and California during **1973** for an album tentatively titled *Human Highway* that never saw the light of day. Songs included Stills' "See the Changes," Nash's "Prison Song," Young's "Sailboat Song," and the proposed title track.

- CSNY's **1974** jaunt was the first stadium trek ever by a rock band. The quartet recorded following the tour, including songs such as "Long May You Run," "The End," "Traces," "Love Art Blues," "Pushed It Over the End," and "Homeward through the Haze" before Young ankled the scene. "He came into the studio and said, 'Great, out of sight. I'll be back tomorrow night' and never showed again," Crosby recalled.

- Young and Stills recruited Crosby and Nash to sing on several songs for their **1976** album, *Long May You Run*. Their vocals were subsequently yanked from finished recording.

- CSNY let bygones be bygones on **July 13, 1985**, when the band played together in public for the first time in ten years at the Live Aid concert in Philadelphia. Monitor problems plagued the set, which included "Only Love Can Break Your Heart" and "Daylight Again"/"Find the Cost of Freedom." Young, with the International Harvesters, and CSN each performed their own sets earlier in the day.

- CSNY's second studio album, **1988's** *American Dream*, was the result of Young's promise to Crosby that he'd do anything Crosby wished if he would clean up the debilitating drug habit that helped land him in a Texas prison earlier in the decade. "And one of the things I wanted was to record with all the guys again," Crosby said. The group did not tour to support the album, however, due to Stills' substance abuse issues. "I don't see us working together until everybody is as strong as they can be," Nash said at the time. "I don't want anyone looking at CSN&Y and saying, 'Look at those four old guys.'"

- Young was lured back into the CSNY fold in **1999**, when he and Stills were working on a Buffalo Springfield box set and Stills played him some songs that CSN was working on in Los Angeles. Young was particularly impressed that the three had left their longtime label, Atlantic Records, and were financing what became *Looking Forward* themselves. He presented the others with a group of songs he had recorded for his own album, *Silver & Gold*, and told them to "take the best ones you think you can do the best job on."

- Young's reaction to the **September 11, 2001**, terrorist attacks was the impetus behind CSNY's 2002 tour. "We got a call from Neil who was talking about that maybe it's a good time to go out and play some music for the folks," Nash said. "It seemed to make sense to us. It was a little earlier than we had kind of planned in our lives but, y'know . . . so what? We're just reflecting the time, like we've always done."

- A CSNY tour was already in motion for **2006** when Young recorded his Grammy Award–nominated album of "metal folk protest music," *Living with War*, and asked the group to make it the focal point of the shows. "I just said to the other guys, 'Listen, this [music] is all I can do. I can't mix this up with anything else,'" Young said. "For us to water it down and sprinkle in our old romantic ballads to try and soften it . . . I said, 'There's no reason to soften it. We should just treat it like journalism and go for it and try to do this.'" His bandmates were wholeheartedly behind the idea. "We saw an opportunity to do what it is we do best," Nash explained, "which is communicate ideas with people, communicate different points of view, communicate subjects that maybe other people don't want to talk about. Obviously Neil could've done [the tour] on his own and created a certain buzz, but it's a different buzz with CSNY. I think we just took advantage of the situation. What happens is if we have a bunch of songs we want to sing, that's an excuse to tour."

- Young called the audience-polarizing Freedom of Speech Tour, which was documented on the **2008** *CSNY/Déjà Vu* film and live album, "the most nerve-wracking tour I've ever done." Nash said it was "the first tour I was on with bomb-sniffing dogs and FBI agents at the gigs."

- At this juncture, Young is considered the leader of CSNY, what Crosby calls the "benevolent dictator" who determines when and how the group works together. "Neil always has a lot of ideas, and they're usually very good, and I'll follow anybody who has a good idea," Nash added. Young himself rejects the leadership mantle, however. "I don't want that responsibility," he said.

CSNY Carry On European Tour, Falkonercentret,
Copenhagen, Denmark, January 16, 1970.
*Photo by Jan Persson/Redferns/Getty Images*

*Germany, 1969. Courtesy Robert Ferreira*

A large part of our job is to just make you boogie, to be a party, but another part of it is to be the troubadour, the town crier—"It's 11:30 and all's well!" or "It's 12 o'clock and there's a chimpanzee loose in the White House and things aren't too good!" That's part of our job, has been for thousands of years.

—David Crosby

This group is like juggling four bottles of nitroglycerin.

—David Crosby

Yeah—if you drop one, everything goes up in smoke.

—Graham Nash

We knew who we were. We knew nobody in the world was doing what we were doing. No one had four guys writing those kind of songs that were also that good as musicians, all at the same time. There was nobody like us. So we were a little punkish about it. We thought we were kings of the world, so it was exciting to us.

—Graham Nash

I don't like to compare us to other bands. We are who we are. When I play in this band, it's a special thing. It goes back to our roots; we've been friends for a long time, Stephen and I, and then the other guys. When they got together with Stephen, and I came and joined them, we already had our history. We already had roots in playing together and developing our music styles and learning how to play guitars together, Stephen and I.

—Neil Young

Our chemistry is really deep respect. We do best when it's the two of us, especially on electric [guitar]. With the Horse he plays differently 'cause he's by himself. When he plays with me, he's really after a balance. It takes us a few rehearsals to get back to our thing, but when we start playing together it's just as cool as when I played with Jimi [Hendrix] and Eric [Clapton] and every other great guy.

—Stephen Stills

We're more than friends. We're brothers. And, unfortunately, brothers fight occasionally. But it's been [more than] 30 years; something's going on.

—Graham Nash

There's a lot of unfinished business. I don't think we really reached our potential, and so we have a lot of things to show and a lot of things to do. This is why it's so exciting. I mean, this band can sing like the Byrds and jam like the Dead . . . and hopefully we can get the audience turned on to what we're doing and have it just be a music thing.

—Neil Young

California, 1969.

The reason I play with CSN is because . . . I don't have to sing every song, because I like playing with them. I like being with guys I've known for [so many] years that have gone through so much with me. It's a rewarding experience. It's fun to look around and see those guys.

—Neil Young

Some of the ridiculous little kid games we used to play with each other . . . were really ridiculous and just beyond belief.

—Stephen Stills

Stephen plays a great guitar. I know how to support his guitar playing. I have no problem finding things that will make him sound better just by finding certain little things underneath it that support it. And when I feel like playing lead, he can support me. That's the way we've always done it. Sometimes we both play lead at the same time. I mean, this band can space out for 45 minutes.

—Neil Young

U.K., 1970. Courtesy Robert Ferreira

Oh, man, we loved him. We loved Buffalo Springfield; that was one of the inspirational bands we tried to copy. I love Neil Young and Crazy Horse and even with Crosby, Stills, Nash & Young, all the stuff they did. He's one of our favorite writers and musicians, and he's just an unbelievable influence to me, inspirational. He's lasted all these years and keeps changing and going forth, then he'll do his old tunes just like he used to and they're still great. He's just saying what he feels, that's all. He's like a rock god.

— *Gary Rossington, Lynyrd Skynyrd*

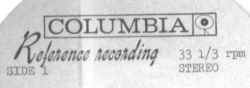

COLUMBIA
*Reference recording*    33 1/3 rpm
SIDE 1                   STEREO

NEIL YOUNG

TELL ME WHY
AFTER THE GOLD RUSH
ONLY LOVE CAN BREAK YOUR HEART
SOUTHERN MAN
TILL THE MORNING COMES

COLUMBIA
*Reference recording*    33 1/3 rpm
SIDE 2                   STEREO

NEIL YOUNG

OH LONESOME ME
DON'T LET IT BRING YOU DOWN
BIRDS
WHEN YOU DANCE I CAN REALLY LOVE
I BELIEVE IN YOU
CRIPPLED CREEK FERRY

Early *After the Gold Rush* sleeve that was printed in the wrong color, 1970. *Courtesy Cyril Kieldsen*

Test pressing of *After the Gold Rush*. Note the Columbia logo. Test-pressing labels with logos of record companies other than those of the artists reportedly were not uncommon. *Courtesy Robert Ferreira*

Recent reissue of the 1970 TWEN-Serie *After the Gold Rush* picture disc originally issued in West Germany, 1970. *Courtesy Cyril Kieldsen*

# SOUTHERN MAN

## *Neil Young's "feud" with Lynyrd Skynyrd*

**WITH 1974'S "SWEET HOME ALABAMA,"** Lynyrd Skynyrd's Ronnie Van Zant threw down a gauntlet between his band—and indeed, all of Southern rock—and Neil Young. And he didn't mean to.

The course of events that led to the non-feud between Young and Skynyrd is easy enough to trace. Young voiced critical sentiments about historical Southern racism in songs such as "Southern Man" and "Alabama." Van Zant, meanwhile, took a bit of contemporary umbrage over his perspective. "I hope Neil Young will remember," he responded in his own song, "a Southern man don't need him around anyhow."

"Yeah, I did attack him in ['Sweet Home Alabama']," Van Zant told one interviewer. He told another that "We thought Neil was shooting all the ducks in order to kill one or two. We're Southern rebels, but more than that, we know the difference between right and wrong."

Former Skynyrd drummer Artimus Pyle explained, "'Sweet Home Alabama' was Ronnie Van Zant saying, 'Don't blame me for something that happened generations back.' He was saying, 'Look, man, don't blame the Southern man now for stuff that happened a long time ago, that our great-grandfathers did. We might not have those attitudes.'"

More recently, Van Zant's younger brother Johnny, who sings in his stead in Skynyrd these days, confirmed that "My brother loved Neil Young. The whole 'Sweet Home Alabama' thing was just a fun kind of song, putting a pun up at Neil Young as far as not being Southern, [but] being Canadian." And guitarist Gary Rossington added, "We love Neil Young. We weren't really trying to cut him down. We were just cutting him down since he cut Alabama, and we loved Alabama."

The Young–Skynyrd "battle" came to take on a certain mythic proportion. VH1 named it one of the Top 40 Celebrity Feuds. Drive-By Truckers' Patterson Hood, meanwhile, turned it into the insightful "Ronnie and Neil" from 2002's *Southern Rock Opera*.

"Neil is amazing, wonderful . . . a superstar," said Van Zant, who was photographed many times wearing a Neil Young t-shirt—including on the original cover of Skynyrd's 1977 *Street Survivors*. "I showed the verse to [former Skynyrd guitarist] Ed King and asked him what Neil might think. Ed said he'd dig it. He'd be laughing at it." And, in fact, Young did, telling *Q*, "Oh, they didn't really put me down! But then again, maybe they did! But not in a way that matters. Shit, I think 'Sweet Home Alabama' is a great song."

Ronnie Van Zant wearing *Tonight's the Night* t-shirt, 1977.
Photo by Ed Perlstein/Redferns/Getty Images

Young also told *Rolling Stone*, "I'd rather play 'Sweet Home Alabama' than 'Southern Man' anytime. I first heard it and really liked the way they played their guitars. Then I heard my own name in it and thought, 'Now *this* is pretty great.'"

The true relationship between Young and Skynyrd took a deeper turn when Young passed a tape of three songs—"Powderfinger," "Sedan Delivery," and "Captain Kennedy"—through archivist Joel Bernstein to then-music journalist Cameron Crowe. He, in turn, gave it to Van Zant to consider the songs for *Street Survivors*. The songs didn't fit on that album, but Van Zant was reportedly interested in recording "Powderfinger" at a later date.

And then, of course, came the plane crash that took the lives of Van Zant and two other band members on October 20, 1977, and there were no later dates. Young paid his own tribute on November 12 at a benefit concert in Miami, when he played a rare rendition of "Alabama" and changed the chorus lyrics to "sweet home Alabama."

A posthumous Van Zant legend has the singer buried in a Neil Young t-shirt, which Rossington believes is true. "He used to always wear that shirt on stage," the guitarist recalled. "It was a Neil Young shirt we got one night we were gonna play with him. Unfortunately, he canceled and somehow didn't make it to the show, but we got the t-shirt for that gig so [Van Zant] wore it a lot. I think he was buried in that, yeah."

(continued from page 53)

vocals, giving Young the sense of immediacy and spontaneity he'd always craved. As if to up the ante, Young asked Lofgren to play piano on the album—something Lofgren didn't know how to do.

With the spare instrumentation, the songs were left to stand on their own, and *Gold Rush* is one of Young's mellowest and most poetic efforts. Among its highlights are the fragile, futuristic title track; a pair of let-you-down-easy breakup tunes, "Only Love Can Break Your Heart" and "Birds"; "Don't Let It Bring You Down," a song guaranteed to do just that, as he'd later joke in concert; and a pair of rockers, "When You Dance I Can Really Love" and "Southern Man." The latter earned Young a musical rebuke from the group Lynyrd Skynyrd, which sang in its hit song "Sweet Home Alabama," "I hope Mr. Young will remember/A southern man don't need him around anyhow." To complete the album, Young pulled a pair of tunes from the sessions with the Horse: the pleading "I Believe in You" and a wonderfully self-pitying cover of Don Gibson's country weeper "Oh Lonesome Me."

Young told *Rolling Stone* that he felt *Gold Rush* "was a strong album. . . . A lot of hard work went into it. . . . *After the Gold Rush* was the spirit of Topanga Canyon. It seemed like I realized that I'd gotten somewhere."

When Young returned to CSNY for another tour, turmoil continued to be the order of the day. Bassist Greg Reeves, emboldened perhaps by his extracurricular adventures with Young, wanted to play some of his own songs with CSNY. Crosby fired him on the spot. Reeves was replaced by Stills' bassist, Calvin "Fuzzy" Samuels. After that, drummer Dallas Taylor, who had never been a favorite of Young's, developed a heroin habit and had to go as well. Johnny Barbata, formerly of the Turtles, stepped in, and the show went on.

A reality check was on the way, however. At Kent State University in Ohio, four students were shot and killed by the National Guard during a Vietnam protest rally. Crosby showed Young the now-famous photo of a female student sinking to her knees, her arms outstretched over a fallen protester. Young wrote the song "Ohio" within minutes. It was quickly recorded and released as a single in just a few weeks. For reasons ranging from the way the song was recorded—live in the studio with the entire band present—to the way it allowed him to use music as a means of reportage, Young called it "the best record I ever made with CSNY."

"Ohio" may have given the group a new sense of purpose, but the tour was the same ego-driven mess as the one before. Several dates were recorded for the bloated live album *4 Way Street*. Young was represented on the set by acoustic renditions of "On the Way Home," "Cowgirl in the Sand," and "Don't Let It Bring You Down," plus electric takes on "Southern Man" and

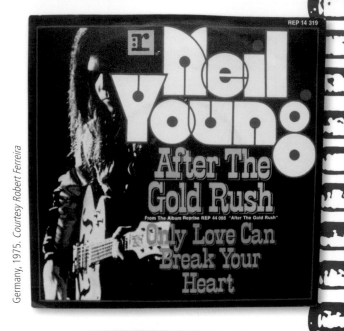

Germany, 1975. *Courtesy Robert Ferreira*

Germany promo, 1970. *Courtesy Robert Ferreira*

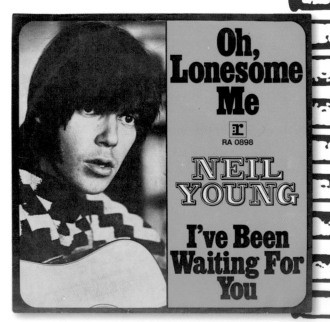

Germany, 1970. *Courtesy Cyril Kieldsen*

# GOTTA GET DOWN TO IT
## *The Making of "Ohio"*

**ON MAY 4, 1970,** U.S. National Guardsmen fatally shot four unarmed students and wounded nine others—not all of whom were part of antiwar protests taking place throughout the first four days of the month on the Kent State University campus in Ohio.

Within weeks, Crosby, Stills, Nash & Young had a hit song protesting the killings.

David Crosby described the sequence of events in the liner notes to the 1991 *Crosby, Stills & Nash* box set: "I was with Neil at a friend's house and handed him *Life* magazine with the Kent State photos. He was silent for a long time, then picked up his guitar and twenty minutes later had this song. I called Stephen and Graham and we immediately booked a studio [the Record Plant on May 21, 1970]. We gave the master to Ahmet Ertegun, who flew it to New York the next day and it was released within the week."

The hard-biting lyrics to "Ohio" spend less time on the political tenor of the incident and more asking questions like "What if you knew her and found her dead on the ground?"

"It's still hard to believe I had to write this song," Young said in the liner notes of *Decade* six years later. "It's ironic that I capitalized on the death of these American students. Probably the biggest lesson ever learned at an American place of learning."

Young called "Ohio" "my best CSNY cut" and recalled that "Crosby cried after his take." Crosby concurred:

> ["Ohio"] was a high point of the band, a major point of validity. There we were, reacting to reality, dealing with it on the highest level we could—relevant, immediate. It named names and pointed the finger. It said "Nixon." I was so moved by it that I completely lost it at the end of the song, in the recording studio, screaming ". . . Four. . . . Why? . . . How many more?"

"Ohio" was also the first CSNY recording to feature the group's new rhythm section of bassist Calvin "Fuzzy" Samuels and former Turtles drummer John Barbata.

When "Ohio" was released on June 4, 1970, CSNY had already put out its debut album, *Déjà Vu*, and was watching Nash's song "Teach Your Children" climb the charts. "We knocked it right off the charts with our own song," Crosby noted, "and Nash never said one word about it, to his great credit. He knew how important it was that this song be out there." "Ohio"

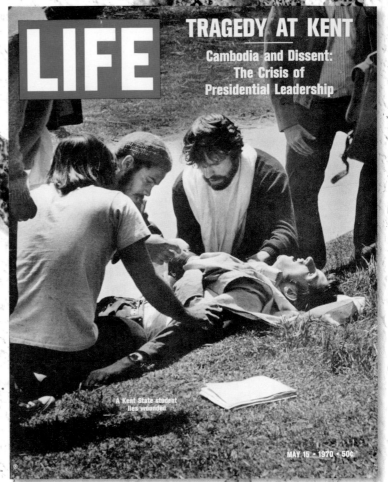

**LIFE**

**TRAGEDY AT KENT**

Cambodia and Dissent: The Crisis of Presidential Leadership

A Kent State student lies wounded

MAY 15 · 1970 · 50¢

*Photo by Howard Ruffner/Time & Life Pictures/Getty Images*

eventually reached No. 14 on the *Billboard* Hot 100, while "Teach Your Children" peaked at 16. "Ohio" was included on the live *4 Way Street* in 1971, but the studio version was never included on an album until 1974's *So Far: The Best of Crosby, Stills, Nash & Young*.

The song has been covered over the years by such artists as the Isley Brothers, Paul Weller, the Black Crowes, Tori Amos, and Gov't Mule.

Young often grappled with the disparity of a hit song about a tragedy and, for a time, felt the song's message was compromised by its popularity. But CSNY was able to reclaim the song again during the group's Freedom of Speech Tour in 2006, a politically polarizing road trek that was spurred by Young's album *Living with War*.

Upon the 2008 release of the *CSNY/Déjà Vu* film documentary of that tour, Young said:

> I've always kind of left ["Ohio"] be. But in a historical perspective . . . it reacquainted people with what the band really was in the first place, and that, I think, is the purpose ["Ohio"] played in the film. It enabled people to understand we've been singing about these types of things for a long time, and what we're doing right now is really no different than what we were doing then. The real difference is in America, not in the band.

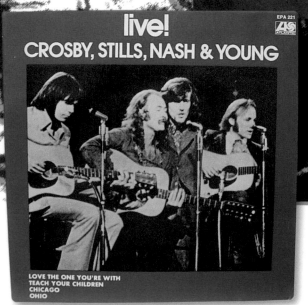

"Ohio." The album was a huge hit, but the squabbling band members went their separate ways when the tour ended. It would be three years before they joined forces again.

Returning to California, Young was determined more than ever to remove himself from the public eye. But he didn't go back to his house in Topanga. Instead, he bought a ranch just south of San Francisco and moved there—without his wife, Susan. Young's unrelenting work schedule had driven a wedge between them, and she was put off by his massive fame. She filed for divorce in October 1970.

Young went on a solo tour that included two sold-out shows at Carnegie Hall. While on the road, he saw the film *Diary of a Mad Housewife*, starring Carrie Snodgress, and, as he'd note in the song "A Man Needs a Maid," he "fell in love with the actress." *Diary* took Snodgress to the peak of her career. She won two Golden Globe Awards for her performance and was nominated for an Academy Award. In a move befitting his status as rock royalty, a smitten Young sent two roadies as emissaries to ask her to call him.

When she did, Young was literally flat on his back. Working on his new property, he'd hurt himself moving a heavy piece of wood. He wound up in a back brace, zoned out on medication. Eventually, he'd require an operation to remove several discs. Still, Young and Snodgress met and quickly fell in love. She moved to the ranch and set about dismantling her career in favor of playing the role of Earth Mother. She became pregnant and even skipped the Academy Awards ceremony. Their son, Zeke, was born in September 1972.

CSNY compilation, Japan, 1971. *Courtesy Robert Ferreira*

CSNY rehearsal, 1970. © Henry Diltz/Corbis

Back on tour, Young stopped in Nashville for an appearance on TV's *The Johnny Cash Show*. While in town, he also booked Quadrafonic Sound Studios to record a raft of new songs. Among the musicians hastily pulled into the sessions were bassist Tim Drummond, a veteran of Conway Twitty's band as well as James Brown's; pedal steel player Ben Keith, who logged time with Faron Young and Patsy Cline; and drummer Kenny Buttrey, who had played on several Bob Dylan records. Young dubbed the assemblage the Stray Gators, a term associated with stoned musicians that Drummond had heard on James Brown's tour bus. But Young's desire for lots of sonic space on his records rubbed some of the Nashville pros the wrong way, especially Buttrey. "He hires some of the best musicians in the world and has 'em play as stupid as they possibly can," he said.

Among the songs they laid down were "Old Man," which Young had written for Louis Avila, the caretaker on his cattle ranch, and "Heart of Gold," which featured guest appearances by fellow *Cash* show guests James Taylor and Linda Ronstadt. In typical fashion, Young handed Taylor a banjo to play, the first time Taylor had ever touched one.

JOHNNY CASH ON CAMPUS

WITH

James Taylor
Neil Young

"THE JOHNNY CASH SHOW" FEB. 17, 1971
WED. 9:00 P.M.   CHANNEL 7   ABC-TV
CHECK LISTINGS FOR LOCAL TIME AND CHANNEL

Broken Arrow Ranch, Redwood City, California, May 27, 1971. © Henry Diltz/Corbis

Young's tour brought him to London, where Jack Nitzsche aided him in recording two songs: the startlingly honest, if chauvinistic, "A Man Needs a Maid" and "There's a World" with the London Symphony Orchestra, adding a new, bombastic, and self-important aspect to his music. After that he returned to Nashville for more tracking and also built a makeshift studio in his barn at the ranch, where he recorded "Words," "Alabama," and "Are You Ready for the Country?" Another key song in the Young canon, "The Needle and the Damage Done," written for Danny Whitten and other Young associates sidelined by hard drugs, was recorded live at UCLA's Royce Hall.

When it was released in February 1972, *Harvest* was an instant sensation, rising to No. 1 even as "Heart of Gold" topped the singles charts. Young described his *Harvest* experience to *American Masters*:

*I can't even remember if I enjoyed it. It was very intense. People saw something in me I didn't see in me. But how many sensitive songs can you write before you're just writing a sensitive song and it's not sensitive 'cause it's not real? And so you can't live up to expectations.*

*The producer of Crazy Horse [David Briggs] felt like that was a sellout record. I did this for everybody else 'cause this is what everybody wanted. The fact is, nobody wanted it. I just did it because I was on tour and I toured and I got to Nashville and I met some people and I went into the studio and recorded the songs I'd done. And then I went home and went into the barn and then I went back to London and recorded with the London Symphony Orchestra. And that was* Harvest, *and I just kept going.*

With Nils Lofgren, Tonight's the Night Tour with the Santa Monica Flyers, London, 1973. © Gijsbert Hanekroot (www.gijsberthanekroot.nl)

Argentina, 1972. *Courtesy Cyril Kieldsen*

Backed with "Sugar Mountain," Portugal, 1972.
*Courtesy Robert Ferreira*

France, 1972.

Japan, 1972. *Courtesy Cyril Kieldsen*

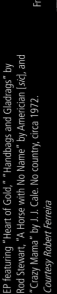

EP featuring "Heart of Gold," "Handbags and Gladrags" by
Rod Stewart, "A Horse with No Name" by Americian [*sic*], and
"Crazy Mama" by J. J. Cale. No country, circa 1972.
*Courtesy Robert Ferreira*

Germany, 1972. *Courtesy Cyril Kieldsen*

Nash & Young, of course, was just right there in my musical development. He's just a fantastic guitar player and a great songwriter and singer.

—Geoff Tate, Queensrÿche

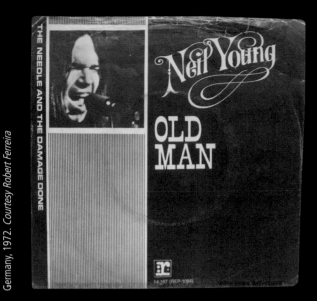

Germany, 1972. Courtesy Robert Ferreira

Japan, 1972. Courtesy Cyril Kieldsen

Japan, 1972. Courtesy Cyril Kieldsen

Germany, 1972. Courtesy Cyril Kieldsen

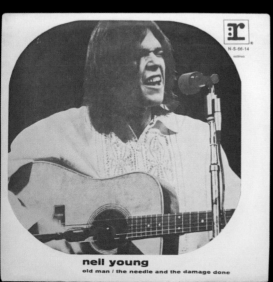

Portugal, 1972. Courtesy Cyril Kieldsen

Japan, 1976. Courtesy Cyril Kieldsen

In fact, fame made Young pull back further than ever. Experimenting with some film equipment he'd bought, Young began working on a loose set of scenes that would become his first filmic adventure, *Journey through the Past*. "I wanted to express a visual picture of what I was singing about," he told *Rolling Stone*. Young filmed documentary footage of himself on tour as well as scenes concocted with some of his oddball neighbors. The process sucked in his CSN partners as well, and no one associated with the film acquitted themselves particularly well.

"It's hard to say what the movie means," Young told *Rolling Stone*. "I think it's a good film for a first film. I think it's a really good film. . . . It does lay a lot of shit on people though. It wasn't made for entertainment. I'll admit, I made it for myself. Whatever it is, that's the way I felt. I made it for me. I never even had a script."

As ever with regard to Neil Young, art imitates life.

original soundtrack recordings
**JOURNEY THROUGH THE PAST**
a film by NEIL YOUNG

se records and tapes

2XS 6480

Film still, *Journey through the Past*, 1972. *Everett Collection/Rex USA*

# Tired Eyes
## 1972-1975

Danny Whitten, circa 1970. *Michael Ochs Archives/Getty Images*

**In the liner notes to his career** retrospective *Decade*, Neil Young famously wrote that his massive hit "Heart of Gold" "put me in the middle of the road. Traveling there soon became a bore so I headed for the ditch. A rougher ride but I saw more interesting people there." A different way to put it, perhaps, is that those who play on the busiest part of the pavement almost always wind up as road kill, and Young wanted no part of that scene. He could already see the bodies piling up.

Danny Whitten, the heart and soul of Crazy Horse, was the first to fall. He had been a drug casualty waiting to happen for several years. Young decided to give the guitarist one last chance, inviting Whitten to join his band from *Harvest*, the Stray Gators, as he undertook his first major tour as a solo superstar. Young must have known he was flirting with disaster, having fired Whitten for being too drug-addled to play once before. When he turned up at Young's ranch for rehearsals, it was obvious things would be no better this time. After several weeks, Whitten was fired and given a plane ticket back to L.A. and fifty dollars.

That night, the call came in: Whitten was dead of a drug overdose.

"I felt responsible," Young admitted to Jimmy McDonough. "But really there was nothin' I could do. I mean, he was responsible. But I thought I was for a long time. . . . Danny just wasn't happy. It just all came down on him. He was engulfed by this drug. That was too bad. Because Danny had a lot to give, boy. He was really good."

Tonight's the Night Tour with the Santa Monica Flyers, Palace Theatre, Manchester, England, November 3, 1973. *Photo by Howard Barlow/Redferns/Getty Images*

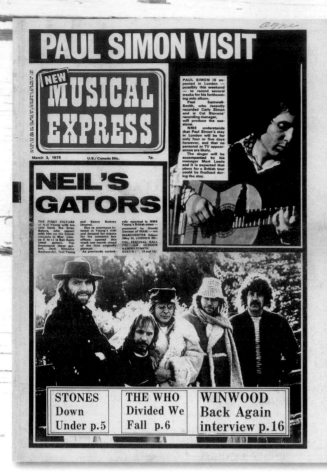

save the tour from being a monumental bummer. A string of shows set for Europe was canceled.

*Time Fades Away*, the live album that emerged from the tour, retains nearly all of those bad vibes, but it also reveals an artist remarkably unafraid to dance out on the edge. Electric songs like the title track, "Yonder Stands the Sinner," and "Last Dance" lumber and lurch, their rattletrap rhythms and unkempt harmonies left untouched. The solo numbers "Journey through the Past" (no relation to Young's film of the same name), "Love in Mind," and "The Bridge" are presented in the same warts-and-all fashion. The album's obvious standout cut is "Don't Be Denied," an unguardedly autobiographical tune that traces Young's life from his parents' divorce to his current dichotomous status as poor in soul but rich in commercial success.

*(continued on page 78)*

Time Fades Away Tour with the Stray Gators, Des Moines, Iowa, February 27, 1973.

Whitten's death shook Young to his core, but there were other things weighing on his mind. Thanks to the success of *Harvest*, the tour was sold out, and the shows were to be held in arenas to boot. Young sensed that the chances of making any real connection with audiences of that size were slim. Worse, the band—Tim Drummond, Ben Keith, Jack Nitzsche, and Kenny Buttrey—was rebelling against him. Buttrey, accustomed to the softer work schedule and substantial salary of a Nashville studio pro, demanded a bigger slice of the financial pie. When the others learned of the drummer's demands, they followed suit. An angry Young agreed to higher wages, but the conflict soured him on the tour before it even began.

Equally problematic was Young's reluctance to serve up a concert filled with the mellow glow of *Harvest*. Having tried and failed to record a new album during the troubled rehearsals, Young decided to tape the concerts instead, shifting the focus of the shows away from his established hits and toward material that was raw, unwieldy, and wholly unfamiliar to the audience. Already isolated from his band and turned off by the large, inattentive crowds, things got even worse for Young when his voice gave out. He was heartened somewhat when David Crosby and Graham Nash came on board to back him on the last few dates, but even that couldn't

# Saddle Up the Palomino
## The Crazy Horse Story

"I ALWAYS WINCE when I see 'Neil Young and Crazy Horse,'" Young mused in the 1998 Jim Jarmusch documentary *Year of the Horse*. "Because it's Crazy Horse. And I know it's really Crazy Horse. For instance, my new jacket doesn't say 'Neil Young' on it. Everybody else's says 'Neil Young and Crazy Horse.' Mine just says 'Crazy Horse.'"

Band or backup band? Crazy Horse is, in fact, a little bit of both. It was a group in its own right—originally known as Danny and the Memories and, when Young started jamming with it in 1968, the Rockets. It has even recorded a few albums on its own and survived the 1972 death of original guitarist Danny Whitten from a heroin overdose.

To any Neil Young fan, however, Crazy Horse is inextricably connected to Young's beck and call. Conventional wisdom says he makes that call when he wants to rock out with heavy feedback and buzzsaw guitars, and he leaves the group on the sidelines when he wants to explore other styles. And Crazy Horse *has* been on hand for some of Young's finest hard rock creations, including *Everybody Knows This Is Nowhere*, *Tonight's the Night* (an elegy to Whitten and CSNY crew member Bruce Berry), *Rust Never Sleeps*, and *Ragged Glory*.

But anyone who's listened to textured, moodier albums—such as *Life*, *Sleeps with Angels*, and *Broken Arrow*, or Crazy Horse's gentle touch on a song like "Lotta Love" from *Comes a Time*—knows that Young can successfully ride the Horse on a wide range of sonic terrain. As Frank "Poncho" Sampedro, who replaced Whitten in 1975, explained, "Whatever moods Neil brings in with the songs, we're there. I don't think any of us individually are . . . virtuoso musicians, but there's a really special chemistry and we play better together than we do by ourselves." Young said of Crazy Horse:

> It really is a band. It's not really me; it's more like an us. It's just big, a lot like classical music, as far as I can tell. It's like a Wagnerian, melodic kind of thing that envelops all kinds of emotions and sweeps through things. It goes off on tangents and returns.
>
> It's like a custom-made vehicle for me. There are no rules of the road in this band. There are places I can go that I don't necessarily get on my own. It's very pure.

Young's longtime manager Elliot Roberts observed in *Year of the Horse*, "When you see

Neil and Crazy Horse, you're seeing a family. You're seeing guys who are intertwined way, way past the music."

When Young was still a teenager navigating the Canadian folk and rock scenes, Crazy Horse started in 1962 in Columbus, Georgia, as a doo wop–style vocal group led by Whitten and dubbed Danny and the Memories. The band moved to San Francisco and then Los Angeles, picking up instruments along the way and renaming itself the Rockets. The group put out an album under that name in 1968, the same year Whitten met Young and invited him to start jamming with the six-piece Rockets at their place in Laurel Canyon.

"They were real primitive, but they had a lot of soul," Young recalled to PBS's *American Masters*. He did, however, feel that "there were too many of them for me" and asked just Whitten, bassist Billy Talbot, and drummer Ralph Molina to back him up on *Everybody Knows This Is Nowhere*, effectively bringing the Rockets' ride to an end. With songs such as "Cinnamon Girl," "Down by the River," and "Cowgirl in the Sand," Crazy Horse clearly gave Young the kind of sympathetic and almost telepathic backing he needed. Stellar reviews and a Top 40 showing on the *Billboard* Pop Albums chart indicated that the audience felt that way, too. Bill Graham dubbed Crazy Horse the third best garage rock band in the world, and Young declared to *Rolling Stone* that "they're the American Rolling Stones, no doubt about it."

"We want to be real," Talbot explained. "Crazy Horse isn't meant to be all slicked up and slicked over. We capture as much as we can of the real stuff."

But Crazy Horse quickly got a lesson in what working with Young would be like. Rather than riding forward to capitalize on the momentum of *Everybody Knows*, released in May 1969, Young joined Crosby, Stills & Nash to form a new supergroup quartet, though he enlisted Crazy Horse's members to play on 1970's *After the Gold Rush*. But Crazy Horse did use its newfound notoriety to launch a separate career for the band in 1971, releasing a self-titled debut that added guitarist Nils Lofgren, a protégé of Young's from the East Coast, to the mix, along with producer Jack

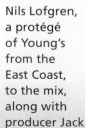

Nitzsche on keyboards. The well-received album included Young's then-unreleased "Dance, Dance, Dance," while other songs such as "Beggar's Day" and "I Don't Want to Talk About It" were covered by artists such as Rod Stewart, Nazareth, Rita Coolidge, and Everything But the Girl. Young himself used a live version of "Downtown" (as "Come On Baby Let's Go Downtown") on his 1975 release *Tonight's the Night*. The group also backed Buffy Sainte-Marie on her 1971 album, *She Used to Wanna Be a Ballerina*.

Whitten was already in the throes of a heroin addiction at this point. In an effort to help him focus and clean up, Young put Whitten on retainer and tried to make him part of the Stray Gators band that would tour to support 1972's *Harvest*. But Whitten wasn't in good enough shape to play with the group—all accomplished Nashville session cats—and was dismissed on November 18. He returned to Los Angeles and suffered a fatal overdose the same day.

That tragedy, along with the overdose death of Bruce Berry, inspired Young to write the dark, raw, grief-channeling songs that became *Tonight's the Night*. Recruiting Talbot, Molina, Lofgren, Nitzsche, and Stray Gators' steel guitarist Ben Keith, Young repaired to Studio Instrument Rentals (SIR) in Hollywood during the late summer of 1973. There, they recorded a harrowing piece of what he called audio vérité that became one of Young's crowning creative achievements and set a standard by which he's still measured. He then took the troupe overseas to play the new material—even though Young's musical machinations and a skittish record company held up the album's release until 1975.

Before *Tonight's the Night* finally came out, Crazy Horse was made whole again with the addition of Poncho Sampedro, whom Talbot met in Mexico and recommended to Molina and Young. Sampedro would go on to become a member of other Young bands such as the International Harvesters, the Bluenotes, the Lost Dogs, the Restless, and Ten Men Working. "Poncho brings us strength," Young once commented. "He has massive amounts of strength . . . just an unbelievable core of strength. When he's there, it's strong." Sampedro, it turns out, had done a lot of jamming to *Everybody Knows*, but

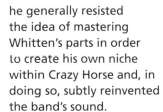

he generally resisted the idea of mastering Whitten's parts in order to create his own niche within Crazy Horse and, in doing so, subtly reinvented the band's sound.

"We start playing and don't ever have arrangements or decide what's going to happen," explained Sampedro. "We start playing long jams, we all just get together in one room, crank up our instruments and play, and that's how they have to record us. It takes a lot of instinct."

The new Crazy Horse debuted on 1975's *Zuma* but really hit its stride on *Rust Never Sleeps* and the companion *Live Rust* in 1979. The group—which released four more albums apart from Young—has had its ups (*Ragged Glory*) and downs (*Life*). There were also more than a few occasions when the band was put on the sidelines, sometimes abruptly, in the midst of an already-started project, or when it contributed small bits to albums such as *Trans* and *Are You Passionate?* "Neil took Crazy Horse and used 'em like sluts, like a component," producer David Briggs said in *Shakey: Neil Young's Biography*, "and they went along with it."

"Let's put it this way: We're always waiting," said Sampedro, who did not join Molina and Talbot in recording 2003's *Greendale* album but did play piano on the tour.

Young, however, told *American Masters* that "it's just a matter of choosing the ride. . . . I don't play with Crazy Horse all the time. You can't wear it out. . . . You have to give it a rest. It's like planting stuff; you've got to let the field rest for a year." At the 2006 South by Southwest Music + Media Conference, Young contended:

*If I played Crazy Horse tours every tour, I'd be dead. There's no way I'd be here. I can remember playing with that band where I'm almost blacking out, hyperventilating. . . . There's something very free about playing with that band, but I couldn't stay there. I wouldn't be here if I stayed there all the time.*

Then again, Talbot, Molina, and Sampedro would probably be delirious if they only had to wait a year between projects. Young has offered no scientific rhyme or reason for the timing of his returns to the Horse.

"I just feel it," he explained. "I can feel my body wanting to play guitar the way I play with Crazy Horse. And then I go for it."

*(continued from page 74)*

The disc was received coolly by fans, yet Young was still able to draw some positives from it. He told PBS's *American Masters*:

> All of those other people that I've been working with are going, "What happened?" And I'm not thinking about that. I'm thinking about what's happening. I'm trying to stay on top of what's going on and I'm recording and I'm mixing and I'm moving. . . . Something to avoid repeating is how I looked at it. I said, "This is good.

> Everybody likes [Harvest]. I could probably make another one, but I'd probably hate myself for it." I didn't want to make another one. . . . I made a record [Time Fades Away] nobody wanted and I put it out and it didn't do nearly as well and people thought I'd failed. But I knew I'd succeeded because I succeeded in moving on. I wasn't dragged down by the success.

In the spring of 1973, Crosby, Stills, Nash & Young convened in Hawaii to discuss a possible album and tour.

Backed with "Don't Be Denied," Yugoslavia, 1973. *Courtesy Robert Ferreira*

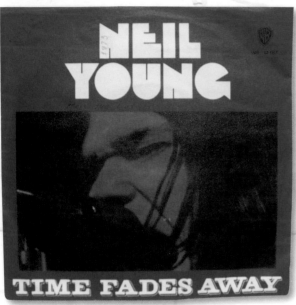

Spain, 1973. *Courtesy Cyril Kieldsen*

Japan, 1973. *Courtesy Cyril Kieldsen*

Promo featuring "Don't Be Denied," "Love in Mind," and "Last Dance," U.S., 1973. *Courtesy Robert Ferreira*

A month later, they were rolling tape at Young's ranch, though its proprietor remained distant and noncommittal. When the group's familiar pattern of ego-charged arguments recurred, Young called a halt to the proceedings.

Meanwhile, the body count continued to rise. Roadie Bruce Berry, a longtime member of the CSNY camp, became another drug casualty, dying of an overdose of heroin and cocaine.

Young responded to the death by heading to the place where Berry had gotten his start: his brother Ken's business, Studio Instrument Rentals, in Los Angeles. There, Young summoned the current Crazy Horse lineup—Billy Talbot, Ralph Molina, Jack Nitzsche, and Nils Lofgren—as well as Ben Keith from the Stray Gators. Young commandeered SIR's rehearsal space, knocked a hole in the wall to run cable, and created a makeshift studio where he and the band recorded *Tonight's the Night*, one of the most harrowing albums of his career—or anyone else's for that matter.

"*Tonight's the Night* is like an OD letter," Young told *Rolling Stone*. "The whole thing is about life, dope and death. When we played that music we were all thinking of Danny Whitten and Bruce Berry, two close members of our unit lost to junk overdoses." The sessions at SIR were loose and liquid. The musicians would turn up in the evening, shoot pool and drink tequila until midnight, then start recording. "We played Bruce and Danny on their way all through the night," Young said.

The songs were suffused with the spirit of the late musicians, and the album's title track mentions Berry by name. A series of candid aural snapshots, the lyrics detail how he drove the van, slept late, and after gigs would pick up Young's guitar "and sing a song in a shaky voice that was real as the day was long." By the time Young confesses the chill that shoots through him with the news of Berry's death, his sense of loss and outrage is palpable.

"I'm sure there's a lot of other people whose friends died and a lot of worse things—people went to war and didn't come back, or came back with half a body," he told *American Masters*. "All of these things happen to people, so I figured it happened to me so I'll write about this, and I'll just write from my heart, and if other people have this happen to them they'll relate to this." Young felt the song so deeply that "Tonight's the Night" is on the album twice, the second version even more harrowing than the first.

If *Time Fades Away* proved that Young preferred to represent the truth of a live recording over the slick perfection technology

afforded, *Tonight's the Night* can only be described as audio vérité. Flubbed lyrics, skewed harmonies, out-of-tune instruments—they're all part of the haunted, unrestrained vibe. The songs themselves range from the woozy, boozy pronouncements of "Speakin' Out" and the stoned sensibilities of "Roll Another Number (For the Road)"— the latter an admission of how distant Young had grown from Woodstock Nation—to desperate pleas for relief such as "Mellow My Mind" and "Albuquerque." Young goes even deeper on "Tired Eyes," the true tale of a Topanga Canyon dope deal gone awry turned into a cautionary tale, albeit one that came too late to save his friends.

On its face, *Tonight's the Night* seemed like an album made by musicians who were at the end of their rope—most likely because they'd smoked the long end of it. But what the album has in spades is pure, unadulterated feeling: It's real.

"I'm not a junkie and I won't even try it out to check out what it's like," Young told *Rolling Stone*, "but we all got high enough right out there on the edge where we felt wide-open to

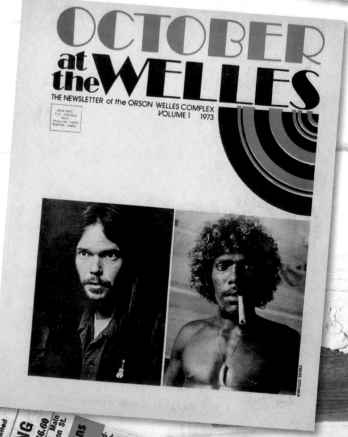

the whole mood. It was spooky. I probably feel this album more than anything else I've ever done."

The release of *Tonight's the Night* seemed imminent. But Young kept toying with the tapes, the song selection, and a string of oddball observations that he inserted between the tunes and later removed. The album, initially recorded in 1973, would not be released for nearly two more years.

Regardless, Young took his new songs on the road. Perhaps to distance himself from the pain of the material—or maybe it was just the Cuervo Gold talking—Young put on the persona of a sleazy nightclub emcee. Wearing a seersucker jacket, patched jeans, and shades, his hair flying every which way, Young greeted most audiences by welcoming them "to Miami Beach. . . . Everything is cheaper than it looks." The band cluttered the stage with a purloined palm tree, a wooden Indian, a collection of platform boots, and anything else they thought would add to the shambolic vibe. Even more so than on the *Time Fades Away* tour, Young eschewed his hit material in favor of the new stuff—much to the audience's displeasure.

Nils Lofgren told *American Masters*:

*We were playing an album that he wanted to turn people on to that hadn't been released yet. [Young] was an icon in England already and everybody wanted to hear him play his hits. And we played the record from beginning to end, starting with "Tonight's the Night" and finishing with "Tonight's the Night" and the English audiences were really not okay with it. They started yelling a lot. They started booing. They started complaining and whining at every show. He'd get to the end of the night and say, "All right, we're gonna play something you've all heard before" and everyone would go crazy thinking it's gonna be "Like a Hurricane" or some Buffalo Springfield hit and we'd play "Tonight's the Night" again.*

Young upped the ante on the confrontational shows during a swing through the United States. His incoherent raps sometimes climaxed with Young shouting about Berry, who'd stolen equipment for drug money, "shooting guitars into his arm." It may have proved personally cathartic, but the tour was not well received. It seemed to many that Young was purposely dismantling his career or possibly was strung out himself. At one point, the BBC even reported that he'd died of an overdose.

With the release of *Tonight's the Night* delayed indefinitely, the album that surfaced instead, *On the Beach*,

was an even more profound downer. Young himself called it "probably one of the most depressing records I've ever made."

Recorded for the most part in Los Angeles with Ben Keith, Tim Drummond, The Band's Levon Helm and Rick Danko, plus guitarist/fiddler and all-around Cajun wildman Rusty Kershaw, the album's lethargic mood was at least in part a result of the sessions' drug of choice: "honey slides," a potent mix of hashish and honey that rendered imbibers near catatonic.

Throughout the album, Young seems isolated and morose. Unmotivated to respond to gossipmongers spreading lies about him, he all but surrenders on the opening cut, "Walk On." Other songs seem like nightmare scenarios come to life. In "See the Sky About to Rain," he plays a silver fiddle for an audience in the South only to have "the man" (and indeed, perhaps *the Man*) break the instrument in two. The title track finds him recoiling from crowds he can't face and being abandoned by a radio interviewer. Caught in a vortex of ennui, Young's only solution is to mosey along.

He gets his back up slightly on the long, rambling "Ambulance Blues," which fires back at critics, albeit laconically, and calls out a man, possibly disgraced president Richard Nixon, for his lies. But it's with more disappointment than disgust that Young delivers to all

Germany, 1974. *Courtesy Robert Ferreira*

Thailand, no date. *Courtesy Robert Ferreira*

Crosby, Stills, Nash & Young Reunion Tour, Oakland Coliseum, Oakland, California, July 13–14, 1974.
© Gijsbert Hanekroot (www.gijsberthanekroot.nl)

his tormentors the album's *coup de grace*: "You're all just pissin' in the wind."

*On the Beach*'s solitary go-for-the jugular moment is "Revolution Blues," a taut, tense rocker inspired by mass-murdering cult leader Charles Manson. David Crosby played guitar on the song, but it hit too close to home. "I played it for Crosby and he said, 'Don't sing about that. That's not funny,'" Young told *American Masters*. "It spooked people. It was spooky times. I knew Charlie Manson, so it spooked the hell out of me. He wasn't what you'd call a songwriter. He was like a song-spewer. But he got . . . turned down by record companies. He got turned down by Reprise, and I remember, I told Mo Ostin, I said, 'This guy, he's good.

He's just a little out of control.' But when he got turned down, that really pissed him off. [He] didn't take rejection well."

Though it seemed like the last thing in the world Young might do, he finally agreed to a full-scale CSNY tour. And never mind Young's disdain of the arena-sized venues he played on the *Time Fades Away* tour. This time they'd be playing *stadiums*, in front of as many as fifty thousand people at a time.

Rehearsals for the shows took place at Young's ranch. "He built this full-size, 40-foot stage in the middle of a grove of redwood and right across from his studios so we could record," Crosby told *Rolling Stone*. "He put half of us up and fed us all, had two chicks working. And the place,

because it's so private and beautiful, was a natural to make us feel great and work hard."

Despite the grand scale of the tour and the decadent spirit that went with it—there were drugs everywhere, hookers (allegedly) on the payroll, and even custom-made pillowcases emblazoned with a sketch of the band drawn by Joni Mitchell—Young chose to remain as low-key as possible. He refused all interview requests and traveled apart from the band in a motor home, his two-year-old son, Zeke, and dog, Art, in tow. The tour pulled in the numbers, but it was an artistic disaster. The sound equipment wasn't adequate for the giant venues, and the four blew out their voices by oversinging. Stills and Young settled their differences with guitars, each trying to play louder and longer than the other. And only Young had any new songs to add to the mix. The others rehashed past glories, reveled in rock-star excess, and collected their substantial paychecks. Crosby nicknamed the endeavor the "Doom Tour."

The ranch recordings and concert tapes left little that was usable for a new album, although Nash was going through the latter again in 2009 with an eye toward releasing something from the '74 tour. "Listen," Young told *Mojo*, "if they'd had new songs with the authority that their old songs had, we could've knocked off four or five of mine so that just the best two surfaced. That would have truly been CSN&Y. But it wasn't to be, so the record never came out." Instead, their label released the warmed-over best-of collection *So Far*.

Young concluded, "Nineteen-seventy-four was the swan song of Crosby, Stills, Nash & Young for me."

*(continued on page 91)*

# Motion Pictures
## Bernard Shakey's Celluloid Adventures

NEIL YOUNG WAS HARDLY WANTING for avenues of creative expression in 1973 when he launched Shakey Pictures with the experimental feature film *Journey through the Past*. He had an active music career, after all, both on his own and in two successful bands: Buffalo Springfield and Crosby, Stills, Nash & Young.

So why film?

"It was something I wanted to do," Young told *Rolling Stone*. "The music, which has been and always will be my primary thing, just seemed to *point* that way. I wanted to express a visual picture of what I was singing about."

As a director and screenwriter (the latter being a somewhat loose term), Young has done that five times, mostly under his *nom de film*, Bernard Shakey. The Shakey nickname, in fact, comes from some of Young's very early filmmaking attempts when, as biographer Jimmy McDonough told NPR's Scott Simon, Young "started making these rather furry home movies. . . . His camera work was none too steady, and thus gave birth to the alter ego Bernard Shakey.

"And if you know the cat, the nickname fits. . . . Nothing is too solid about the guy."

Young's film work has tested the faith of his fans and critics even more than his prolific and eclectic musical output. He's eschewed conventional plots and scripting; he told one interviewer that, when it came to screenplays, "I can never write more than a half a page at a time," preferring a more spontaneous approach. "Once in a while I like to do something that has a chance of failing," he noted, which is not necessarily what producers and studios like to hear.

Young has both succeeded and failed as a filmmaker, but most feel that the filmography of Mr. Shakey, who subsequently practiced his camera skills shooting commercials for the Hyatt House Hotel, is nothing if not interesting:

*AFTER THE GOLD RUSH* (1972): Based on a script by actor Dean Stockwell, Young and company took this proposed disaster flick to Universal Pictures, but it never made it off the drawing board.

*JOURNEY THROUGH THE PAST* (1973): Shakey Pictures' first real venture, an impressionistic and widely panned $350,000 project, was described by Young as "a collection of thoughts" after its screening at that year's U.S. Film Festival in Dallas. "Every scene meant something to me—although

with some of them, I can't say what," Young noted. Even Fred Underhill, *Journey*'s co-producer, revealed that "I keep asking Neil what it's about, too." There's certainly a post-hippie, kitchen-sink flavor to the film. Concert footage is mixed with vignettes featuring David Crosby, Graham Nash, and Stephen Stills, as well as real-life footage of Jesus rallies on Hollywood Boulevard and the Reverend Billy Graham and President Richard Nixon singing "God Bless America" at a youth rally. There are scenes of a junkie preparing to shoot up and of Young and his girlfriend, Carrie Snodgress, smoking a joint (which reportedly cost the actress her contract with Universal Pictures). Young's neighbor Richard Lee Patterson resides at the center of the film as a metaphysical character called "The Graduate," tooling around in a pickup truck; in one scene he's descended upon by hooded horsemen who bring him a bible containing a syringe (which got *Journey* banned in Britain). "I think it's a good first film," Young told *Rolling Stone*. "I just made a feeling. . . . It wasn't made for entertainment. I'll admit, I made it for myself."

*RUST NEVER SLEEPS* (1979): Shakey hit pay dirt with what some rightly consider one of the best concert films ever made. Filmed on October 22, 1978, at the Cow Palace in San Francisco, *Rust* captures Young and Crazy Horse at full gallop, emboldened by a batch of strong new songs from the album of the same name and fortified with favorites from Young's previous releases. The show is a conceptual stitch, too: At the end of the opening acoustic segment, Young "falls asleep," only to awaken to a stage full of giant amplifiers and equipment cases, *Star Wars*–like "Road-eyes" moving gear and switching instruments, sound men dressed like *Saturday Night Live* Coneheads, and producer David Briggs as the white-coated "Dr. Decibel."

*HUMAN HIGHWAY* (1982): Shakey returned to the experimental fold with a comedy, this time sinking $3 million and spending more than four years of non-continuous shooting on a Hollywood soundstage and in Taos Pueblo, New Mexico. Taking its title from a 1974 CSNY song, the film has an (extremely) loose plot set on Earth's last day in a fictional town located in the shadow of a nuclear power plant, whose workers are played by members of the band Devo. Young stars as Lionel Switch, an auto mechanic who dreams of being a rock star. Dean Stockwell co-directed the film and appears along with Russ Tamblyn, Dennis Hopper, Sally Kirkland, Young's wife, Pegi, and his manager Elliot Roberts. *Human Highway* premiered in June 1983 in Los Angeles, where it bombed. It did not surface on video for another dozen years.

**MUDDY TRACK** (1986): This proposed concert film never saw the light of day, though some footage wound up in Jim Jarmusch's 1997 Crazy Horse documentary, *Year of the Horse*.

**GREENDALE** (2003): Shakey tried his hand at rock opera with this parable about tradition and change in small-town America, with some anti-media and pro-environment messages tossed in. Built around ten lengthy and largely instrumental songs, the film featured a cast combination of actors and Young cronies—including his wife, Pegi, musician Ben Keith and his wife, Elizabeth, and members of the rock band Echobrain—lip-synching the lyrics. It's homespun and low budget; the Internet Movie Data Base termed it "essentially a feature-length music video." But Jonathan Demme, who directed the 2006 Young concert film, *Silver & Gold*, called it "one of my favorite American movies. It looks like it was done

on an absolute shoestring . . . but the imagination was unlimited. It charted incredible new ground on every front, and I just thought it was such a triumph and such a challenge to filmmakers: 'Can you do something this original that works?'"

**CSNY/DÉJÀ VU** (2008): Shakey's most fully realized film may well be this documentary of 2006's politically polarizing Freedom of Speech Tour, whose conceptual center was Young's forceful *Living with War* album. "I thought it was a good subject for a film, a documentary," Young explained when it was released. "I took it on like a journalistic endeavor and tried to be balanced as much as I could with the material we were able to gather." Young enlisted TV journalist Michael Cerre to "embed" with CSNY during the tour, interviewing fans and foes alike for an admirably even-handed view of the varying audience reactions to the show—which, among other things, called for the impeachment of President George W. Bush. Cerre, who had been on assignment in Iraq, also helped Young hook up with war veterans from Iraq, Afghanistan, and Vietnam, as well as family members of slain troops. The film culminates in a resonant sequence featuring CSNY performing "Roger and Out" and "Find the Cost of Freedom" amid images of survivors mourning their loved ones.

With filmmaker Jim Jarmusch, Broken Arrow Ranch, Redwood City, California, circa 1997. *Michael Ochs Archives/Getty Images*

Crosby, Stills, Nash & Young Reunion Tour, Wembley Stadium, London, September 14, 1974. *© Tolca/Sunshine/Retna UK*

*(continued from page 83)*

was crumbling, too, and he asked that she vacate the ranch. Whatever he couldn't bring himself to say in person he poured out in a series of stark, confessional songs that he began recording in Nashville: "Frozen Man," "Separate Ways," "Homefires," and "Love Art Blues." The songs were compiled into an album titled *Homegrown*, and everyone who heard it felt like it would be a blockbuster along the lines of *Harvest*.

Well, nearly everyone.

As the album was wrapping up, Young held a party at the Chateau Marmont in Hollywood that was attended by Crazy Horse members Ralph Molina and Billy Talbot and The Band's Richard Manuel and Rick Danko, among others. They listened to the finished *Homegrown* album, followed by the unreleased *Tonight's the Night*, which was on the same reel of tape.

"No comparison," Young recalled thinking. He ordered *Homegrown* scrapped and released *Tonight's the Night* instead. But first came more tinkering. Several songs—including "Lookout Joe," "Borrowed Tune," and "Come On Baby Let's Go Downtown" (featuring Danny Whitten on lead vocals)—were rescued from an abortive Broadway play based on Bruce Berry's life, titled *From Roadie to Riches*. They were added to the Studio Instrument Rentals tracks, and Young's darkest but most enduring classic was born.

The songs were compiled into an album titled *Homegrown,* and everyone who heard it felt like it would be a blockbuster along the lines of *Harvest.*

# Like a Hurricane
## 1975-1979

## 5

**Eventually, Young broke free** from the dark period that included the deaths of Danny Whitten and Bruce Berry; the grim, disconsolate albums referred to as his "ditch trilogy" (*Time Fades Away*, *On the Beach*, and *Tonight's the Night*); and his split with Carrie Snodgress. "I feel like I've surfaced out of some kind of murk," he told *Rolling Stone*.

Young moved to Malibu, lived the bachelor life, and began writing and recording at a frenetic pace. "I've got all these songs about Peru, the Aztecs, and the Incas," he said. "Time travel stuff. We've got one song called 'Marlon Brando, John Ehrlichman, Pocahontas and Me.' I'm playing a lot of electric guitar and that's what I like best. Two guitars, bass, and drums. And it's really flying off the ground, too. Fucking unbelievable."

Best of all, he got his favorite band back. Young reconvened Crazy Horse when Billy Talbot and Ralph Molina informed him they'd found a new guitarist that he simply had to hear.

Manuel Frank "Poncho" Sampedro was a Virginia native, born to Spanish immigrants, and grew up in Detroit before moving to California. He was a ladies'

Malibu, California, 1975. © *Henry Diltz/Corbis*

OPPOSITE: Crazy Horse Tour, Hammersmith Odeon, London, March 28–31, 1976. *Photo by Dick Barnatt/Redferns/Getty Images*

With Crazy Horse (from left), Frank Sampedro, Bill Talbot, and Ralph Molina, Malibu, California, 1975. © Henry Diltz/Corbis

man, a player in every sense. He would become Young's primary foil in the band as well as a mainstay of other projects not involving the Horse.

Sampedro recalled being brought into the fold in the film *Year of the Horse*:

> *I wasn't playing in a band when* Everybody Knows This Is Nowhere *came out. And I used to sit around and jam to that quite a bit. . . . I was smokin' pot every day, and I'd put on the old record and break out my guitar and play along. I think the funniest thing that happened, you know, as I was playing with these guys, and Billy would say, "You should check out the record, Poncho, and learn Danny's part better." And I would tell him, "You know, man, I've listened to that record probably more than you when I played along with it." Neil would make the comment, "You know what, Billy? He's listened to it a lot, and he plays both our parts." I never just followed one guy. I played Danny's part for a while, Neil's part for a while. . . . But it definitely wasn't all of Danny's style. I never*

> *really sat down and studied his parts. I didn't like to do that.*
>
> *But it is kind of interesting. When I first joined the band, I was doing heroin and a lot of dope myself. And probably through having a job and making the money I had and having the success I had helped me along the road to finally end up quitting all that stuff. So we kinda like lost one guy and saved another guy.*

At the time, Sampedro's swearing off was still somewhere down the line, but that was true of Crazy Horse in general. The band members partied and played like lunatics during the *Zuma* sessions, but they bonded all over again. As evidence of what a closed fraternity Crazy Horse became, consider that, decades later, Sampedro is still hazed for his lack of seniority. In *Year of the Horse*, Young smirks and says, "He's our new guy."

*Zuma* is rife with stories of callous behavior, jealousy, and betrayal, but it crackles with energy and renewed spirit. There's a straightforward melodicism to its nine songs, something Young had not concerned himself with much since *Harvest*.

The album opening "Don't Cry No Tears" reworks "I Wonder," a song from Young's days with the Squires. Though he wrote it more than a decade earlier, the subject matter of a relationship gone bad fits perfectly with Young's suddenly single status. What's remarkable—and somewhat disturbing—is the icy calculation with which he tells his ex to stop blubbering and move on. Another breakup song, "Pardon My Heart," is a naked acoustic number originally intended for the abandoned *Homegrown*. "Stupid Girl" is a vicious putdown of an old flame. "Drive Back" is equally detached, summarily dismissing an overnight guest. Even the relatively cheery bachelor song "Lookin' for a Love" takes note of his "darker side" and stands as a warning to whomever Young might hook up with next.

The album's true standouts, though, are "Danger Bird" and "Cortez the Killer." The former is a mythic tale whose title character is determined to fly, "though his wings have turned to stone." What really drives the song forward is Young's searching guitar solo, which swoops and soars, borne aloft by Crazy Horse's hazy group harmonies. Despite its degree of impenetrability, "Danger Bird" stands as one of Young's most audacious and breathtaking works.

Japan, 1975. *Courtesy Cyril Kieldsen*

Right alongside it is "Cortez," a story of the Spanish conquistador who found Aztec king Montezuma wandering magnificent halls. The song catalogues the idyllic civilization that the natives had built, only to have it wantonly destroyed by the Spaniards. The final verse adds an additional dimension as Young shifts into first person narration and sings about an unspecified woman who lives there and "loves me to this day."

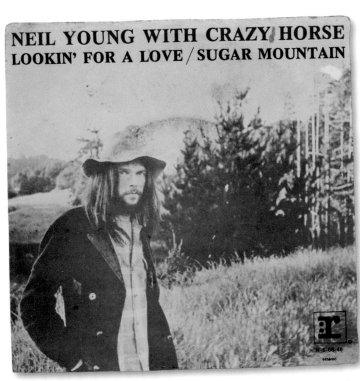

Portugal, 1975. *Courtesy Cyril Kieldsen*

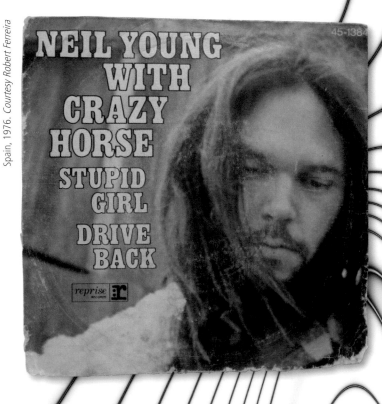

Spain, 1976. *Courtesy Robert Ferreira*

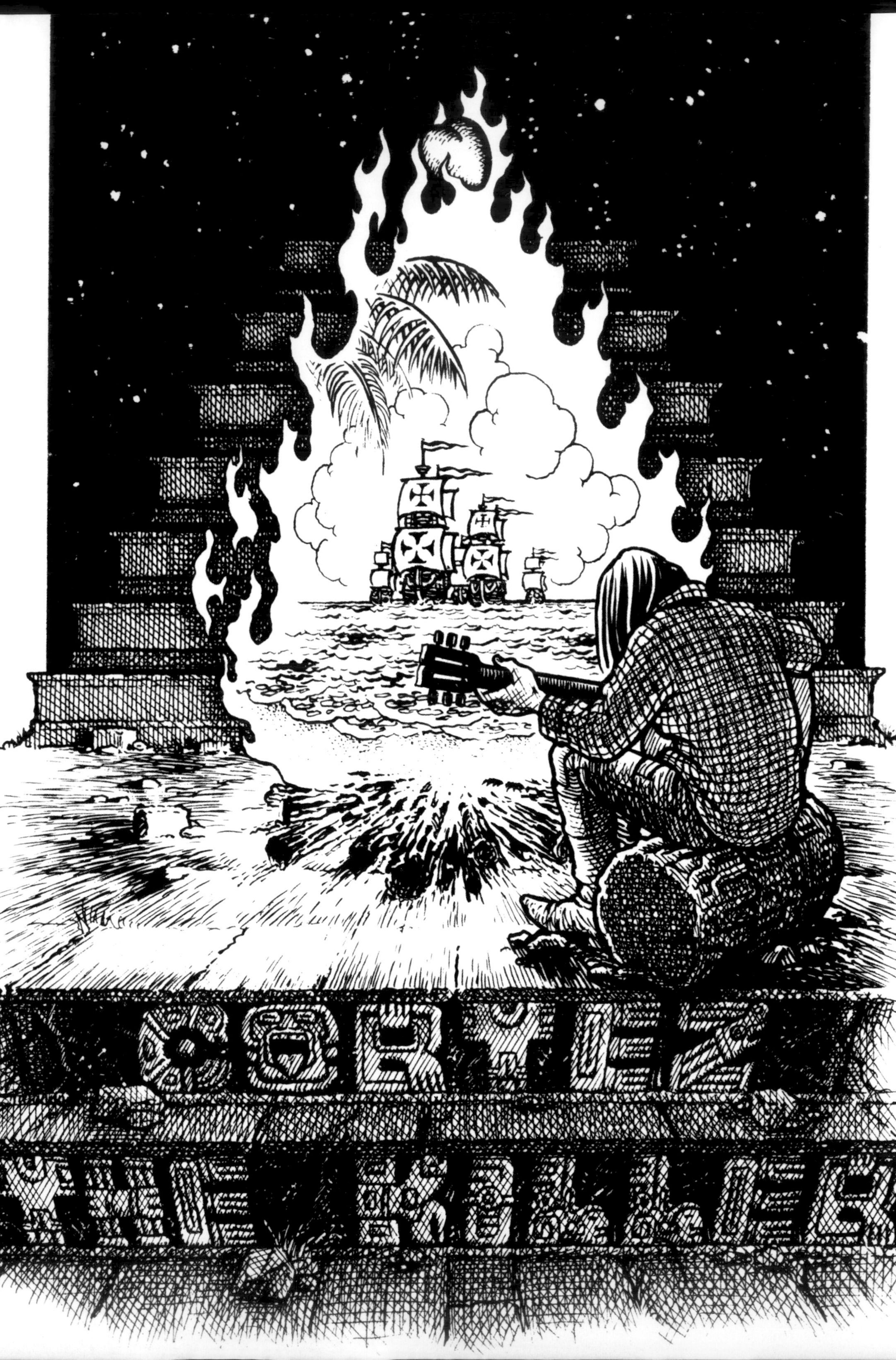


Artist: Peter Pontiac (www.peterpontiac.com)

Like "Danger Bird," "Cortez" is marked by long, lyrical guitar passages that have made it a perennial fan favorite. Young quipped in the liner notes to *Decade* that the song was "banned in Spain."

After *Zuma*'s release, Young led the band through a string of small, unannounced gigs at bars near his ranch, followed by a chaotic, large-scale tour of Japan and Europe. But just as the Horse was primed to take America by storm, Young shifted gears dramatically and canceled the dates.

Instead, he renewed his partnership with Stephen Stills and flew to Miami to record the album *Long May You Run*. For the sessions, held at Criteria Studios, the partners used Stills' band: percussionist Joe Lala, keyboardist Jerry Aiello, bassist George Perry, and drummer Joe Vitale. But the principals rarely shared studio time. Young turned up bright and early, with Stills stumbling in when the spirit moved him, and they didn't collaborate at all on material.

*With Crazy Horse, Copenhagen, Denmark, 1975. © Gijsbert Hanekroot (www.gijsberthanekroot.nl)*

BILL GRAHAM PRESENTS

SAT MARCH 10 / BERKELEY COMMUNITY THEATRE
**AMERICA**
JOHN DAVID SOUTHER

THURS MARCH 15 / BERKELEY COMMUNITY THEATRE
**SEALS & CROFTS**
ENGLAND DAN & JOHN FORD COLEY

FRI-SAT MARCH 16-17 / WINTERLAND
**STEVE MILLER BAND**
**DOOBIE BROS. / DR. HOOK & THE MEDICINE SHOW**

SUN MARCH 18 / BERKELEY COMMUNITY THEATRE
**BETTE MIDLER**
TWO SHOWS 7 & 10 P.M.

FRI-SAT MARCH 23-24 / WINTERLAND
**MAHAVISHNU ORCHESTRA**
W/ JOHN McLAUGHLIN

FRI-SAT MARCH 30-31 / WINTERLAND
**FRANK ZAPPA**
& THE MOTHERS OF INVENTION
**FOGHAT**
RUBEN & THE JETS

SAT MARCH 31 / BERKELEY COMMUNITY THEATER
**JOHN DENVER**

SAT MARCH 31 / OAKLAND COLISEUM
**NEIL YOUNG**
LINDA RONSTADT

FRI APRIL 6 / WINTERLAND
**SANTANA**

SAT APRIL 7 / WINTERLAND
**YES**

SUN APRIL 8 / BERKELEY COMMUNITY THEATRE
**SANTANA**
TWO SHOWS 6 & 9 P.M.

FRI-SAT APRIL 13-14 / WINTERLAND
**THE KINKS**
**DAN HICKS AND HIS HOT LICKS**
MASON PROFFIT

FRI-SAT APRIL 20-21 / WINTERLAND
**SHA NA NA**
**COMMANDER CODY AND HIS LOST PLANET AIRMEN!**

SAT APRIL 28 / OAKLAND COLISEUM
**DEEP PURPLE**
**FLEETWOOD MAC**
RORY GALLAGHER

SAT-SUN APRIL 28-29 / WINTERLAND
**THE JEFF BECK GROUP**
WITH JEFF BECK · TIM BOGART · CARMINE APPICE

WINTERLAND TICKETS $4.00 ADVANCE $4.50 AT DOOR, BERKELEY TICKETS $3.50, $4.50, $5.50 TICKETS ARE NOW ON SALE FOR ALL SHOWS AT TICKETRON OUTLETS INCLUDING THE DOWNTOWN CENTER BOX OFFICE. FOR INFO CALL 642-2121. TICKETS ARE ALWAYS AVAILABLE AT THE DOOR. WINTERLAND 6:30 P.M. THE EVENING OF THE SHOW. FOR OAKLAND COLISEUM TICKETS INFORMATION PLEASE CALL 635-7800.

Despite such obvious signs of trouble, the sessions almost blossomed into a full-blown CSNY reunion after Young played some of the tracks for Crosby and Nash and asked if they thought something was missing.

"Yeah, us," Crosby replied, and off they went to Miami. Several of the Stills-Young tracks were given the CSNY treatment, and a number of other songs were completed as well. But when Crosby and Nash departed to continue work on their own album, *Whistling Down the Wire*, Stills and Young decided to can the reunion and wipe their partners' vocals from the tape. The move cut Nash to the quick. He swore he'd never work with them again.

"They're in it for the wrong reasons," he seethed to *Rolling Stone*. "They're in it for the bucks, the manipulation and the career moves, and I'm in it for the great music."

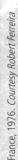

Holland, 1976. *Courtesy Robert Ferreira*

France, 1976. *Courtesy Robert Ferreira*

Portugal, 1976. *Courtesy Cyril Kjeldsen*

Italy, 1976. *Courtesy Robert Ferreira*

Alas, either with Crosby and Nash or without them, there wasn't much great music to be had on *Long May You Run*. Young acquitted himself nicely with the title track, a valentine to Mort, his legendary hearse, as well as the shimmering "Midnight on the Bay," plus "Ocean Girl," "Let It Shine," and the sardonic "Fontainebleau." Stills, whose solo career was hitting the first of many troughs, offered only lackluster songs that could have used a boost from Crosby and Nash.

Despite their lackluster performance in the studio, it seemed likely the pair could still shoot some sparks in concert. Joe Vitale told *Mojo*:

> *Neil and Stephen are so different, and yet so alike, that when they play together they're better than when they don't. They inspire each other, they play off of each other, and they just fulfill each other's live needs. There's never a dull moment playing with them. It's just because the two of those guys have a chemistry. It's fabulous to watch them go at it together. They're both very competitive, but they're also both respectful of each other. You've got two lead singers and two lead guitar players there. Sometimes it works incredibly, but sometimes, it gets a bit too intense.*

The pair hit the road, but the road hit back. The tour was plagued by bad reviews that often set the partners against one another, almost always to Young's advantage: "Young's Hot, Stills's Not" read one headline from *Rolling Stone*. A frustrated Stills teed off on crew members, sometimes onstage, enraging Young.

Having had his fill of the scene after only two weeks, Young vanished, leaving Stills holding the bag and a telegram that read, "Dear Stephen, funny how some things that start spontaneously end that way. Eat a peach, Neil."

Staggered, Stills blurted to a reporter, "I have no future."

His actions over the previous several months scored a rare trifecta for even the notoriously capricious Young: He'd burned Crazy Horse by pulling out of their American tour; burned Crosby and Nash by removing their contributions to the would-be reunion album; and burned Stills, one of his oldest friends, with perhaps the coldest kiss-off in rock history.

Eat a peach, indeed.

Young told biographer Jimmy McDonough:

> *Well, that was an easy way of doin' it—but I still did it. I still went from place to place, and I just left a trail of destruction behind me, y'know. But the older you get, the more you realize how much that hurts people. On the other hand, at that age, what I woulda had to do to talk to all those people and go through all that would've replaced three or four of those records in energy. Those records wouldn't be there— and those people would still be as pissed off as they were in the first place. I chose to put the energy into the records.*

Amends with Crazy Horse were made, allowing Young to make good on the abandoned Stills-Young dates. He also guested at the Last Waltz, The Band's 1976 gala farewell concert at San Francisco's Winterland Palace, joining Bob Dylan, Joni Mitchell, Muddy Waters, Van Morrison, Eric Clapton, and a host of others. But the main takeaway from that show regarding Young is not what was seen in Martin Scorsese's legendary concert film—a weary Young delivering a ragged take of "Helpless"—but rather what was not seen: a giant hunk of cocaine dangling from Young's nostril during the performance. Mercifully, it was removed from the final cut of the film.

*(continued on page 106)*

His actions over the previous several months scored a rare trifecta for even the notoriously capricious Young: He'd burned Crazy Horse by pulling out of their American tour; burned Crosby and Nash by removing their contributions to the would-be reunion album; and burned Stills, one of his oldest friends, with perhaps the coldest kiss-off in rock history.

BOTH: Crazy Horse U.S. Tour, L.A. Forum, Los Angeles, November 4, 1976. © Doug Allsop

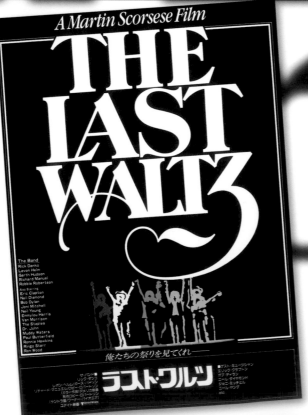

A Martin Scorsese Film

# THE LAST WALTZ

The Band
Rick Danko
Levon Helm
Garth Hudson
Richard Manuel
Robbie Robertson

Also Starring
Eric Clapton
Neil Diamond
Bob Dylan
Joni Mitchell
Neil Young
Emmylou Harris
The Staples
Van Morrison
Dr. John
Muddy Waters
Paul Butterfield
Ronnie Hawkins
Ringo Starr
Ron Wood

俺たちの祭りを見てくれ――

ラスト・ワルツ

*Empezó como Concierto*

Una Película de Martin Scorsese

# EL ULTIMO ROCK

Eric Clapton

Joni Mitchell

Neil Diamond

Neil Young

Bob Dylan

Emmylou Harris

Protagonizada por
**La Banda**

Rick Danko  Levon Helm  Garth Hudson  Richard Manuel  Robbie Robertson

*Se Convirtió en Celebración*

Van Morrison  The Staples  Dr. John  Muddy Waters
Paul Butterfield  Ronnie Hawkins  Ringo Starr  Ron Wood

Una Película de MARTIN SCORSESE
## El Ultimo Rock
[The Last Waltz]

Diseño de Producción por
BORIS LEVEN

Productor Ejecutivo
JONATHAN TAPLIN

Director de Fotografía
MICHAEL CHAPMAN

Producida por
ROBBIE ROBERTSON

Cinematografía por
LASZLO KOVACS, A.S.C. and VILMOS ZSIGMOND, A.S.C.

Dirigida por
MARTIN SCORSESE

DOLBY STEREO

Distribuida por
United Artists

[The Last Waltz] SPANISH

With Paul Butterfield, Eric Clapton, and Ron Wood, *The Last Waltz,* Winterland, San Francisco, November 25, 1976. *Photo by Ed Perlstein/Redferns/Getty Images*

Japan, 1977. *Courtesy Cyril Kieldsen*

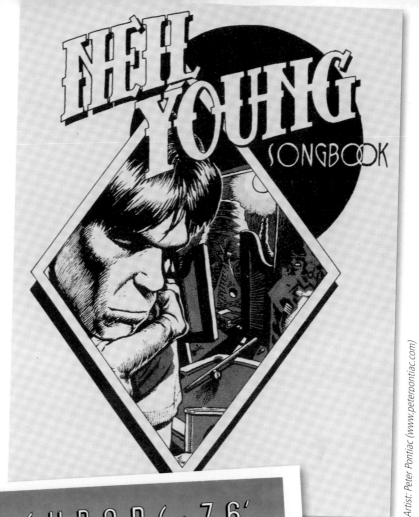

*Artist: Peter Pontiac (www.peterpontiac.com)*

Köln, Germany, 1976.

# Cowgirls in the Sand
## Neil Young's Female Collaborators

Though testosterone has dominated Young's bands and recording sessions, his world has not been exclusively a boy's club. These five women have made significant contributions since the early 1970s.

### Emmylou Harris

Emmylou Harris, 1978. *Photo by Richard McCaffrey/ Michael Ochs Archives/Getty Images*

After being discovered by Gram Parsons in the early '70s and then starting her solo career in 1975, Emmylou Harris became the founding queen of Americana music—though it's likely she didn't realize what she was creating at the time. That and her unwavering individuality made her a kindred spirit to Neil Young, and it is somewhat surprising that they waited as long as until the mid-'70s to start working together.

"He's a little bit of a fearless leader for us all," Harris said. "He's such an original. I don't think anybody else compares, really." Except, perhaps, Harris herself.

The two first met on creative ground in 1974, when Young was working on his ill-fated *Harvest* follow-up, *Homegrown*, and asked Harris to contribute harmony vocals to "Try" and "Star of Bethlehem." She was also part of *Silver & Gold* in 2000 and *Prairie Wind* in 2005 and performed at the Ryman Auditorium concerts in Nashville that Jonathan Demme filmed for 2006's *Neil Young: Heart of Gold*. Harris also covered the Stills-Young Band's "Long May You Run" on her 1982 live album, *Last Date*. Her cover of "After the Gold Rush" with Trio—a collaboration with Linda Ronstadt and Dolly Parton—won a Grammy Award in 1998 for Best Country Collaboration with Vocals.

Young, meanwhile, wrote the title track for Harris' 1995 album, *Wrecking Ball*, and performed on it, as well as on Harris' version of Lucinda Williams' "Sweet Old World."

### Nicolette Larson

Nicolette Larson, 1979. *Photo by Julian Wasser/ Time & Life Pictures/Getty Images*

Young hired Larson—on the recommendation of Ronstadt and several others—to become part of the Saddlebags backing chorus for his *American Stars 'n Bars* album in 1977. She also wound up working on 1978's *Comes a Time*, which led to a deal with Warner Bros. Records and her 1978 debut, *Nicolette*, that featured the Young-penned Top 10 hit "Lotta Love." She was hailed as a newcomer but in truth was well-seasoned even before she met Young.

Born in Helena, Montana, Larson moved around quite a bit due to her father's position with the U.S. Treasury Department. San Francisco eventually became home base, though her professional singing debut was opening for Eric Andersen in Vancouver. In 1975, she wound up singing with Commander Cody, which led to sessions with Rodney Crowell, Jesse Colin Young, Jesse Winchester, and Emmylou Harris, among others. She recorded eight solo albums, none of which equaled *Nicolette*'s success, and continued to do sessions for Ronstadt, Jimmy Buffett, Graham Nash, Rita Coolidge, Dolly Parton, Carlene Carter, the Georgia Satellites, and Weird Al Yankovic.

She was also the maid of honor for actress Valerie Bertinelli's wedding to Eddie Van Halen in 1981.

Larson, who had a brief romantic fling with Young during the '70s, later rejoined him for *Harvest Moon* and *Unplugged*, and she sang on the two tracks Young contributed to 1994's *Seven Gates: A Christmas Album by Ben Keith and Friends*.

Larson died on December 16, 1997, in Los Angeles following a cerebral edema at the age of forty-five. Her husband, drummer Russell Kunkel, organized a pair of tribute concerts in 2007 and 2008.

### Linda Ronstadt

Linda Ronstadt grew up in a music-loving family in Tucson, Arizona, and played with two of her siblings in a folk and roots trio variously called the New Union Ramblers, the Union City Ramblers, and the Three Ronstadts. But Ronstadt was drawn to rock 'n' roll as well. In 1964, she moved to Los Angeles and co-founded the rock group Stone Poneys, which released three albums in fifteen months during 1967 and 1968. She set off on her own in 1969—among her first works was a commercial with Frank Zappa for Remington shavers—and the musicians from one of her early backing bands went on to form the Eagles.

Linda Ronstadt, 1974. *Photo by Julian Wasser/Time & Life Pictures/Getty Images*

Ronstadt and Neil Young were both part of the same burgeoning California rock/folk/country scene, so it was probably inevitable that they'd wind up working together. "I've always felt that Neil had a great deal of really uncanny prescience in his writing," she told biographer Jimmy McDonough. "As strange and surreal as a lot of Neil's lyrics are, they're very clear. . . . There's a clarity that grabs you by the collarbones and just shakes you." Their initial recorded encounter was not planned, though; Ronstadt, along with James Taylor, happened to appear on the same episode of Johnny Cash's TV show, which taped in Nashville while Young was recording *Harvest*. After the show, Young invited her to his studio to provide backing vocals for the album. Ronstadt subsequently opened for Young on his 1973 *Time Fades Away* tour and had a Top 5 country hit with Young's "Love Is a Rose" in 1975.

Ronstadt's association with Young continued as part of the Saddlebags with Nicollette Larson for *American Stars 'n Bars* (1977), and she also sang on *Freedom* (1989), *Harvest Moon* (1992), and *Silver & Gold* (2000)

Ronstadt has been dubbed the Queen of Rock, the First Lady of Rock, and Rock's Venus. Her career includes thirty-two studio albums, twenty Top 40 singles, and eleven Grammy Awards. She's recorded not only rock and country but also mariachi as well as a three-album dip into the Great American Songbook with Frank Sinatra collaborator Nelson Riddle. Ronstadt formed the popular group Trio with Emmylou Harris and Dolly Parton, which won a Grammy Award for its cover of Young's "After the Gold Rush." Ronstadt also earned Tony Award and Golden Globe nominations in 1980 for her turn in *The Pirates of Penzance* on Broadway and in New York's Central Park.

After a prolific musical career, Ronstadt has spent most of the twenty-first century in semi-retirement, raising her two children in Arizona.

## Astrid Young

Neil Young gave his half-sister—the daughter of his father, Scott Young, and his second wife, Astrid Mead—her first amplifier. This gift put her on a path to the '80s bands Ohm and the Secret Sources and Sacred Child. Astrid Young also sang backing vocals for Blackthorne, Dramarama, and Heart's Nancy Wilson. She first recorded with her brother on 1992's *Harvest Moon* and was part of the following year's tour with Booker T. & the MGs and the MTV *Unplugged* session. She also appears on the *Road Rock V1* live set and the 2002 studio album *Are You Passionate?*

Astrid has released two albums of her own: *Brainflower*, which she released independently in 1995, and *Matinee* on the Inbetweens Records label in 2002. She also paints and has written several screenplays as well as a book, *Being Young*, published in 2008.

## Pegi Young

Pegi Young, 2007. *Photo by Gary Gershoff/ WireImage/Getty Images*

Pegi Young has loved music all her life and started writing songs when she was in high school. But outside of occasionally busking, her first performance was in 1994—at the nationally televised Academy Awards ceremony, singing backup for her husband, Neil Young, on his Oscar-nominated song, "Philadelphia."

"It was, 'OK, let's just plunge in,'" she recalled with a laugh.

The plunge has only gotten deeper. Pegi became a backup singer in her husband's touring bands, and—starting with longtime Young associate Ben Keith's Christmas album, *Seven Gates*—began hitting the studio, singing and playing the occasional acoustic guitar. She has contributed to albums including *Greendale*, *Prairie Wind*, *Chrome Dreams II*, and *Fork in the Road*. She also took photographs for *Silver & Gold* and CSNY's 1999 comeback album, *Looking Forward*.

And in 2007, she released her own album, *Pegi Young*, produced by Elliot Mazer of *Harvest* fame, with backing by Keith, Spooner Oldham, Rick Rosas, Marty Stuart, the Jordanaires, and, of course, her husband. "It's very different," Pegi said of stepping into the spotlight after years in the background. "It's completely different. There's that wonderful anonymity of being the background singer. You just hope you're adding to what's going on, but they're not all looking at you. When it's *you*, it's definitely a different experience."

Beyond the music, Pegi's greatest achievement has been the Bridge School, which she co-founded in 1986 to help children with severe physical and speech impairments. She and Young have a son, Ben, with cerebral palsy, while Zeke, Young's son from his relationship with actress Carrie Snodgress, also has the disorder. The school, which Pegi said has grown "way beyond my expectations," is promoted by an annual concert hosted by Young. Pegi said:

*I really didn't know what to expect, but the global impact that we're having. . . . We've had people that come from different countries around the world and they come and mentor at the Bridge School for a year and get different opportunities for ongoing professional development and then go back to their countries and begin to effect their change.*

*It's having a global impact. That was my dream, but to actually be realizing it is huge.*

(continued from page 99)

Young's trail of destruction led to his record company as well. At the last minute, he halted the release of his long-planned multivolume retrospective, *Decade*, opting instead to proceed with the album that eventually became *American Stars 'n Bars* but just as easily could have become the still-unreleased set with which it shares some tracks, *Chrome Dreams*. The primary difference between the two albums is a handful of rollicking country rock tunes that Young recorded in a single day at his ranch, aided by the Horse, Ben Keith, fiddler Carole Mayedo, and a pair of backup singers known as the Saddlebags: superstar Linda Ronstadt and her friend (and Young's soon-to-be girlfriend) Nicolette Larson.

Those songs are as much fun to listen to as they likely were to make. You can hear laughter between tracks as Young uncorks goofy lines like "If you can't cut it/Don't pick up the knife" on "Saddle Up the Palomino." But the album's latter half, cobbled together from various sessions over the previous few years, is another story: The songs include the somber "Will to Love," one of Young's most extraordinary works, if only for the way it was recorded: in front of a crackling fire (which you can hear in the background) on a boombox, taping over a Stills-Young Band cassette. The lyrics are a revelation as well, as Young uses the metaphor of a fish swimming upstream to explain his complex feelings about life, love, and art.

Of course, the song that defines *American Stars 'n Bars*—and perhaps this entire period of Young's artistry—is "Like a Hurricane," a track dating back to 1975. Written for a woman Young spied in a bar (but who proved unattainable), "Hurricane" is one of his most impassioned performances, his frenzied guitar filling in whatever emotions of need, lust, and yearning that his lyrics fail to convey. It remains one of Young's signature songs.

Feeling the itch to play live in an unfettered atmosphere, Young popped up in Santa Cruz, California,

NEIL YOUNG IS FEROCIOUS—obviously a free spirit and, when the mood strikes him, he shifts gears. He can almost be a bit elusive, but the things he emotes in his music are so palpable. I'm sure he's complicated like a lot of artists, but his music's got so much heart. I remember we were playing on the H.O.R.D.E. Fest with him, maybe in Pittsburgh. There was a huge storm that blew in, pouring down buckets of rain, and the wind was actually blowing the rain up into the stage. Neil Young and Crazy Horse were playing, all in these big yellow rain jackets, and I'm standing on the side of the stage next to Neil's son [Ben], and watching water drip off the headstock of Neil Young's guitar. He was singing "Like a Hurricane," but he was facing sideways and just looking at his son and, man, it was very moving, very heavy, and very intense. I read into the lyrics in a totally different way watching him with rain dripping off his hood and his guitar just singing that song to his son. It blew me away. I've never thought about him the same way. I thought, "Wow, that's a guy with a big heart."

— Chris Phillips, Squirrel Nut Zippers

The Ducks Tour, Santa Cruz, California, August 1977. The Ducks comprised Young, Bob Mosley (bass), Jeff Blackburn (guitar), and Johnny Craviotta (drums). *Photo by Richard McCaffrey/Michael Ochs Archives/Getty Images*

in 1977, playing a series of unannounced gigs with the Ducks, a local band that featured ex–Moby Grape bassist Bob Mosley and guitarist Jeff Blackburn, a friend of Young's from the Buffalo Springfield days. Young played a few originals, but for the most part he was content to stay in the background, sitting in on the other band members' originals and covers of '50s rock 'n' roll tunes.

Even as Young moved relentlessly forward in his career, he fastidiously kept track of his footprints, ever aware that there would be a time to look back. Determined to offer a musical autobiography that was true to his own vision, he released in October 1977 the long-delayed *Decade*, a carefully selected compilation that traced his journey from the Springfield and CSNY years through his solo career, including blockbuster material as well as unreleased tracks, among them "Sugar Mountain" (heretofore only released as a B-side); "Love Is a Rose," which had been memorably covered by Linda Ronstadt;

His songs tell a story like few can. I identify with the rebel in him.
—Paul Rodgers

and "Campaigner," a curious acoustic number that asserts, "Even Richard Nixon has got soul." The sprawling collection gave weight to Young's reputation, but it merely scratched the surface in terms of the wealth of unreleased material that some fans knew existed even then.

Young repaired to Miami, where he cut an album's worth of solo acoustic material that would morph into *Comes a Time*. When his label heard it, they suggested he flesh the recordings out a bit by adding a backing band. Usually loathe to accept direction under any circumstances, Young acceded for once, heading to Nashville where he assembled a crew that included Ben Keith, Tim Drummond, drummer Karl Himmel, noted

*(continued on page 110)*

Outside the Mabuhay Gardens, San Francisco, May 27, 1978.
© Chester Simpson (Rock-N-RollPhotos.com)

I Saw NEiL ★ At The Boarding House In SanFrancisco
May 24-28, 1978

*Courtesy Cyril Kieldsen*

Playing the Blow Job arcade game at the Mabuhay Gardens, San Francisco,
May 27, 1978. After his show at the Boarding House, Young went to the
punk club to shoot scenes for *Human Highway* with Devo. Young was
reluctant to have his photo taken until photographer Chester Simpson
showed him the machine and offered him quarters to play it.
© Chester Simpson (Rock-N-RollPhotos.com)

(continued from page 107)

songwriter and session keyboardist Spooner Oldham, Cajun fiddler Rufus Thibodeaux, and a horde of guitarists and string players. He dubbed the aggregation the Gone with the Wind Orchestra.

Lush and accessible, *Comes a Time* turned out to be one of Young's most inviting albums. Its recording coincided with his brief relationship with Nicolette Larson, whose harmony vocals shadow Young throughout, reflecting a mood of happiness and contentment. "There's something there that's me, that record," Young told Jimmy McDonough. "It tells a story."

From the opening track, "Goin' Back," the album drifts in a pool of warm nostalgia, where love is lost, but life goes on. Elsewhere, there's "Already One," a loving tribute to his son, Zeke; a solo stab at the old CSNY track "Human Highway"; the boldly optimistic "Field of Opportunity"; and "Motorcycle Mama," a raunchy bit of comic relief. Young also brought in two tracks featuring a much-subdued Crazy Horse: "Look Out for My Love" and "Lotta Love," the latter of which would become a disco-tinged Top 10 hit for Larson.

The closing song, a cover of Ian Tyson's "Four Strong Winds," was a chance to revisit an important musical moment from his youth. Young recalled in the film *Heart of Gold*:

> When I was just a kid, sixteen years or seventeen years old, I went to this place near Winnipeg where I grew up, and it's called Falcon Lake. And it's just one of those first times when you really got away from home and are on your own. I was just kinda feelin' it for the first time. And there was this little kind of a restaurant place with a jukebox in it that was there, and I used to go there, and I think I spent all my money playing ["Four Strong Winds"] over and over again. It was the most beautiful record that I've ever heard in my life, and I just could not get enough of it.

*Courtesy Cyril Kieldsen*

"LOTTA LOVE"

REP-14.492

Limited-edition "Comes a Time" backed with "Motorcycle Mama," U.S., 1978.
*Courtesy Cyril Kieldsen*

Neil Young — Comes A Time
SIDE 2
Season's Greetings 1978
Kent Crawford
Warner Bros. Records

注目の女性シンガー、ニコレット・ラーソンとの共演で蘇ったブラザース・フォーの大ヒット曲!!
傑作アルバム「カムズ・ア・タイム」からの話題のニュー・シングル!!

STEREO
P-415R

**風は激しく**
FOUR STRONG WINDS

歌・演奏：ニール・ヤング
NEIL YOUNG

45RPM
¥600

ヒューマン・ハイウェイ
HUMAN HIGHWAY

*Japan, 1978. Courtesy Cyril Kieldsen*

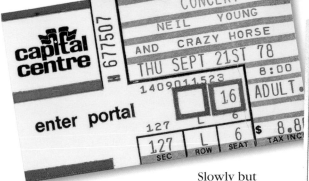

Despite the album's easygoing feel, the actual release of *Comes a Time* proved problematic. Britain's New Musical Express was reported to have joked that Young was awarded a gold record solely for the number of test pressings he'd ordered. Even after the album was shipped, Young discovered a flaw in the mix and paid $200,000 out of his own pocket to have it recalled. In *Neil and Me*, Scott Young recalled seeing boxes of LPs stacked in one of his son's storage buildings. "Each case of albums had been fired at with a rifle," he wrote, "piercing each record and making it unusable."

To promote his gentle, country-inflected album, Young, changeable as ever, hired Crazy Horse to go out on the road with him. But there were other, more significant changes afoot as well. Having split with Larson, Young met Pegi Morton, a local who had caught his eye while waitressing in a diner near his ranch. They married in August 1977, and their son, Ben, was born the next year.

By that time, Young was up and running on several projects, including a film titled *Human Highway*, which bore no relation to the track from *Comes a Time* nor the aborted CSNY album of the same name. Initially conceived as an improvisatory film based on Young and the mad swirl of hippies and hangers-on that surrounded him, it evolved into something else entirely.

The film had a basic repertory company that included Young, Dean Stockwell, Russ Tamblyn, Dennis Hopper, and Sally Kirkland. What it lacked was a script. The project was taken to another dimension, though, when Stockwell turned Young on to a band of oddball art-punks from Akron, Ohio, known as Devo.

With their yellow radiation suits, red plastic "energy dome" hats, and herky-jerky rhythms, Devo was everything that Neil Young was not. Or so they thought. "When we met him, we just thought he was the grandfather of granola," bassist Gerald Casale told PBS's *American Masters*. "And as soon as we talked to him, we realized all our perceptions of him were wrong. He was really far out. I mean really loopy, almost like a mad scientist. So when he asked us to participate in the movie and he said he wanted us to be nuclear waste workers, any resistance we had was gone."

Slowly but surely, a series of improvised scenes emerged. Young played Lionel Switch, a hapless mechanic, and Tamblyn played his clueless friend. Hopper was a jabbering short-order cook and Kirkland a fired waitress who refused to leave the premises. Stockwell was their evil boss, Otto. The members of Devo, who toil at the local nuclear plant, glow red from radiation poisoning.

Wackiness ensues, but not much of the film is coherent. Conked on the head by a wrench, the unconscious Switch dreams of rock stardom in a psychedelic sequence that includes a scene in which Devo's Booji Boy—frontman Mark Mothersbaugh in a rubber baby mask—sits in a crib and sings a bizarro-world version of Young's soon-to-be anthem, "Hey Hey, My My (Into the Black)." "It went on and on and on," Casale recalled.

With Dennis Hopper on the set of *Human Highway*, July 1, 1978.
© Caterine Milinaire/Sygma/Corbis

Young got more than a whacked-out movie scene from Devo. While they jammed, Mothersbaugh intoned the phrase "rust never sleeps," a slogan the band members, in their days as graphic artists, created for Rust-Oleum, a protective spray paint.

Young took the idea and ran with it. *Rust Never Sleeps* became the title of his next album and the concept behind the tour with Crazy Horse (which itself would become a concert film wholly separate from *Human Highway*). To stave off complacency, the disease that attacks veteran rockers like creeping rust, Young presented a show that surveyed his past, reenergized his present, and revealed a brace of new songs as forward-looking and defiantly loud as anything he'd ever done.

The *Rust* tour turned the concert stage into a theater of the absurd, with roadies replaced by hooded "road-eyes," whose look was borrowed from *Star Wars'* Jawas. There was a giant prop microphone, tuning fork,

amplifiers, and road cases that dwarfed the performers. The soundmen wore makeshift Conehead costumes, while producer David Briggs donned a lab coat and became Dr. Decibel.

In the show, Young, who is first spied sleeping atop one of the amplifiers, wakes up and grabs his guitar, playing a solo acoustic set that eventually gives way to the thundering Horse. Signature sound bites from Woodstock add another layer of theatricality, while a cheesy emcee adds a Dadaist twist by instructing the audience to put on prop "Rust-O-Vision" glasses he says will enable them to watch the band decay before their eyes.

But the real triumphs of *Rust Never Sleeps* have less to do with concept than content. Young turned Devo's comical slogan into an overarching statement about guarding against creative decay, remaining committed as an artist, and bridging the gaps between genres and generations. At the time of its release—most of

the album was recorded live, then overdubbed in the studio—it was shocking to hear the line "The king is gone but he's not forgotten/This is the story of Johnny Rotten" from "My My, Hey Hey (Out of the Blue)." Few artists of Young's stature would dare to connect the snot-nosed, self-destructive Rotten with the sainted, only recently dead Elvis Presley. But Young used the song to open the discussion: Is it more profound to be a survivor, to hang on and make rock a career, like it's some sort of middle management desk job (and by extension, die on the crapper, full of Moon Pies and a prescription drug pharmacopeia)? Or should an artist say his/her piece and move along, making way for the next band, the next trend, the next idea that's waiting to take hold?

Young put this all more succinctly, of course, asserting, "It's better to burn out/Than to fade away," a sentiment that, a decade and a half later, was taken with dead certainty by Kurt Cobain, who quoted the couplet in his suicide note.

*(continued on page 117)*

Rust Never Sleeps Tour, 1978. *Michael Ochs Archives/Getty Images*

113

*Rust Never Sleeps* promo poster, 1979.

# Aerosmith's Joe Perry on Neil Young

ONE OF MY FAVORITE ARTISTS as a whole. He's a songwriter's songwriter. There are people who get into this business for a lot of different reasons—some of them have to write and some of them have to perform. Some of them use the writing as a form to get to some other things; sometimes it's the lifestyle, sometimes it's the lure of the money and the glamour and all that. But he's like Dylan; he has to write—he *has* to—and he's constantly changing, like Springsteen. He just knew he was doing it forever, and he's doing it, constantly coming up with stuff. I love listening to his stuff. It's one of those things on my playlist. I'm constantly listening to his stuff.

He tells the truth and he's transparent. There's no guile. What he feels emotionally, musically, and what he puts down with his guitar and through the microphone, it's as simple as that, and there are very few people who can be as untainted as he is. He's amazing like that. You can just tell by the choices he's made in his career he has no care for the business. I'm sure he's a smart businessman, and I'm sure he's nobody's fool when it comes to that, but it's probably a vast annoyance to him, as it is to most of us.

He's so musical, and it just comes out of him. You can just feel what he's feeling. He pays absolutely no attention to technique; it sounds like you'd imagine what it sounded like the first time he picked up a guitar. And when he has something to say he says it and he does it in such a way that it's just so unadorned. In its simplicity it's just fantastically complex; you can talk about it for hours and hours and hours. It's just transparent. He doesn't let anything get between how he feels and what he lays down. Even though he's not a great technician, he just puts so much into, like, those one-note solos. It stops you in your tracks. These songs that are so simple and yet they are brilliant.

"Rockin' in the Free World" is probably one of the best rock songs ever written. Again, it's simple but it's so powerful. It's an anthem. It's iconic, and it works for all time. And the [guitar] solo on it is just

beyond. . . . I was fortunate enough to see [Crosby, Stills, Nash & Young] on the last date [of the 2006 Freedom of Speech Tour]. The whole show was great, and then he did this solo at the end where he just got the whole band together and the solo was really the whole band playing with the solo—it was kind of like putting a stamp on it, just after all the music and all the lyrics it just cut loose and was about three minutes of manic chaos and everybody was involved and he just led the charge. Strings were breaking on his guitar and it was really amazing. I have to say that was probably one of the best solos I've ever seen, because it was like he took all the stuff he'd been feeling and just had to get it out that way and finish it off.

It's the same with his singing style. They talk about his singing style is like Dylan's, they just don't get it. It's all about expression, and it all comes from *here*.

I got another chance to see him play in Pittsburgh a couple of tours ago. We were there, and I think they were playing the next night so we stayed the next night to see him. I got to go on his tour bus, his fabled tour bus, which is unbelievable. It looks like a throwback to 1968. It looks like it was hand-built by hippies, like real craftsmen, and it's a bus like they haven't made them in 15 years. It's been totally rebuilt, and he's got this Studebaker half in the front and a Studebaker half on the back and there's skylights and the inside is all hand-carved wood and it smells like a head shop from 1968 and it's just beautiful. The downstairs where they usually put the bags is a playroom for the kids, so he opened this hatch up in the lounge area and we climbed down there and there were couches and TV and places for kids to play. And he said that is where he sleeps most of the time because it's a comfortable ride even though he's got the double bed and all that in the back. You can just tell he plans on being out there forever.

—*As told to Gary Graff*

It's really just about the songs; he has so many songs that are so good, and no matter when they came out I feel like people would feel the same way about them. If a new band came out with "Hey Hey, My My," I feel like everyone would lose their minds about it, still. He taps into some kind of, like, primal vein, these songs that feel like they were discovered more than written. I also love what he's been able to do without too much complicated music theory stuff. He's able to conjure up these kind of landscapes with the melodies, but not with these complicated chords or being too cute about what he's doing with the music. It's not needlessly intellectual; it's obviously smart music, but it's not like you stroke your chin over it. That's something to aspire to in your own music.

—Robin Pecknold, Fleet Foxes

Brazil, 1979. *Courtesy Robert Ferreira*

*(continued from page 113)*

Young had still more arrows in his quiver. "Thrasher" unceremoniously cuts down his partners Crosby, Stills & Nash, albeit poetically and never by name. You can almost imagine him ending the song with "eat a peach."

Deeper in the album, Young unleashes the Horse on the furious "Powderfinger," narrated from beyond the grave by a young rifleman killed in the act of defending his family. "Welfare Mothers" adds a bit of low comedy to the proceedings, while "Sedan Delivery" reveals a punkier version of a song that, like "Powderfinger" and the time-traveling acoustic number "Pocahontas," was originally meant to appear on *Chrome Dreams*. Finally Young burns down the house with "Hey Hey, My My (Into the Black)," which authoritatively asserts, "Rock and roll will never die."

Young claimed the album's music and take-no-prisoners attitude were not directly inspired by punk rock, but he told *Rolling Stone* that he was aware of punk's emergence:

*I first knew something was going on when we visited England a year and a half ago. Kids were tired of the rock stars and the limousines and the abusing of stage privileges as stars. There was a new music the kids were listening to. As soon as I heard my contemporaries saying, 'God, what the fuck is this. . . . This is going to be over in three months,' I knew it was a sure sign right there that they're going to bite it if they don't watch out. And a lot of them are biting it this year. People are not going to come back to see the same thing over and over again. It's got to change. It's the snake that eats itself. Punk music, New Wave. You can call it what you want. It's rock and roll and to me, it's still the basis of what's going on.*

Young proved his devotion to reinvention with *Rust Never Sleeps* and the *Live Rust* album and concert film that followed closely on its heels. As for *Human Highway*, Young's tortured opus wouldn't see the light of day until 1982, and even then it didn't find a distributor. It was finally released on home video in 1995 with a cover blurb from Young's booking agent that spoke volumes: "It's so bad, it'll be huge!"

*Comes a Time*

NEIL YOUNG
International Harvesters

MY, MY, HEY HEY
NEIL YOUNG UGA
FEB. 3, 1983

STONE CITY ATTRACTIONS Presents
A SOLO EVENING With
NEIL YOUNG
AUSTIN MUNICIPAL AUDITORIUM
AUSTIN, TEXAS
FRIDAY
14
8:00 P.M.

WHERE THE BUFFALO ROAM

**Following the critical** and commercial triumphs of *Comes a Time, Rust Never Sleeps*, and *Live Rust*, the 1980s are widely viewed as Neil Young's lost decade. The period is marked by an acute artistic restlessness that found him flitting from one genre to another, resulting in inconsistent and sometimes slapdash records that, in turn, led to feelings of confusion, frustration, and downright anger in even his most ardent fans. Record sales plummeted.

Predictably, Young has a different perspective.

"I feel really good about what I've done in the '80s," he told the *Village Voice*. "Even though I've taken a lot of shit for it. Everything I did made sense to me, yet everywhere I went people were telling me, 'What the fuck are you doing? Why are you doing this? You're systematically dismantling your record sales.' There was this huge abyss between me and everybody else."

What the public didn't know—because Young forbade his camp to divulge it—was that the music he made during the period was, to some degree, a response to various crises he was facing in his personal life.

His son Ben, born to Young and wife Pegi in 1978, was diagnosed with cerebral palsy. Young's older son, Zeke, born to actress Carrie Snodgress, also suffers from the disorder. But Ben's condition was more severe: he was spastic, quadriplegic, and nonoral.

"I remember looking at the sky, looking for a sign, wondering, 'What the fuck is going on?'" Young told the *Voice*. "'Why are the kids in this situation? What the hell caused this? What did I do? There must be something wrong with me.'"

In 1980, there was another emergency on the horizon. Pegi required brain surgery to repair an arterial

Young supplied the musical score for Art Linson's film
*Where the Buffalo Roam*, based on the life of Hunter S. Thompson, 1980.

problem that, left unchecked, could have killed her. She recovered fully in a matter of months, but one can only imagine the strain the family's health problems placed upon Young.

To be sure, both situations would impact his music in the '80s, most strikingly on *re·ac·tor* and *Trans*, which offered Young's artistic response to Ben's monotonous, repetitive therapy. But first came *Hawks & Doves*, which showed the artist already adrift creatively, casting about for new genres to work in and navigating the shifting political and cultural tides around him.

With vocalist Hillary O'Brien of the Hawks & Doves Band, Bread & Roses Festival, Greek Theatre, Berkeley, California, October 3, 1980. © Henry Diltz/Corbis

*Hawks & Doves* is a minor effort that Young himself called a "transitional" album, although he also defended it to *Mojo* as "a funky little record that represents where I was and what I was doing at the time."

Funky? Not so much. But little it is, clocking in at barely half an hour.

The album is roughly split along the lines of opposing acoustic "dove" tunes and electric "hawk" songs. The two opening numbers are leftovers from Young's abandoned *Homegrown* album. "Little Wing" is a short, sweet song about a nurturing woman, which is given new relevance by Young's nesting with Pegi. "The Old Homestead," which takes up almost a quarter of the album's run time, is a nearly impenetrable allegory that seems to describe Young's warring creative impulses.

"Lost in Space" is another song yearning for domesticity, albeit in an unusual setting: the ocean floor. In one of his loopier moments on record, Young manipulates the tape to make his voice sound like he's joined by an underwater chorus. In stark contrast, "Captain Kennedy" offers a blast of harsh reality, detailing a sailor's last few minutes before going into battle.

The album's electric tunes were newly minted for *Hawks & Doves* but depart wildly from the take-no-prisoners rock that Young pursued on the *Rust* albums. Instead, they're country songs, as pure and unfiltered as Young had ever offered, led by Ben

Keith's swooping steel guitar and Rufus Thibodeaux's sawing fiddle. At the time, some of them, like "Stayin' Power" and "Coastline," seemed slight and somewhat tossed off. But, in retrospect, it's possible to view them in the context of Young's longstanding relationship with Pegi and the steadfastness with which they faced down their hardships. In the latter, he boasts, "We don't back down from no trouble."

Of course, the *Hawks & Doves* songs that are most remarked upon are the last three, each of which hints at an unexpected shift to the political right. In "Union Man," Young lampoons the musicians' union (and by extension

Neil and Pegi Young, the Ritz, New York City, March 2, 1981. © Bob Leafe (bobleafe.com)

other bloated and ineffective unions that did little to make life better for the rank and file). "Comin' Apart at Every Nail" is a blue-collar anthem that exults in patriotism even as the nation unravels. This was the time, recall, of Jimmy Carter's "malaise," the Iranian hostage crisis, and the dawn of the age of Ronald Reagan. If Young's brethren from Woodstock Nation were aghast at his sudden rightward tilt, they must have been floored by the album's title track, which blatantly spoiled for war. In it, Young even volunteered his life, or at least his checkbook, for service. It was a far cry from "Ohio." But it was nothing compared to what would come further down the road.

Young was unable to tour to support either *Hawks & Doves* or its follow-up, *re·ac·tor*, which he recorded with Crazy Horse in the fall and winter of 1980 and the summer of 1981. By that time, he and Pegi had enrolled Ben in a radical therapy program designed by the Institute for the Awareness of Human Potential. The demanding program required the couple's total commitment, twelve hours a day, seven days a week. It also altered Young's work schedule, forcing him to record only during breaks in the afternoon, when it had been his natural inclination to howl at the moon.

You can feel Young's desire to break free and rock out on *re·ac·tor* tracks such as "Opera Star"; the stuttering, slobbering "Rapid Transit"; and the character-driven "Surfer Joe and Moe the Sleaze." "Get Back On It" expresses a desire to head back out on the road but nebulously hints that he's otherwise engaged. Still, the album contains enough social commentary to suggest that Young's attention could be at least temporarily drawn outside the demands of Ben's program. "Southern Pacific" is a chugging rocker about a railroad worker who gave his life and good health to his profession, only to be cast aside when he reached the age of mandatory retirement. "Motor City" is a scriocomic rant about the American automobile industry, which even then was being savaged by imports. The album-closing "Shots," meanwhile, is dominated by intense sound effects of automatic weapons fire, and it pairs two topics seldom discussed simultaneously: suburban lust and international ultraviolence.

For both good and ill, *re·ac·tor*'s standout track is "T-Bone," a thudding nine-and-a-quarter-minute composition whose repetitiveness is thought to have been inspired by Ben's therapy. Its sole lyrical content is a koan that most found a bit too Zen for the room. "Got mashed potatoes," Young declares. "Ain't got no T-bone."

With no public acknowledgment of his personal situation, Young's fans weren't sure just what to make

of "T-Bone" or the rest of *re·ac·tor*, though at least the album found him kicking out some *Rust*-style jams. But those who paid attention to album art must have known something was up. The back cover was inscribed with Reinhold Niebuhr's Serenity Prayer, which has been adopted by Alcoholics Anonymous and other twelve-step recovery programs: "God grant me the serenity to accept the things I cannot change; Courage to change the things I can; And wisdom to know the difference."

Maintaining the requisite level of mystery, however, Young had the prayer printed in Latin.

He must have taken the prayer's wisdom to heart, however, because in short order, he drastically changed a number of aspects of his life to help him regain control of it:

☆ On the personal front, he and Pegi quit Ben's demanding program and opted for another, less pressure-filled form of therapy designed by the National Academy for Child Development.

☆ Professionally, Young, who was frustrated by the lack of promotional oomph behind *re·ac·tor*, left Warner/Reprise, his record label for nearly a decade and a half. He turned down a more lucrative deal with RCA in order to sign with David Geffen's eponymous label, which offered him a huge advance for each album and complete artistic freedom.

☆ Musically, Young purchased two devices that would change the course of his work for the foreseeable future: a synthesizer/sampling unit called the synclavier (first heard on *re·ac·tor*'s finale, "Shots") and a vocorder, a device that radically altered the sound of the human voice.

"I was looking for ways to change my voice," Young told the *Voice*. "To sing through a voice that no one could recognize and it wouldn't be judged as being me."

Young began recording a handful of songs that would eventually wind up on *Trans*. One of them was a robotic take on his Buffalo Springfield hit, "Mr. Soul," made to blow the minds of his fellow Springfield bandmates, who were considering a reunion. But when the Geffen deal was signed, Young set the tracks aside and, with Springfield bassist Bruce Palmer in tow, headed for Hawaii to make an album called *Island in the Sun*.

That album, which also featured Ben Keith, Ralph Molina, Nils Lofgren, and CSNY percussionist Joe Lala, was intended as a commercial album that would please Young's new label. "It was a tropical thing all about sailing, ancient civilizations, islands and water," Young told *Mojo*. But Geffen rejected it. So much for artistic freedom.

In his usual taciturn fashion, Young returned to the mainland and revived *Trans*, which deals even more explicitly than *re·ac·tor* with the demands of Ben's original program. To handle the pressure, Young said, he completely shut himself down emotionally.

"I closed myself down so much that I was *makin'* it, doin' great with *surviving*," he told the *Voice*. "But my soul was completely encased. I didn't even consider that I would need a soul to play my music, that when I shut the door on pain, I shut the door on my music."

Young attempted to lay bare his crippled emotional state but to do it anonymously, hiding himself in a cast of characters created by the vocorder's many voices. It took years for him to let his fans in on the album's subtext:

Trans *was about all these robot-humanoid people working in this hospital, and the one thing they were trying to do was teach this little baby to push a button. That's what the record's about. Read the lyrics, listen to all the mechanical voices, disregard everything but*

# TRAIN OF LOVE

**NEIL YOUNG'S A MODEL TRAIN GUY**—has been since age five, when he got his first set, a Marx Santa Fe diesel on an L-shaped track layout in a basement prone to flooding. He never lost his locomotive jones and for a time wound up running the most famous model train manufacturer in the world.

Young's association with Lionel LLC came from his passion for the product as well as his desire to bond with his sons, Zeke and Ben, both of whom have cerebral palsy. Young owns one of the most extensive model train collections in the world, rolling them around an elaborate layout in a separate barn on his property in Redwood City, California. The spread is decorated with landscapes made from real redwood trunks, living plants watered by an internal irrigation system, ponds stocked with real goldfish, handmade wooden trestles, and a variety of accessories acquired during his travels.

Biographer Jimmy McDonough described the train barn as "a refuge for Neil: no band members flubbing notes, no producers storming off, no surprises outside of the occasional derailment." But the ability to connect further with his sons is what truly enriched the experience for Young and inspired him to pursue model trains on a larger scale.

Young had set up a train layout for Zeke, and when Ben—whose CP is more debilitating—was old enough, Young began "inventing all these gizmos

Flying the Lionel flag, Ahoy Hall, Rotterdam, the Netherlands, May 27, 1987.
*Photo by Rob Verhorst/Redferns/Getty Images*

*that computerized thing, and it's clear* Trans *is the beginning of my search for communication with a severely handicapped* nonoral *person. "Transformer Man" is a song for my kid. If you read the words to that song—and look at my child with his little button and his train set and his transformer—the whole thing is for Ben.*

In its released form, however, *Trans* is a mix of Young's inscrutable computer music and three songs from the *Island in the Sun* sessions: "Little Thing Called Love," "Hold On to Your Love," and "Like an Inca." True, songs like "Computer Age," "Sample and Hold," and "Transformer Man"—the latter of which, in its new context, seems more sweet than foreboding—didn't go anywhere that the German electronic band Kraftwerk didn't go first. But the album represented an incredibly bold, risky move for an artist of Young's stature.

Far riskier, though, was Young's decision to take the Transband (as it was dubbed) on the road before the album's release. Unlike the *Rust* tour, whose backdrop was

*(continued on page 127)*

# TRAVELS ON THE LIONEL LINE

so he can run the train set with it." The inventions are mostly simple devices that allow Zeke to regulate the flow of train traffic around the tracks. Young formed his own short-lived company, Yardmaster, in the late 1980s and then worked for a time with Quinn-Severson Industries (QSI) to develop new and more realistic sound systems for the trains.

But all roads led to Lionel.

Young met Lionel's owner and CEO, Richard P. Kughn, through QSI. Even as Young's relationship with the latter derailed—and wound up in court—he and Kughn, a self-professed "Bing Crosby fan," developed an alliance and a surprising friendship. "Neil is a very, very bright individual when it comes to electronics," Kughn noted, "and he happens to be a very, very fine human being as well as a very talented guy. He's a very warm and caring human being."

Young and Kughn partnered in a new venture called Liontech Trains LLC to bring the technology he'd invented at home to the masses. "We believe that the experience of controlling a miniature world can help the physically challenged improve their confidence and self-esteem and their perspective," Kughn explained. And having Neil Young involved in the company—especially as he was at a music career high with the *Freedom*, *Ragged Glory*, and *Harvest Moon* albums—boosted morale at Lionel, too. One staffer noted:

*It's kind of wild, because he does not have the typical corporate look. Just to see a table full of suits and this guy standing up there talking, saying, "Here's the game plan," makes it pretty interesting. But nobody's going, "Who the hell is this guy?" He knows what he's talking about, and when he talks, you listen. . . . And he loves trains, which kind of makes you part of the family out here.*

Young eventually became a father figure in that family. In 1995, when Kughn was unable to hang on to Lionel, Young joined a partnership that purchased controlling interest in the company, with his share a reported 20 percent.

In a world increasingly dominated by video games, however, the model train industry suffered. Lionel filed for bankruptcy in 2004, following a number of cost-cutting measures—including layoffs and moving some production out of the United States—as well as a $38.6 ruling against the company in a suit filed by rival MTH Electric Trains. The reorganization led to new ownership by the private-equity firm Guggenheim Corporate Funding and the estate of the late Martin Davis, who was one of Young's partners in the 1995 purchase.

Lionel administration has said that Young retains some interest in the company, primarily via a continued joint venture between Lionel and Young's Creative Trains LLC in Liontech.

Transband, the Catalyst, Santa Cruz, California, July 13, 1982. © *Robert Matheu*

Trans Band Tour, Wembley Arena, London, September 26, 1982. *Andre Csillag/Rex USA*

The label on the record reads:

MADE IN U.S.A. REPRISE RECORDS, A DIVISION OF WARNER BROS. RECORDS INC., 3300 WARNER COMMUNICATIONS COMPANY

RE·AC·TOR
NEIL YOUNG & CRA·ZY HORSE
PRODUCED BY DAVID BRIGGS, TIM MULLIGAN & NEIL YOUNG
WITH JERRY NAPIER
MASTERED BY
DAVID GOLD AT GOLD STAR STUDIOS, HOLLYWOOD, CALIFORNIA
RECORDED AT MODERN RECORDERS, REDWOOD CITY, CALIFORNIA

RPSP 49895
(YCA 9750 S)

STEREO
33⅓ RPM

From the Reprise Album HS 2304 RE·AC·TOR

MO·TOR CIT·Y    3:11
(Neil Young)

Published by Silver Fiddle—ASCAP
© 1981 Warner Bros. Records Inc.
for the U.S. & WEA International Inc.
for the world outside of the U.S.

re·ac·tor
south·ern pac·i·fic
b/w mo·tor cit·y

neil young    cra·zy horse

(continued from page 123)

comically outsized for effect, everything about Young's European trek was literally too big. It was over budget, used too much equipment, was booked into halls he couldn't fill and was too technically complex. Some of the dates were canceled. Several ended in riots. The shows left audiences puzzled and Young awash in red ink.

On *Live Berlin*, a video compiled from the tour's last two shows, you can see the band—especially Molina (a basher at heart) and Palmer (who'd been suspended from the tour earlier for boozing too much)—fail in its attempt to gel with a tangle of backing tapes, synched-up synclaviers, and Young and Lofgren's vocorders. It was all too much, especially given that the audience was completely unfamiliar with the new material.

Even had that not been the case, it's hard to say how much difference it would have made. Young admitted that, bottom line, the songs he was singing were about a communication breakdown that can't be repaired.

"It was very obscure," Young said. "[The audience] didn't have a fuckin' chance in the world. The whole thing is. *Trans* is about communication, but it's not getting through. And that's what my son is. You gotta realize—you can't understand the words on *Trans*, and I can't understand my son's words. So feel *that*."

Back in the United States, Young jettisoned the band and pared the show down to a solo outing dubbed "A Very Special Evening with Neil Young." It opened with an acoustic set and ended with an electric one, as Young put to better use the electronic backing techniques he debuted in Europe.

The tour's true innovation, though, was "Trans TV," a live in-house video broadcast hosted by anchorman "Dan Clear" (actor Newell Alexander). Clear showed video clips and interviewed the crew, members of the crowd, and even Young himself, who offered a halftime assessment of his performance.

As with so much of Young's output in the '80s, such hijinks were, for some fans, an acquired taste.

Anxious once again to move on to the next thing, Young took a brief break from performing to record in Nashville with familiar faces Ben Keith, Tim Drummond, Rufus Thibodeaux, and Spooner Oldham, among others. The result—as much of an about-face as was possible after *Trans*—was *Old Ways*, a country record that went even further afield than side two of *Hawks & Doves*. Among the songs recorded were the working-class anthem "Depression Blues" and the title track, on which Young vowed to stop drinking and doping.

Young returned to the road but canceled the tour after

he collapsed backstage in Louisville, Kentucky. Things worsened when Geffen rejected *Old Ways*, requesting a rock 'n' roll album instead. Young told PBS's *American Masters*:

> They said, "Hey Neil, you've got to make a rock
> and roll record, you just have to." I said, "Do
> you know what rock and roll is?" and there was
> kind of a silence and then I tried to figure out
> what it was. And then I thought in my mind,
> "Rock and roll, what the hell is rock and roll?
> Let's go back in time to when rock and roll
> started and try to see what it is."

Young slicked his hair back, donned a hep-cat suit and tie, and recorded a quick collection of rockabilly and '50s-style pop tunes that was, in its own way, as puzzling as *Trans*. His band was called the Shocking Pinks and featured Keith, Drummond, pianist Larry Byrom, drummer Karl Himmel, and vocalists Anthony Crawford and Rick Palombi.

Clocking in at less than twenty-five minutes, *Everybody's Rockin'*, beyond being a genre exercise and a peek into the kind of music on which Young grew up, is mostly forgettable. A notable exception is "Payola Blues," which asserts that pay-for-play radio (and, indeed, MTV) was as prevalent a problem then as in the days of '50s deejay Alan Freed. The title track, meanwhile, affirms Young's Republican bona fides, surreally imagining "Ronnie and Nancy" boogying on the White House lawn.

Young got deeply into the *Everybody's Rockin'* character and took the Shocking Pinks on tour, but the album stiffed. Who could blame his fans for wondering if this was just another put-on?

However sincere his retro trip, Young put the Shocking Pinks to rest and attempted a reunion with Crazy Horse, which produced a pair of explosive shows at the Catalyst in Santa Cruz, California, but fell apart in the studio. He then formed the International Harvesters, a country band featuring Keith, Drummond, Himmel, Thibodeaux, Oldham, and Crawford.

But then came a move that no one was looking for, and for once it wasn't perpetrated by Young.

Disappointed and confused by Young's increasingly outré activities, Geffen slapped him with a $3.3 million lawsuit, claiming his records had become "unrepresentative" of his previous output. Rather than bow to the pressure of the lawsuit, Young simply dove deeper into his latest country excursion. He swore off rock, booked tours with Waylon Jennings and other country artists, and even played the Grand Ole Opry.

*(continued on page 131)*

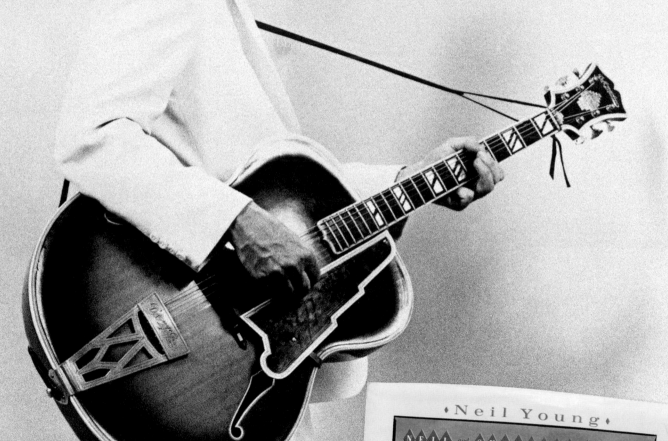

*Everybody's Rockin'* promo photo, August 1983. *AP Photo*

•Neil Young•

NEIL and the SHOCKING PINKS

Wonderin'

A 3581

Backed with "Payola Blues," the Netherlands, 1983.
*Courtesy Robert Ferreira*

ADMIT ONE
Mon., July 4, 1983-8:00 PM
Weldon, Williams & Lick—Ft. Smith, Ark.
Admission $12.25
PRICE INCLUDES 25¢ USERS FEE

with NEIL YOUNG
Presented by Contemporary Presentations
S. & C. Fair

NEIL YOUNG
A Solo Evening
MONDAY 8:00 P.M.
ASSEMBLY CENTER
OMAHA, NEBRASKA
Schon Productions presents
A-Z-92 Concert Celebration
WEDNESDAY 8:00
Wed., July 13, 1983-8:00 PM
OK, OKLAHOMA

$12.50
NO REFUND — NO EXCHANGE

JULY
4
1983

SEC/BX K
ROW F
SEAT 2

RESERVED

NO REFUND-NO EXCHANGE
*****RESERVED*****
TKT. NO. 9179
CIVIC AUDITORIUM
GENERAL

# Throw Your Hatred Down
## The Feud with David Geffen

**WHEN FORMER ASYLUM RECORDS** founder David Geffen returned to the music industry in 1980 to start Geffen Records with $25 million in startup money from parent label Warner Bros., he began loading up on stars: John Lennon, Elton John, Donna Summer, Joni Mitchell, Peter Gabriel. He wanted to sell lots of records. That's one of the reasons he signed Neil Young for $1 million per album and total creative freedom.

And that's why Geffen and Young wound up in one of the most notorious feuds ever between an artist and his record company.

"They didn't look at me as an artist," Young told *Rolling Stone* after the dust had settled and he was back with Warner's Reprise imprint. "They looked at me as a product, and this product didn't fit in with their marketing scheme."

To be fair, Young did present Geffen with some of his most ambitious and challenging—some would say just plain weird—music: 1983's *Trans*, his foray into electronic music, and *Everybody's Rockin'*, a short (25-minute) rockabilly celebration that came out later that year. But, Young counters, he also presented the label with albums he felt were definitely saleable that Geffen ultimately rejected, including the tropical-flavored *Island in the Sun* and a version of *Old Ways* that he described as *Harvest II*. "I really tried to do my best during that period, but I felt I was working under duress," Young said. "It was blatant manipulation. It was just so different from anything I'd ever experienced."

The situation exploded in November 1983, when Geffen sued Young in Los Angeles Superior Court for $3.3 million, accusing him of making albums that were "not 'commerical' and . . . musically uncharacteristic of Young's previous recordings." Young countersued for $21 million. Needless to say, the rapport between them was a bit . . . tense.

"To get sued for being noncommercial after 20 years of making records, I thought was better than a Grammy," he told *Musician*. He related to *Q* that he told Geffen executives to "back off or I'm going to play country music forever. And then you won't be able to sue me anymore because country music will be what I always do so it won't be 'uncharacteristic' anymore. . . . I'll turn into George Jones."

The stalemate ended on April 1, 1985, with both parties dropping their respective suits. Young volunteered to restructure his deal with Geffen, reducing the per-album fee to $500,000. After the legal swords were sheathed and Geffen personally apologized, Young was charitable in his comments, empathizing with the financial pressure of running a label and telling biographer Jimmy McDonough that Geffen took Young's low sales "personally—that I was making these weird records just to make him look like an idiot." He noted that Geffen was "still my friend."

He was not Young's boss for much longer, however. Young recorded several more studio albums for Geffen, including an even more country-flavored *Old Ways* in 1985 and a set with Crazy Horse, *Life*, in 1987, as well as the 1993 compilation *Lucky Thirteen*. And, if it made Geffen feel any better, Young's first release back with Reprise was the brassy blues set, *This Note's for You*.

In 1990, David Geffen sold Geffen Records to MCA Music Entertainment for an estimated $800 million in stock, which multiplied when Matsushita Electric Industrial Co. Ltd. bought MCA the following year. Geffen stayed with the company until 1995, when he joined forces with Jeffrey Katzenberg and Steven Spielberg in the multimedia DreamWorks SKG.

*(continued from page 127)*

"I miss the feeling of community that rock had in the '60s," Young told *Rolling Stone.* "But I got back that feeling when I started hanging out with country guys."

Eventually, the suit blew over. Young agreed to take a smaller advance for future recordings, and Geffen agreed to release his previously rejected country album, albeit in a completely revamped form.

*Old Ways* bore little resemblance to its earlier version. Only a couple of the original songs survived, including the title track, which was recast as a duet with Willie Nelson. In place of some of the other cuts were epic overproductions, including a schmaltzy remake of "The Wayward Wind," a '50s hit for Tex Ritter and Gogi Grant, and the string-laden "Misfits," which proved Nashville hadn't quite wrung all of the hippie out of him. The song imagines the inhabitants of the space station watching "re-runs of Muhammad Ali."

More damning, though, was Young's replacing the cadre of trusted sidemen he had brought to the earlier sessions with a host of Nashville pros, whose approach to music had little to do with Young's vibe-dependent technique. In short, the album became another case of style over substance.

As before, it was difficult to tell where the real Neil Young ended and the role he was playing began. In interviews, Young trashed rock music and its fans, touted Ronald Reagan, and toed country's conservative line on subjects such as patriotism, welfare, and foreigners—never mind that Young, who had never given up his Canadian citizenship, was one himself.

If Young's pronouncements hurt his reputation at home, they all but destroyed it in Europe, where he also canceled a tour due to fear of Libyan terrorism (then on the rise following the bombing of Pan Am flight 103 over Lockerbie, Scotland). Indeed, it would take Young years to rebuild his relationship with his fans abroad.

That doesn't mean he turned his back on the rest of the world, however. In 1984, Young's third child was born, a daughter named Amber. And in early 1985, Young took part in the charity single "Tears Are Not Enough," the Canadian collective Northern Lights' equivalent to USA for Africa's "We Are the World" and Band Aid's U.K. effort "Do They Know It's Christmas?" Young performed twice at the Live Aid concert for Ethiopian famine relief: first in a set backed by the International Harvesters, then in a surprise return with Crosby, Stills, Nash & Young.

Under-rehearsed, plagued by monitor problems, and thrown off by a drug-addled Crosby, the two-song CSNY reunion was a disaster. Though fans continued to long for a new album and tour from the supergroup, the Live Aid performance made clear how unfortunate such an endeavor would be if Crosby didn't pull himself together. Young even made that a condition of any future get-together.

Trade ad, 1985 Australia tour.

**I actually did meet Neil, and, of course, the Bob Dylans and Neil Youngs and Willie Nelsons, and all those guys from that era are fantastic poets, songwriters. You just don't see very many guys being successful in this day that do what they do, which is too bad. I expected Neil to probably not dig my patriotic image, but he's one of those guys that don't take an issue with you being patriotic. They really don't put being patriotic into the political category; they just view you as an artist out doing your own thing, and that's the way Neil was.**

**—Toby Keith**

International Harvesters Tour, Pacific Amphitheatre, Costa Mesa, California, October 24, 1984. © Robert Matheu

The "Tears Are Not Enough" famine-relief single recorded by Canadian artists, February 10, 1985.

Live Aid, JFK Stadium, Philadelphia, July 13, 1985. *AP Photo/George Widman*

Crosby would indeed clean up, but he wouldn't do it willingly. He entered and abandoned numerous treatment programs and established a substantial rap sheet along the way. By year's end, he was in the Texas State Penitentiary on drug and gun charges. The only way he would quit hard drugs, it seemed, was by doing hard time.

At Live Aid, Bob Dylan made an offhand pronouncement that he'd like to see some of the money raised go to help pay the mortgages of American family farmers. Willie Nelson took that ball and ran with it, joining with Young and John Cougar Mellencamp to make Farm Aid a reality. The first of many such concerts was held at the University of Illinois' Memorial Stadium and featured thirty-eight acts—Bob Dylan among them—raising millions of dollars and, perhaps more importantly, awareness for the plight of the family farmer.

Not everyone was in such a charitable mood, however. Geffen rejected the idea of Young releasing a five-song EP to benefit Farm Aid.

Whether to placate his increasingly difficult label chief—which is unlikely—or because he sensed his time as a country artist was at an end, Young returned to the studio to record a rock album, *Landing on Water*. But rather than hire Crazy Horse for the task, he brought in two studio pros: drummer Steve Jordan, whose credits included numerous jazz, rock, and funk sessions, and guitarist/co-producer Danny Kortchmar, best known as a veteran sideman and songwriting partner of Don Henley and Jackson Browne.

Initially, Young was fired up. "That album was like a rebirth," he told *Rolling Stone*. "Something came alive; it was like a bear waking up."

*(continued on page 136)*

With (from left) Anthony Crawford, Waylon Jennings, and Rufus Thibodeaux, Farm Aid I, Memorial Stadium, Champaign, Illinois, September 22, 1985. © *Robert Matheu*

# Field of Opportunity
## Farm Aid

Farm Aid–organized protest to support the Freedom to Farm Act, U.S. Capitol, Washington, D.C., September 13, 1999. *Photo by Michael Smith/Getty Images*

**ON JULY 13, 1985**, some of the world's top music stars had spent nearly fifteen hours at seven sites around the world singing to raise money for the people of famine-ravaged Ethiopia. As the "global jukebox" known as Live Aid drew to a close, Bob Dylan stepped up to the microphone at JFK Stadium in Philadelphia and said, "I hope that some of the money . . . maybe they can just take a little bit of it, maybe . . . one or two million, maybe, and use it, say, to pay the mortgages on some of the farms . . . the farmers here owe to the banks."

The comment angered Live Aid organizer Bob Geldof, but the idea stirred Willie Nelson, who subsequently enlisted Neil Young and John Mellencamp as the artistic muscle behind a new venture called Farm Aid. All three remain members of Farm Aid's board of directors and were joined by Dave Matthews after the 2001 concert.

Nelson brought the idea to Young first, a few days after Live Aid at the video shoot for "Are There Any More Real Cowboys?" from Young's forthcoming *Old Ways* album. Enlisting Mellencamp and country singer John Conlee, they made the first Farm Aid a reality, with thirty-eight acts playing on September 22, 1985, at the University of Illinois' Memorial Stadium in Champaign-Urbana.

Prior to the concert, Young wrote an open letter to President Ronald Reagan, which was published as a full-page ad in *USA Today* and read aloud at the concert. In it, Young told Reagan, who he called "in many ways . . . a great leader," that it was time to aid family farmers both in the U.S. and around the world. He argued that America's food exportation "undercut the family farmers in those countries, forcing them out of business." He told Reagan that his administration's policies would "deal a fatal blow" to America's family farm community and also send "a tremor of fear through every small family business in America. What will this do to the American spirit?"

The issue, of course, was a bit harder to sell to the masses than, say, feeding people in Africa. Nevertheless, the first Farm Aid raised an estimated $10 million. Today, Farm Aid lobbies on behalf of family farm interests—it's credited with the passage of the 1987 Agricultural Credit Act to help family farms facing foreclosure—provides legal and financial assistance, and educates the public about the importance of family farms. Young has remained an outspoken proponent at each of the concerts, including a memorable diatribe against Vice President Al Gore and Secretary of Agriculture Mike Espy for not attending the 1993 show in Ames, Iowa. "Why aren't they here to hear this?" Young raged. "We shouldn't be doing this for seven, eight, ten, fifteen, twenty-five, thirty years. Farm Aid is not an American tradition. It's a band-aid. We ought to get rid of it. We want *more* from Washington!"

Farm Aid concerts have taken place annually—except for 1988—and have moved from large-scale stadium spectacles to more modest but still impactful amphitheater shows. Young has performed solo as well as with Crazy Horse and CSNY. His "Mother Earth (Natural Anthem)" from 1990's *Ragged Glory* was recorded during Farm Aid IV at the Hoosier Dome in Indianapolis.

"Farm Aid has been great," Young told biographer Jimmy McDonough. "We've done alotta things. The shortcomings of Farm Aid are many, and the accomplishments are many. It's just one of those things—you believe in it, you keep goin' and you keep tryin' to make it better."

With John Fogerty, Keith Richards, and Chuck Berry, First Annual Rock and Roll Hall of Fame Awards, Waldorf-Astoria Hotel, New York, January 24, 1986. *AP Photo/Frankie Ziths*

Solo performance at Greenpeace Rainbow Warrior Music Festival, Auckland, New Zealand, April 23, 1986.

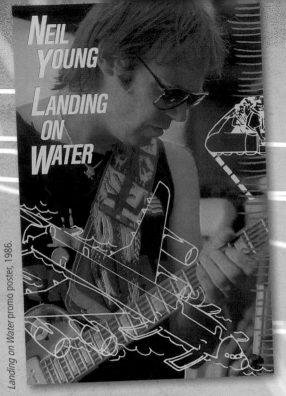

*Landing on Water* promo poster, 1986.

*Neil Young in Berlin* film poster, 1986.

(continued from page 133)

Young revived some of the songs he'd tried to record with Crazy Horse in 1984, including "Touch the Night" and "Violent Side," but his approach this time was very different. Instead of employing the Horse's shoot-from-the-hip spontaneity, the songs this time were tightly produced and heavily overdubbed, emphasizing Jordan's drums and all manner of percussive clinks and clanks. And while Young's guitar rings out in ways that it hadn't in years, the album is dominated by synthesizers instead. In its attempt to sound utterly contemporary, the album sounds positively stuck in the '80s. It's *dated*—one of the very few Neil Young albums to wear that particular badge of shame.

Eventually, even Young turned on it, admitting to the syndicated radio show *Rockline* that *Landing on Water* is "a piece of crap."

Having already spearheaded one long-running charity in Farm Aid, Young turned his attention to raising funds and awareness for a cause even closer to home: The Bridge School is a Mountain View, California, institution dedicated to aiding severely impaired children with physical and communication issues. Pegi Young was one of the school's founders. The first Bridge School Benefit was held at Shoreline Amphitheatre and featured acoustic performances from Young, Bruce Springsteen, Nils Lofgren, CSNY, Don Henley, and Tom Petty. The show became an annual event, and the involvement of Young and other noted musicians has raised millions of dollars for the cause.

Despite having cast Crazy Horse aside for the recording of *Landing on Water*, Young hired them to go on tour in support of it. The shows mixed high concept

and low comedy, evidenced by a stage set that brought back some of the oversized props from the *Rust* era with a few new twists. Billed as the "Third Best Garage Band in the World," Young and the Horse played as if they were just that. Along the way, they were forced to endure the same type of indignities as a genuine garage band: a mother who phoned in, asking that the music be turned down; household pests, including mechanical insects and giant talking mice (actually a couple of roadies in rodent costumes); and a team of exterminators who interrupted the proceedings.

The tour took on an even more ambitious dimension as Young attempted to record *Life*, an entirely new set of songs, in concert (later to be finished in the studio á la *Rust Never Sleeps*) and document the entire process with a film that was to be titled *Muddy Track*. But Young hadn't yet gotten the synthesizers out of his system, nor his taste for right-wing politics. "Mideast Vacation" and "Long Walk Home" take note of how isolated America had become from the rest of the world—a predicament

He's really one of our last true artists left that follows his muse wherever it leads. He's got some incredibly beautiful records and records that are unlistenable and downright confusing. Yet he makes them and he puts them out and seems to love them all equally. It's really an extraordinary journey by an extraordinary guy. I don't work with anybody who doesn't think Neil's the best thing ever. He doesn't compromise; you don't see a beer ad or a party on a boat with Neil Young. He's always maintained a true and full artistic credibility. And he was incredibly nice to us when we did the Bridge School thing; there were 18 million people playing there, and he made everybody who came feel like they were his favorite band and he was as happy as could be to have them there. That's one more telling act of a very gracious man.

—Steve Berlin, Los Lobos

NEIL & YOUNG
CRAZYHORSE
1986
ALL AREAS
OTTO

Spain, 1987.
*Courtesy Robert Ferreira*

**Ever anxious to get into the music by playing a character, Young slipped into a ratty suit coat, fedora, and some shades and transformed himself into a bluesman known as Shakey Deal.**

to which Young could no doubt relate. "Inca Queen," meanwhile, is a poor cousin of precursors "Cortez the Killer" and "Like an Inca." Still, "Prisoners of Rock 'n' Roll" shows a bit of spirit, railing against "taking orders from record company clowns," Young's most pointed reference to his Geffen overlords. "When Your Lonely Heart Breaks," an emotionally charged ballad, could have been one of Young's standout tracks from the 1980s, but its indifferent arrangement and placement deep in the album all but buries it.

More than anything, *Life* seems like a missed opportunity. Why spend time on heavy-handed production, mechanized beats, and endless overdubs when you've got Crazy Horse standing around?

The *Muddy Track* film, incidentally, has yet to be released.

Also unheard is an album that Young was allegedly going to use to fulfill his contractual obligation to Geffen: a New Age/ambient sound collage called *Meadow Dusk*. It's impossible to know how serious he was about the album, but he never got a chance to test the already outraged Geffen's mettle. Young was unceremoniously dumped from the label.

He wasted no time in rejoining Warner/Reprise, a move that contractually cleared the way for the CSNY reunion Young had promised if Crosby cleaned up. But

even as that process began, Young went back on the road, heading to Europe for a dismal tour that proved he had yet to regain his star power overseas.

Returning to the United States, Young inserted into his concerts an impromptu blues interlude, featuring guitar tech Larry Cragg on saxophone. The idea captured Young's imagination, and eventually Crazy Horse gave way to the Bluenotes, a nine-piece band boasting a six-man horn section. Ever anxious to get into the music by playing a character, Young slipped into a ratty suit coat, fedora, and some shades and transformed himself into a bluesman known as Shakey Deal.

Assembling a quick batch of songs, Young hastily recorded *This Note's for You*, which is unquestionably the best of his genre excursions. But the prevailing wisdom about the Bluenotes is that the band's best work was done in concert, evidenced by several choice bootlegs from the period. Among the officially released album's better tunes are the haunting "Coupe de Ville," the trenchant "Life in the City," and, of course, "This Note's for You," an anti–corporate sponsorship rant that earned widespread infamy when its video swung a satirical ax too close to MTV's purse strings. The video channel banned it, but after being embarrassed by the obvious overreaction, reversed course and not only played the video but awarded it honors as the Video of the Year.

Life Tour, Philadelphia, 1987.

In changing musical styles radically in the '80s, Young became viewed by many as "his generation's consummate weirdo," according to *Rolling Stone*. Young's own perspective, though, was that whatever he did, whenever he did it, he meant every word, every note. He told *Q*:

> *It's a very stupid thing to assume that I'm making different kinds of music to draw attention to myself. I made* Trans *because I wanted to. I did the Shocking Pinks and the International Harvesters because I wanted to and I'm doing the Bluenotes because I want to, and if you don't like that shit, fine. What are these guys saying? That the cool thing is just to do the same thing over and over again and not be a weirdo? Because if Neil Young did do the same thing over and over and over again and wasn't a weirdo, then these guys would be going, "Oh, Neil Young, he's so boring . . . ." You can't win.*

With the Bluenotes. *Photo by Al Pereira/Michael Ochs Archives/Getty Images*

Back on the CSNY front, David Crosby had fulfilled Young's reunion requirement that he clean up. But he was still in horrific physical shape and, indeed, would eventually be diagnosed with hepatitis C and require a liver transplant. Stills, too, was in a bad way. Though *American Dream* was eventually completed and released, the album was doomed from the beginning.

The quartet recorded at Young's home studio with his right-hand man, Niko Bolas, manning the controls. Young contributed three songs—the title track, "Name of Love," and "This Old House"—and co-wrote two others with Stills. But it's a bland, milquetoast record and nothing resembling the bold return to form that CSNY fans—and certainly certain members of CSNY—hoped for.

Young likely knew it was a blind alley. As the decade neared its close, he found himself once again looking for a new direction. Though he'd spent the better part of the '80s doing projects that interested *him*, he seldom fully engaged his fans. And what magic he did create, onstage or off, during those years was rarely made manifest in the studio.

But at a time when many were ready to dismiss Young as a hippie star who had long ago lost his way, Young set his course for a major comeback that found him stripping his music back to an elemental level: guitar, bass, drums.

Both freedom and ragged glory awaited.

*Courtesy Robert Ferreira*

*Courtesy Cyril Kieldsen*

Certainly I think he's one of the most influential artists of the last 30 or 40 years . . . . I think in many ways he's had the sort of career that I think most artists, myself included, would kill for. He's able to just do as he pleases and go from country to rock and folk and blues and do all these things and sort of tie them in seamlessly. It's been really beautiful to watch. I think artists like him are not affected by downturns in the music business; they're just kind of immune to it because they exist in their own worlds. That's the key to success is to do exactly that. In many ways I admire him not only for his music and his creative spirit but also for his entrepreneurial spirit and his philosophical spirit . . . . When he sticks to something that he believes in, it's full-on commitment, and I think we need more of that. I think he's a very brave artist.

—Raul Malo

# Sponsored by Nobody
## This Note's for You

NO ONE WOULD HAVE CALLED NEIL YOUNG an MTV darling in 1988 when he delivered the clip for the title track of his new album, *This Note's for You*, to the video music channel. He hadn't made many music videos to begin with, and the network gave only sparing play to those he did for the *Everybody's Rockin'* album in 1983. So it wasn't noteworthy for MTV not to air Young's videos. But it became a major news story when MTV banned one.

"This Note's for You" is a pointed jab at the wave of music artist endorsements that were proliferating during the mid-'80s. The Julien Temple–directed video poked fun at Eric Clapton's Michelob ad and Calvin Klein's Obsession perfume (introducing Young's faux Concession fragrance), and had a Whitney Houston look-alike pour beer on a Michael Jackson look-alike's flaming scalp. The clip finishes with Young toasting the camera with a beer can bearing the label "Sponsored by Nobody."

In July of 1988, MTV's legal department gave the clip a thumbs-down, ostensibly because it made direct reference to real products and brand names. "They had problems with trademark infringement," MTV spokesman Barry Kluger told *Rolling Stone*. Young, not surprisingly, had problems with the decision— especially since he and Temple had submitted a script prior to shooting the video that MTV had approved, and since Reprise Records, his label, had offered to indemnify the network against any lawsuit. Young and Temple even offered to re-edit the clip.

"Then they came back and said, 'It's the song we're worried about,'" Young told *Rolling Stone*. "It's sort of like dealing with spineless twerps. . . . They're supposed to be rebellious but haven't got enough guts to show something that's not middle-of-the-road." Young also wrote an open letter in which he asked, "What does MTV stand for: music or money?" And he appeared on an MTV News segment, telling Kurt Loder, "Your bosses or whatever, they really messed up. . . . I just want to get my video on the air so people can see it."

Ironically, "This Note's for You" won the Music Video of the Year trophy at that year's MTV Music Video Awards. The broadcast's audio feed temporarily dropped out during Young's acceptance speech—which was surely a coincidence.

You can't say, "Oh, I know what he does. *That's* why I really like him." His reputation has not changed in that he does exactly what he wants to do and he says exactly what he wants to say. He just pays no attention to public opinion; he wants to do it, he does it. He's really a character, man. He's unique. There's no question about it. He's one of a kind.

--Felix Cavaliere, Young Rascals/Rascals

The '80s were a rough ride for Neil Young on all fronts. But a funny thing happened on the way to the '90s. Young had often spoken of destroying his career in order to save it, casting off fame in favor of his artistry. A decade of what seemed, to some, to be mere genre exercises and indifferent efforts had nearly done the trick. But even as he was being abandoned by casual fans and staunch supporters alike, Young was gathering support in an altogether unlooked-for quarter: the generation of alternative rockers who were supplanting established stars and re-energizing rock 'n' roll in the process.

A wide array of the underground scene's movers and shakers—including Sonic Youth, the Pixies, Dinosaur Jr., the Flaming Lips, and Nick Cave— supplied tracks for *The Bridge: A Tribute to Neil Young* in 1989. Sonic Youth bassist Kim Gordon confirmed Young's status as an influence and inspiration for younger musicians. "Oh yeah, I think he is for a lot of people," she said, "musically, and as a guitar player and a songwriter. And his attitude has always been—he's a very perverse, complicated person. I mean, he's the only sort of person from his generation who our peer group still thinks has any kind of integrity."

Young may have appreciated a tip of the cap from the kids, but he wasn't ready to accept a gold watch just yet. He was already on the road to proving he could still make music that was as vital as anything he'd done. To do so, he cut his big band, the Bluenotes, back to just two pieces: bassist Rick Rosas and drummer Chad Cromwell. They entered New York's Hit Factory to record an album

*Courtesy Cyril Kieldsen*

of brutally loud, electric-guitar-based rock that was to be titled *Times Square*. He called the band Young and the Restless.

The music proved that Young had regained his musical footing, but—perhaps gun shy from all of the second-guessing he'd experienced over the last ten years—he pulled the record back. While on tour in Australia, New Zealand, and Japan, Young distilled *Times Square* to the five-song EP *Eldorado* and released it in a limited edition available only overseas. He told the *Village Voice*:

*I thought people were so used to me doing a style they might think I was just doing a style. I think it was a paranoid kind of a thing. Just the fact I'm worried about what people think is completely wrong, completely fucked. Thank God I didn't let that bother me on* Eldorado. *I did that for me. . . . What I did was take all the sweetness out of* Times Square *and made it more abusive than it already was and put it out of reach. . . . I put* Eldorado *out so people would know I was still here. There's something about the way things have gone for me that made me want to put it out and make sure my handwriting was on it. Pick the artwork, do everything with my friends, and put out this little record. But then, I'm sick. I only made 5,000. I said, "That's all, that's it." That's the way I did it—it reemerged. Just like I'm reemerging from myself. It's a funny thing. I feel my feelings coming back.*

Having indulged his electric side, Young balanced his approach with a solo acoustic tour of the United

Muziektheater Stopera, Amsterdam, the Netherlands, December 10, 1989.
*Photo by Rob Verhorst/Redferns/Getty Images*

States and worked on new music that balanced the two extremes. The resulting album, *Freedom*, was easily his best effort since *Rust Never Sleeps*. Like that album, it was bracketed by two versions of the title track, the first one acoustic and the second a barnburning rocker. The song itself is one of Young's best. Its anthemic chorus begs to be shouted along with, while ambivalent verses offer a complex vision of the state of the world. In between are several songs from *Eldorado*, including Young's savage breakup tune, "Don't Cry," and a thundering version of the Drifters' "On Broadway," plus two from the Bluenotes era: "Crime in the City (Sixty to Zero Part 1)" and "Someday."

Young cemented his comeback status with an incendiary performance of "Rockin' in the Free World" on *Saturday Night Live*. His appearance was a surprise, given his hostility toward performing on television and the fact that his backup band—Crazy Horse guitarist Frank "Poncho" Sampedro, bassist Charley Drayton, and drummer Steve Jordan—was assembled just for the occasion. For its sole appearance, Young dubbed the assemblage YCS&P (Young, Charley, Steve & Poncho).

The trade ads that accompanied Young's next release trumpeted "Feedback is back," and it wasn't just hype. For *Ragged Glory*, his most guitar-centric and jam-heavy studio effort since *Everybody Knows This Is Nowhere*, Young summoned Crazy Horse, though he'd sworn several years before not to work with them again. But "it seemed like the right time," he explained to *Rolling Stone*. "I try to savor those times I play with Crazy Horse and I space them out so that we don't wear ourselves out." In truth, though, Young first had to patch up hurt feelings with Billy Talbot and Ralph Molina for having excluded them from various projects while continuing to work with Sampedro.

The two tracks that lead off the album, "Country Home" and "White Line," are older tunes that had been heard in concert, in somewhat different form, as far back as the '70s. Elsewhere, Young borrows from familiar folk songs: The ecological hymn "Mother Earth (Natural Anthem)" is a rewrite of the standard "The Water Is Wide," while "Days That Used to Be" reworks Bob Dylan's "My Back Pages." The latter song and "Mansion on the Hill" are nostalgic trips back to '60s culture, where "Peace and love

*(continued on page 148)*

Smell the Horse Tour, L.A. Sports Arena, Los Angeles, April 26, 1991. © *Robert Matheu*

*(continued from page 144)*
live" and "Psychedelic music fills the air." But the songs are tinged with sadness, too, as on "Days," where Young notes, "There's very few of us left, my friend, from the days that used to be."

"Farmer John" is a cover of the Premiers' mid-'60s garage-band favorite. Young's treatment of the tune is less than genteel, however. He blasts through it with gale-force guitar and proto-punk attitude. The newer songs on *Ragged Glory* take up where that one leaves off. "F*!#in' Up" is angry, frustrated, and hilarious at the same time. But the true heart of the album can be found in three extended jams: "Over and Over," "Love to Burn," and "Love and Only Love," which clock in at eight-and-a-half minutes, ten minutes, and ten-and-a-quarter minutes, respectively. Young told *Rolling Stone*:

> *I purposely wanted to play long instrumentals because I don't hear any jamming on any other records. There's nothing spontaneous going on on records these days, except in blues and funkier music. Rock & roll used to have all that. People aren't reaching out in the instrumental passages and spontaneously letting them last as long as they can. I love to do that, but I can only really do it well with one band. I tried it a little on* Freedom, *but that kind of music is better for me with Crazy Horse.*

Young was suitably jazzed by the results on *Ragged Glory* to take Crazy Horse on the road for a series of concerts stressing full-bore, electrified rock. For the occasion, he invited some of his younger admirers, including Sonic Youth and Social Distortion, to open the shows. "We've been mentioned in so many reviews of Neil Young's album and shows," Kim Gordon said. "I guess it makes a lot of sense for us to be there." For his part, Young told *Rolling Stone* that Sonic Youth has "got this thing happening that I enjoy. It's soothing to me; it was very soothing before I went onstage to hear that feedback through the cement walls."

The tour was marked by two sad events, though: the passing of Young's mother at age seventy-two and the beginning of the Persian Gulf War, which Young adamantly opposed. "That war really left a mark on me," Young said. "We were playing so raucously, so violently, really like a bombardment. It was like we were there. It was very military sounding at times—big machinery, unbelievable power and destruction. That was our sound."

The two-disc live album *Weld* resulted from the tour and, upon first encounter, seems superfluous. After all, among its sixteen songs, five were repeated from *Ragged Glory* and six—including the long guitar showcases "Cortez the Killer," "Powderfinger," and "Like a Hurricane"—had already been captured in concert on *Live Rust*. But on *Weld*, Young rocks harder, longer, and louder than you'd think a middle-aged man would have cause to do. And his cover of Dylan's "Blowin' in the Wind," complete with air-raid sirens and the sound of explosions, made clear that Young had not yet lost his capacity to rage—against war, injustice, the inherent unfairness of life, or any questioning of his own continued relevance.

The intensity of the performances was so great that Young—allowing his perverse/playful nature to surface once again—spliced together *Arc*, a thirty-five-minute sound collage consisting of waves of guitar feedback and white noise that flowed from the stage. Listening to it, one can conclude that, if nothing else, it certainly creates its own space—like, say, the work of post-bop jazz geniuses Miles Davis and John Coltrane, often overlooked as a source of Young's cacophonous guitar excursions. Young told *Mojo*:

> *My guitar improvisations with Crazy Horse are very, very Coltrane-influenced. I'm particularly taken by works like "Equinox" and "My Favorite Things." Miles I love just because of his overall attitude towards the concept of "creation," which is one of constant change. There's no reason to stay there once you've done it. You could stay for the rest of your life and it would become like a regular job.*

Young's electrified albums and tours had restored his reputation, but it came at a price. Playing so loud and then mixing the *Weld* album damaged Young's hearing to the point where he had little choice but to tone it down in the studio as well as in concert. For *Harvest Moon*, Young reconvened the Stray Gators—the band that took him to unprecedented commercial heights on *Harvest* only to disintegrate on the *Time Fades Away* tour. The ensemble comprised Kenny Buttrey, Tim Drummond, Ben Keith, and Spooner Oldham (sitting in for Jack Nitzsche), with backup singers Linda Ronstadt, James Taylor, Nicolette Larson, Larry Cragg, and Young's half-sister, Astrid. "It's unique to have a new record that allows you to refer back to another work that goes back so far," Young explained. "It's a unique perspective to look at the musicians and singers and hear how voices and talents have changed."

With Steve Cropper, Bob Dylan 30th Anniversary Concert, Madison Square Garden, New York, October 16, 1992. *AP Photo/Ron Frehm*

My God, he's incredible. I have a lot of respect for him as a songwriter over the years. He's always managed to ride all of the trends and phases. He's a true singer-songwriter, and I think one of the most important people that's been on the scene, the music scene. He's always been able to come up with something pretty fresh. He's interested in all kinds of music, and I think he's been a guiding light to a lot of musicians and writers.

—Mick Jones, Foreigner

Cleveland, Ohio, 1992.

I think time's been good to Neil Young, and Neil Young's been good to time. He's made no attempt to cling to his 25-year-old self; he seems quite comfortable with having grown up, if you like. He doesn't have to deal with being the voice of a generation like Bob Dylan does. Bob Dylan seems to kind of have to wrestle with his past a lot, whereas Neil Young sort of steadily built up. He's gone through different phases, but it's always felt like him. I'm always happy whenever one of his songs comes on. My favorite of his is actually "Harvest Moon"; that's the one I spent the most time with, and I love the feeling of that song. He was obviously hugely influenced by Dylan, but I think Dylan helped Neil Young become himself and unrepentantly more Neil Young. He's just got a terrific identity and playlist, and you can rely on it.

—Robyn Hitchcock

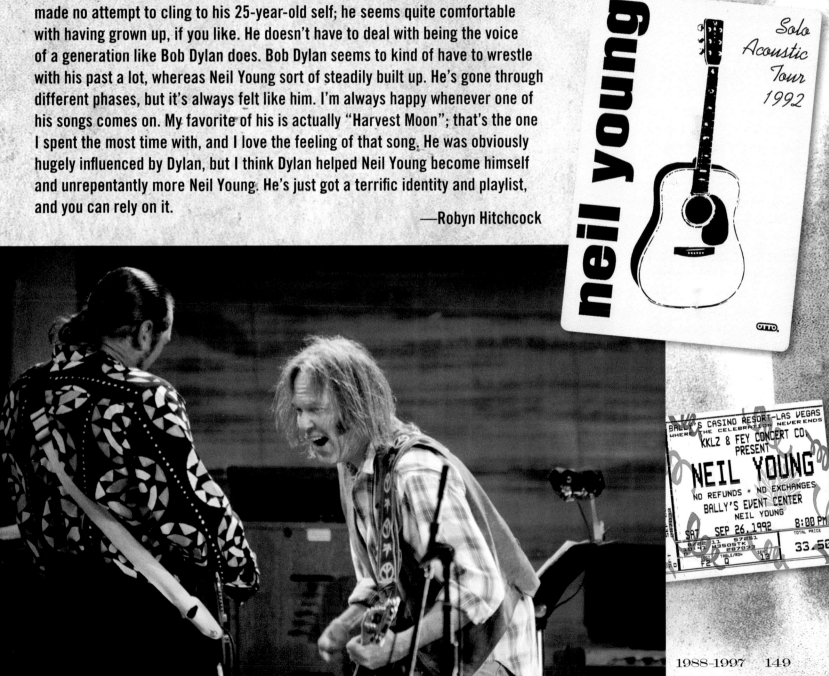

The album fulfilled the longtime desire of fans who never understood why Young didn't follow up the massive success of *Harvest* with more of the same. Young said:

> Fans would stop me on the street and say, "[Harvest] is my favorite record of yours. Will you ever do another record like that?" That's nice to hear, but you can't really go home and write music like that. It's all dictated by the songs I write . . . and they're not based in logic. I don't get a concept going and then try to write a song. Every time I do that, the songs are terrible.

Like its predecessor, *Harvest Moon* is a mostly mellow, acoustic-based effort, but it skips the grand orchestral works that threw *Harvest* out of kilter. Young waxes nostalgic on "From Hank to Hendrix" and "One of These Days," and he is sweetly sentimental on the unabashed love songs "Harvest Moon" and "Such a Woman." But there's an edge—a carryover from the war-fueled rage of the Crazy Horse tour—to tracks such as "War of Man" and "Dreamin' Man." "I'm singing about the same subjects but with 20 years more experience," Young told *Rolling Stone*. "What this album is about is this feeling, this ability to survive and continue and grow and get higher than you were before. Not just maintain, not just feel well. Not just 'I'm still alive at forty-five.' You can be *more* alive."

Sated fans made the album Young's biggest commercial success since *Rust Never Sleeps*.

Promotional harmonica issued for *Unplugged*, 1993. *Courtesy Cyril Kieldsen*

**He's a giant, really, to other musicians and other pros, an example of how to handle a career and have the courage to say "no" to some things as well. I don't know anybody who doesn't have the greatest respect for him. His song about Hank Williams' guitar ["This Old Guitar"] is just a masterpiece, a little masterpiece.**

**—Justin Hayward, Moody Blues**

Performing "Farmer's Song" with Willie Nelson, Farm Aid VI, Jack Trice Stadium, Ames, Iowa, April 24, 1993. *Photo by Ebet Roberts/Redferns/Getty Images*

The Stray Gators, however, were doomed, and once again it was money that did them in. This time it was Drummond who broached the subject of higher pay. Young had asked the band to accompany him on MTV's popular *Unplugged* show, recorded live on a soundstage in New York. A cloud came over Young, and he hated the performance so much that he paid the production costs rather than allow the show to be aired. Another try was attempted several months later with a revamped band, and this time it took. Young dipped deep into his songbook for the show, singing "The Old Laughing Lady," "Mr. Soul," "Helpless," and the seldom performed "World on a String." Two radically reworked songs are the standouts: a pump-organ take on "Like a Hurricane" and "Transformer Man," which, stripped of the electronic effects of *Trans*, is startlingly lovely.

In the meantime, Young had joined a superstar cast that included George Harrison, Eric Clapton, Willie Nelson, Johnny Cash, Eddie Vedder, and others at the Bob Dylan thirtieth anniversary celebration at Madison Square Garden, which Young tagged "Bobfest." His performance of Dylan's "All Along the Watchtower" turned out to be one of the highlights of the night.

Young also released *Lucky Thirteen: Excursions into Alien Territory*, which closed the book at last on his contentious 1980s sojourn with Geffen Records. The subtitle, which is half promise/half threat, tells the story. The album mixes previously issued tracks along with alternate takes and live versions of "Depression Blues" from the *Old Ways* sessions, "Get Gone" (with the Shocking Pinks), and "Don't Take Your Love Away from Me" and "Ain't It the Truth" (with the Bluenotes). Young had once commented that his '80s work might be better understood if it were looked at as one long, continuous album, which may be true. Distilled on one normal length disc, though, it produces a case of stylistic whiplash.

*(continued on page 155)*

# Mansion on the Hill
## Neil Young and the Rock and Roll Hall of Fame

Tenth Annual Rock and Roll Hall of Fame induction ceremony, Waldorf-Astoria Hotel, New York, January 12, 1995. *AP Photo*

**NEIL YOUNG'S RELATIONSHIP** with the Rock and Roll Hall of Fame has been like many of the others in his musical life: great moments marked by disappointments for both parties.

He has been an enthusiastic participant, inducting the Everly Brothers in 1986, Woody Guthrie as an Early Influence in 1988, the Jimi Hendrix Experience in 1992, Paul McCartney in 1999, and, along with Paul Simon, Warner Bros. executive Mo Ostin in 2003, also taking part in the show-closing all-star jams. But he made a late decision not to turn up for Buffalo Springfield's 1997 induction in Cleveland, ostensibly unhappy that the event had turned into a tightly scripted TV show rather than the loose and spontaneous gathering it had been to that point.

"So, Rich, he quit again," Springfield bandmate Stephen Stills said to Richie Furay onstage, referencing Young's decision to leave their group in 1967 just as it was preparing for an appearance on NBC's *The Tonight Show*.

Young did show up for his own induction two years prior, on January 12, 1995, at the Waldorf-Astoria Hotel in New York, ironically the first ceremony to be broadcast, by MTV. Young was accompanied by wife Pegi, manager Elliot Roberts, longtime producer David Briggs, attorney Irwin Osher, the members of Crazy Horse, brother Bob, and half-sister (and occasional backing vocalist) Astrid.

Pearl Jam's Eddie Vedder made the induction speech, proclaiming that Young's example "taught us a lot as a band about dignity and commitment and playing in the moment. . . . I don't know if there's been another artist that has been inducted into the Rock and Roll Hall of Fame to commemorate a career that is still as vital as he is today. Some of his best songs were on his last record." Young then accepted his trophy, joking that Roberts was "managing this speech" by telling him whom to thank from the side of the stage. He told Pegi he loved her, had Briggs and Crazy Horse take bows, and thanked record executives Ahmet Ertegun and Mo Ostin as well as the late Kurt Cobain "for giving me the inspiration to renew my commitments." Acknowledging fellow inductees the Allman Brothers Band, Young noted, "I wish I had a bunch of people up here with me. . . . it's a solo thing, though."

Musically, Young played a new song, "Act of Love," with Crazy Horse, then added members of Pearl Jam for the *Ragged Glory* track "F*!#in' Up." Later in the evening he joined Led Zeppelin for a run-through of "When the Levee Breaks," into which Robert Plant snuck a bit of "For What It's Worth." Backstage, Young needled Plant and Jimmy Page to remember John Paul Jones' phone number after the Zep bassist sarcastically thanked them for remembering to call him for the Hall of Fame induction after "losing" his digits for their *Unledded* reunion the previous year.

Young did stir things up again at the 2003 ceremony. While inducting Ostin in the nonperformer category, Young made mention of the impending war in Iraq, noting that:

> *We're having a good time tonight, but we're going to kill a lot of people next week. So let's not forget about that. I don't want to ruin this, but it's too real not to mention it. And music used to be about this. And it still is about this. It's a human thing. And these are human beings over there, and we're making a big mistake. I feel like I'm riding in a giant gas-guzzling SUV, and the driver's drunk as a fucking skunk. He's drunk on power.*

BMI PROUDLY CONGRATULATES OUR 1995
Rock & Roll
Hall of Fame
INDUCTEES

We are proud to represent more than 75% of
the members of the Rock & Roll Hall of Fame.

Frank Zappa'

Neil Young'

Martha & The Vandellas

Al Green

The Allman Brothers Band

**94**
The Animals (PRS)
Duane Eddy
John Lennon (PRS)
Elton John (PRS)
Willie Dixon
Johnny Otis

**89**
Otis Redding
The Rolling Stones
(PRS)
The Temptations
The Ink Spots
The Soul Stirrers
Phil Spector

**88**
The Beach Boys
The Beatles (PRS)
The Drifters
The Supremes
Woody Guthrie
Leadbelly

**87**
Eddie Cochran
Bo Diddley
Aretha Franklin
B.B. King
Clyde McPhatter

**86**
Chuck Berry
James Brown
Ray Charles

Ahmet Ertegun
Jerry Wexler

# ROCK
## AND
# ROLL

The *Tenth* Annual Induction Dinner

# HALL
## of
# FAME

THE ALLMAN
BROTHERS BAND
AL GREEN
JANIS JOPLIN
LED ZEPPELIN
MARTHA AND
THE VANDELLAS
NEIL YOUNG
FRANK ZAPPA
PAUL ACKERMAN
THE ORIOLES

Neil Young is an artist. He's just one of those guys. I like the way he plays guitar, with abandon. He's a great songwriter. I like his falsetto. He's cool. I remember listening to his stuff with Buffalo Springfield back then, in the '60s, and I thought he should've won an Oscar for that one song ["Philadelphia"] instead of Bruce Springsteen. I thought his song was great in that.

—Robert Cray

With Booker T. & the MGs, Schuttorf Festival, Gildehaus, Germany, 1993.

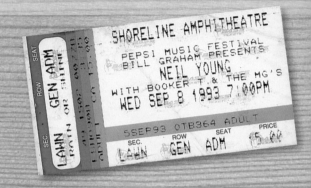

With Booker T. & the MGs, Finsbury Park, London, 1993.

I was talking with this guy Joel Bernstein, who's a friend of Neil's, a comrade and coworker who was cataloging all of Neil's tapes from over the years for a box set. . . . and Neil and I were standing in this room, and we were looking at all these [tapes], and I thought he was maybe gonna take one down, and we were gonna play it. He looked around, and he said, 'I gotta get outta here.' I saw a man overwhelmed by his body of work.

—Eddie Vedder,
Neil Young's Rock
and Roll Hall of Fame
induction speech

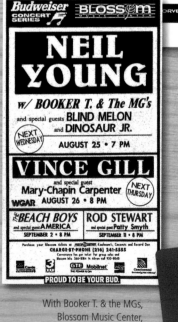

With Booker T. & the MGs,
Blossom Music Center,
Cuyahoga Falls, Ohio, 1993.

*(continued from page 151)*

Young supplied the despondent anthem "Philadelphia" to Jonathan Demme's emotional film of the same name. The song earned Young an Academy Award nomination, and he performed the song at the Oscar ceremony, though he lost the trophy to Bruce Springsteen, who was nominated for "Streets of Philadelphia" from the same film.

What happened next was a tragedy that had little to do with Young but pulled him in nonetheless. Nirvana frontman Kurt Cobain killed himself, which was bad enough. But in his suicide note, he quoted Young's song "My My, Hey Hey (Out of the Blue)," stating, "The worst crime I can think of would be to rip people off by faking it. I don't have the passion anymore, and so remember, it's better to burn out than to fade away."

Already deep into a long set of sessions with Crazy Horse, Young paid tribute to Cobain's death, however obliquely, on *Sleeps with Angels*. "He really, really inspired me," Young said of Cobain in *Mojo*. "He was so great. Wonderful. One of the best, but more than that. Kurt was one of the absolute best of all time for me." Crazy Horse was present again for the first time since *Ragged Glory*, but the band's sound is measured and brooding, matching the downcast feel of the album, which deals with loss ("Sleeps with Angels," "Blue Eden," "Train of Love," and the epic "Change Your Mind") but also comments on urban paranoia ("Driveby" and "Safeway Cart") and consumer angst ("Piece of Crap"). *Sleeps* doesn't pack quite the same emotional wallop of Young's previous musical elegy, *Tonight's the Night*, but it still taps into a melancholy sense of waste and bereavement pervading both the music industry and fans in the wake of Cobain's death.

With Booker T. & the MGs, Shoreline Ampitheatre, Mountain View, California, September 8, 1993.
*Photo by Tim Mosenfelder/ Getty Images*

Photo by Ebet Roberts/Redferns/Getty Images

**ALTHOUGH SONIC YOUTH HAD LOBBIED** to have Nirvana as the other opening act on Young's *Ragged Glory* tour with Crazy Horse, Young himself professed to only have become familiar with the group and its music shortly before frontman Kurt Cobain killed himself in April of 1994, invoking the line "it's better to burn out than to fade away" from Young's "My My, Hey Hey (Out of the Blue)" in his suicide note.

That single gesture inextricably linked Young and Cobain for all time, but the connection was already in place before that, despite the fact that the two men had never met.

By 1994, Young had already been labeled "the godfather of grunge," an acknowledged influence on the Northwest music scene from which Nirvana had emerged. Young had taken Soundgarden on tour as an opening act and played with Pearl Jam at the 1993 MTV Music Video Awards. Pearl Jam and the Melvins were among the many "grunge" bands who'd covered Young—especially his anthem "Rockin' in the Free World"—in concert. Cobain himself acknowledged Young as an influence and once told a concert crowd at the Seattle Center Coliseum that he'd been banned from the venue for

drunken, disorderly conduct during an unspecified Young show there.

The connections are not hard to hear. That generation of rockers clearly drew from the distorted, feedback-drenched, electric intensity of Young's work with Crazy Horse, as well as the dark but cathartic lyrical tones of *Tonight's the Night* and the broad stock-taking of *Rust Never Sleeps*. "I think [Young's] songs really spoke to a lot of us," Soundgarden's Chris Cornell said. "The message I got from his music was that letting those emotions out really made you feel better."

Young was certainly tapped into by this group of younger artists who saw him as a musical mentor— and he, in turn, gleaned inspiration from them, especially Cobain and Nirvana. "He really, really inspired me," Young told *Mojo*. "He was so great. Wonderful. One of the best, but more than that. Kurt was one of the absolute best of all time for me." He also told *Spin*, "I really could hear his music. There's not that many absolutely real performers. In that sense, he was a gem." Young also identified with the debilitating ambivalence Cobain felt about the dichotomy between his creative and public life, commenting to *Spin*, "He was bothered by the fact that he would end up following schedules, have to go on when he didn't feel like it, and be faking, and that would be very hard for him because of his commitment."

Young was aware of Cobain's personal problems, including a heroin addiction and a decision, just before he committed suicide, to leave rehab and return to Seattle. Young and his management office even tried to track down Cobain a few days before his death. "I read something and someone told me a few things that made me think he was in trouble that week," Young, who was working on *Sleeps with Angels* at the time, told *The Guardian*. "I had an impulse to connect. Only when he used my song in that suicide note was the connection made. Then, I felt it was really unfortunate that I didn't get through to him. I might've been able to make things a little lighter for him, that's all. Just lighten it up a little bit."

For a long time, Young was reticent to comment about Cobain's use of "it's better to burn out than to fade away" in his suicide note. Immediately afterward, he told biographer Jimmy McDonough "that's just another interpretation of it. It's just one of those lines. There's so many levels to take it on. . . . I just feel badly to see it in that light, but it was appropriate in his situation. There was nothing else for him to do. There was nowhere else to go." Young later said to Britain's *New Musical Express* that "obviously his interpretation should not be taken to mean there's only two ways to go and one of them is death."

Young's principal comment, however, was the title track to *Sleeps with Angels*, a mournful ode whose chorus declares, "He sleeps with angels (Too soon)." Young scratched out the idea for the song on a matchbook during a celebrity golf tournament hosted in Los Angeles by Eddie Van Halen and recorded it with Crazy Horse on April 25, 1994, at the Complex—including a twenty-one-minute-long version that remains in the vault. A week was spent editing the track, according to McDonough. Young also told McDonough "what that suicide has done is return me to my roots. Makes me go back and investigate where I started. Where I came from. Why am I here and why is he not here? Does my music suffer because I survived?"

There were initially erroneous reports that Young said he would never play "My My, Hey Hey" again. He did, in fact, perform it less than six months after Cobain's death, on October 1 at the Bridge School Benefit concert—pointedly playing it after "Sleeps with Angels." "It just made it a little more focused for awhile," Young told McDonough. "Now it's just another face to think about while you're singin' it." And when Young performed "The Needle and the Damage Done" from the Rock and Roll Hall of Fame and Museum for the 1996 MTV Video Music Awards, he was surrounded by photos of late musicians whose deaths were drug-related, including Cobain.

Pukkelpop Festival, Hasselt, Belgium, 1995.

European Tour with Pearl Jam, Reading Festival, Reading, England, 1995.

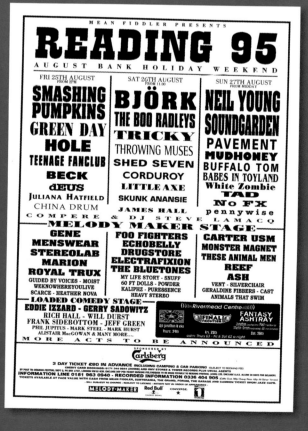

# Mirror Ball
## Neil Young and Pearl Jam

With Pearl Jam's Eddie Vedder and Mike McCready, Tenth Annual MTV Awards, Universal City, California, September 2, 1993. *AP Photo/Kevork Djansezian*

**NEIL YOUNG WORKS FAST**. That's not news.

But his 1995 collaboration with Pearl Jam, on the album *Mirror Ball* and subsequent tour dates, was swift even by his standards.

It started at Young's Rock and Roll Hall of Fame induction on January 12. Pearl Jam frontman Eddie Vedder did the honors, and Young played an unreleased song, "Act of Love," that night with Crazy Horse. The members of Pearl Jam taped it on cassette from their table at New York's Waldorf-Astoria hotel, just for posterity—a fortuitous move since both acts were playing pro-choice benefit shows on January 14 and 15 in Washington, D.C., and wanted to do something together. Young suggested "Act of Love," and, he recalled, "It was great."

"I said, 'Maybe we ought to record it. It sounds good.' They were thinking the same thing," Young said. "So we set a date to go in and record. I wanted to have more than one song, so I came in with three songs in hand."

He came out with nine songs that appeared on *Mirror Ball*, plus another couple on which Vedder sang lead and that were held for Pearl Jam's use. The sessions were fast, taking place over four days in January and February with Pearl Jam producer Brendan O'Brien at Heart's Bad Animals Studio in the band's home base of Seattle. Save for "Act of Love" and "Song X," Young noted that the songs "were written the day before they were recorded." There was no demoing or rehearsals, either. "The beauty of the thing is that hardly any talking had to happen at all," Young explained. "I'd bring the song in and run it down, then everybody would play it. I don't think we did more than five takes on anything. We all knew what we had to do. Everybody was together."

Pearl Jam guitarist Mike McCready recalled the sessions as particularly heady. "We'd be jamming, and I'd look over and say to myself, 'That's Neil Young, and he's playing leads. That's the shit!' I could only wish to be that good."

McCready added that Pearl Jam was "honored [Young] says he's into us. I think he just likes where we're coming from. He sees a lot of honesty in our music."

Young had already developed a kinship with Pearl Jam dating back to appearances at the 1992 Bob Dylan tribute in New York and the 1992 Bridge School Benefit concert, as well as a 1993 performance of "Rockin' in the Free World" together at the MTV Video Music Awards. "We're sympathetic," Young explained. "They're definitely old souls—they've been around. Musically there's youthful energy, but without the sound of inexperience. And our musical styles are compatible—it's like a big wall of sound with a lot of nuances in there."

That seems to be not unlike Crazy Horse, but Young contended Pearl Jam was an entirely different beast. "It's hard to compare them. They have different rhythms. Both are very sincere, very intense, very real, and very raw. But they are different."

Artist: Peter Pontiac (www.peterpontiac.com)

**DINOSAUR SENIOR**

*Crazy Mole COMIX*

THE SULTAN (1963)

THE TRICK OF DISASTER

THE LONER

THE VOCODER

AND DOZENS OF COUSINS!

PONTIAC

PEPNO

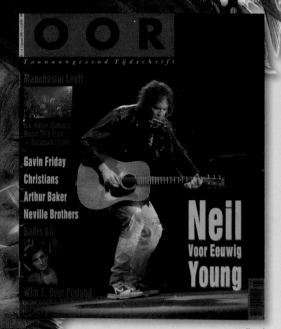

# OOR
*Toonaangevend Tijdschrift*

Manchester Leeft:

Gavin Friday
Christians
Arthur Baker
Neville Brothers

Radio 80:

Wim T. Over Pleinp!

## Neil
Voor Eeuwig
## Young

# Histoire du Rock

LA PREMIÈRE
ENCYCLOPÉDIE DU ROCK
EN 42 NUMÉROS

NEIL YOUNG: Un groupe solitaire
THE ALLMAN BROTHERS
BAND: Près de la rivière Styx
CHARLES MANSON: Les dessous de Sharon Tate
PLUS: Gilbert O'Sullivan, George Martin, Help

NO 33
CHAQUE
SEMAINE

CANADA 95c    FRANCE 4F    BELGIQUE 35FB    SUISSE 3,20FS

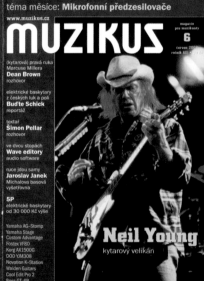

# THE HISTORY OF
# ROCK
90p

89

FOREVER
YOUNG

Aus $2.15 NZ $2.65 SA R2.45 IR £1.15

|   |   |   |
|---|---|---|
| Holland | France | Australia |
| Finland | Holland | Czech Republic |

## RUMBA
*ROCKIN AJANKOHTAISLEHTI*

14/95    28.7.—10.8.    14 mk

FESTIVAALIRAP
Rääkkylästä
Rock Summe
Roskildesta
Ruisrocki

# NEIL
# YOUNG
Don Grungo

Beautiful South
Future Sound Of London
Iron Maiden
RAMONES
gabba gabba bye bye?

# Platenblad

Voor platen/cd
verzamelaars

Verschijnt 10 keer per jaar - Nr 98
25 januari t/m 28 februari 2002
Los nummer € 2,40

Favoriete
Neil Young
Albums
Het ultieme
Popjaar '66
Yes
Kurt Cobain
Elektra Label
en met
Robbie van Leeuwen
Townes Van Zandt

Plus: Lijstjes beste Albums 2001 - De Omgevallen Platenkast
Columns - Platen/CD Beurswijzer - Recensies
Veel Vraag en Aanbod van LP's, Singles, CD's, Promo's enz.

téma měsíce: Mikrofonní předzesilovače
www.muzikus.cz

# MUZIKUS
magazin
pra muzikanty

6

(kytarová) pravá ruka
Marcuse Millera
**Dean Brown**
rozhovor

elektrické baskytary
z českých luk a poli
**Buďte Schick**
reportáž

textař
**Šimon Pellar**
rozhovor

ve dvou stopách
**Wave editory**
audio software

ruce jdou samy
**Jaroslav Janek**
Michalova basová
vyšetřovna

**5P**
elektrické baskytary
od 30 000 Kč výše

Yamaha AG-Stomp
Yamaha Stage
Custom Advantage
Fostex VF80
Korg AX1500G
DOD VM306
Novation K-Station
Walden Guitars
Cool Edit Pro 2
Boss GT-6B
RME Hammerfall DSP
Clavia Nord Electro

## Neil Young
kytarový velikán

Broken Arrow Tour, 1996. *Photo by Larry Hulst/Michael Ochs Archives/Getty Images*

Broken Arrow European Tour,
Duren Badesee Festival, Duren, Germany, 1996.

NEIL YOUNG with CRAZY HORSE · Dave Matthews BAND
GIN BLOSSOMS · FRIDAY, SEPTEMBER 6 · 93

Broken Arrow North American Tour,
New World Music Theatre, Tinley Park,
Illinois, 1996.

Broken Arrow European Tour, Phoenix
Festival, Stratford upon Avon, England,
1996.

I like Neil. I buy everything he puts out. Neil's really unique because he does have an innocence to some of his writing that others don't, and that innocence can be looked at as being, "Hey, is that a good song?" There are some things I've heard Neil do where I've gone, "Man, is that any good?" because he slaps it on the table. There isn't any editing going on with Neil; you don't feel like he sat there and angsted over it much. But after repeated listenings you go, "Of course it is," because it's like every song is part of a symphony. That gives other writers like myself a lot of confidence. It's great to see because you just kind of say, "Well, if Neil's doing it, aw, fuck, I'll do it! I'll do something like that."

—Stan Ridgway

H.O.R.D.E. Festival, Portland Meadows, Portland, Oregon, 1997.

H.O.R.D.E. Festival, Fiddler's Green, Englewood, Colorado, 1997.

H.O.R.D.E. Festival, Deer Creek Music Center, Noblesville, Indiana, 1997.

Poster for Malmö, Sweden, June 12, 1997, one of the Crazy Horse European Tour shows that was canceled after Neil cut his finger while making a sandwich.

Oh, I think he's great. I owe him something. I didn't know all that much of Neil's music until I toured with him for a while. I must've done 40 dates with Neil, and he taught me something just by sitting side-stage and watching his shows. All us whippersnappers were trying to make small clubs feel like a coliseum, and there he was making these coliseums and big, Blockbuster Pavilion kind of places into living rooms. I thought that was much more powerful. There's a vibration about what he does that's so pure and has so much integrity that I think it just transcends. He can write a bad song and it's OK. It's like old blues artists or something; they're not sitting there going through every lyric and every note. It's more about the bigger picture.

—Ben Folds

## Briggs had guided many of Young's best and most significant projects. He is part and parcel of the artist's legacy.

(continued from page 159)

Young and Crazy Horse suffered an immeasurable loss in 1995 when producer David Briggs succumbed to cancer. Briggs had guided many of Young's best and most significant projects. He is part and parcel of the artist's legacy. Young says in the film *Year of the Horse*:

> David Briggs is so important. And luckily he was with us long enough so that we learned from him. And really, he's a guy who taught us more about ourselves at the same time as he was learning it. He just kept things coming back and kept me moving along. He was a really close friend and in some ways my closest friend. . . . He left enough for us to go on. We know what to do.

Determined to carry on in a fashion they thought Briggs would approve of, Young and Crazy Horse barnstormed small clubs and billed themselves as the Echos. They also repaired to Young's ranch to record the raw, unpolished *Broken Arrow*. On the opening track, "Big Time," Young defiantly declares, "I'm still livin' the dream we had/For me it's not over." But as much as the album attempted simultaneously to restate the band's purpose and to play Briggs home, it just didn't have, in Crazy Horse parlance, "the spook."

If *Dead Man*—the film or the soundtrack—didn't exactly ignite the public's imagination, it at least allowed Young to meet counterculture director Jim Jarmusch. Together they conceived the film *Year of the Horse*, a documentary of the most recent tour with Crazy Horse, plus interviews, (unintentionally) hilarious footage (some of it salvaged from the abandoned *Muddy Track*) of backstage arguments, and, ahem, horseplay, such as nearly setting a restaurant on fire with candles and table napkins.

The *Year of the Horse* soundtrack is perhaps the least dynamic of Young's live albums: Crazy Horse is unusually flat-footed throughout, and Young himself is wobbly as well. The most significant moment occurs in the album's first few seconds. An obviously dissatisfied audience member shouts at the stage, "They all sound the same."

Not missing a beat, Young steps to the microphone and deadpans, "It's all one song."

In 1997, Buffalo Springfield was inducted into the Rock and Roll Hall of Fame, but Young was a no-show. He protested the ceremony's shift from a Friar's Club–style insider's party to a VH1 broadcast. "So, Rich," Stephen Stills quipped to bandmate Richie Furay at the podium, "he quit again."

Young, it turned out, was intent on celebrating the Springfield in another fashion. For years he had been working on his magnum opus, a multi-disc box set that was originally titled *Decade II* but eventually came to be known as *Archives*. In an act of ego that would qualify as a delusion of grandeur had he not gone on to do such great work, Young had saved all his recordings so one day he'd be able to piece together his own musical history rather than rely on someone else to do it. Of course, that history included Buffalo Springfield, so he sifted through the band's material with an eye toward compiling a box set separate from his own. He invited Stills to his ranch to hear what he'd done. The two "laughed, cried, and hugged each other," Young recalled.

At some point, Stills brought out a guitar and played a song he'd just written. Young liked it so much that he volunteered to play guitar on it, and a full CSNY reunion blossomed from there. Young recalled:

> *I came into the studio and discovered that they were in here working on a record by themselves, and they weren't using a record company. They had to finance it themselves, so obviously they were really into it. That's the only real good reason to play music. So it was just a good feeling again; it was three guys who have been making music together for thirty years, and they*

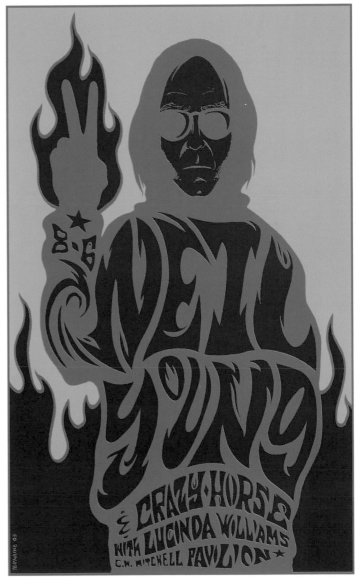

Artist: Jermaine Rogers (www.jermainerogers.com)

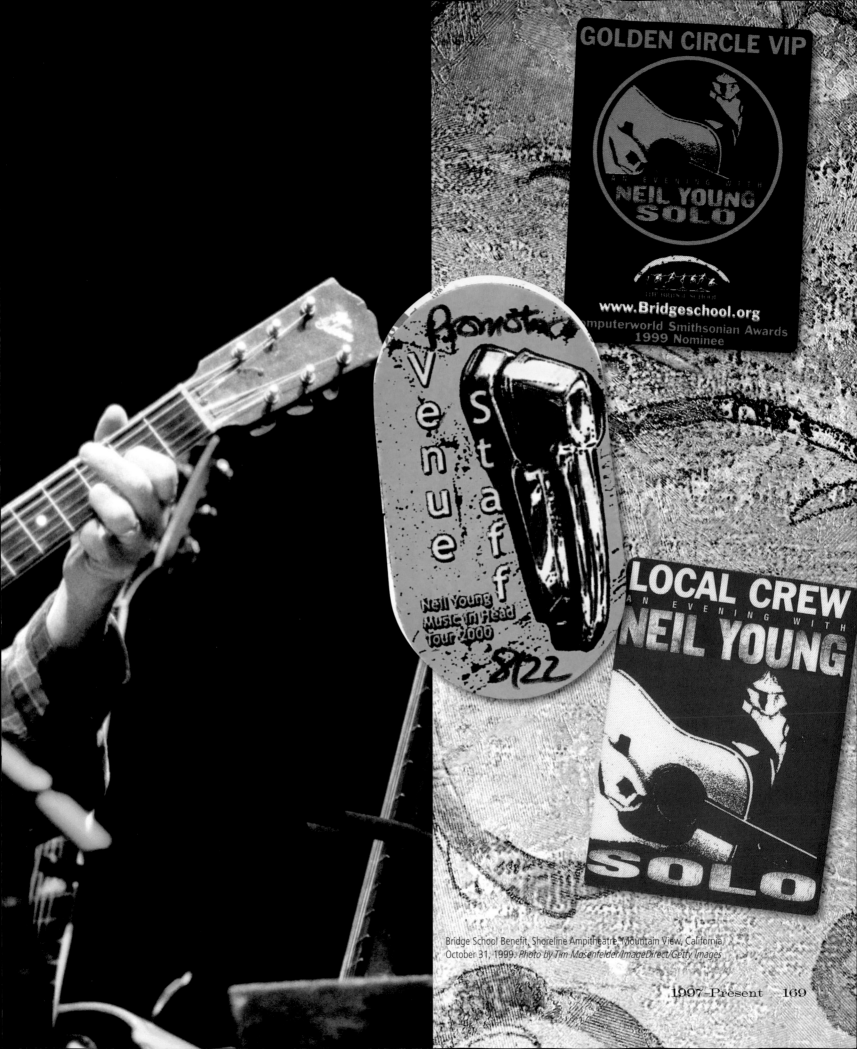

GOLDEN CIRCLE VIP

AN EVENING WITH
NEIL YOUNG
SOLO

THE BRIDGE SCHOOL

www.Bridgeschool.org

Computerworld Smithsonian Awards
1999 Nominee

Promoter

Venue Staff

Neil Young
Music In Head
Tour 2000

8/22

LOCAL CREW
AN EVENING WITH
NEIL YOUNG
SOLO

Bridge School Benefit, Shoreline Ampitheatre, Mountain View, California,
October 31, 1999. *Photo by Tim Mosenfelder/ImageDirect/Getty Images*

*still want to do it enough to take out bank loans or whatever. That's why someone would want to be involved in that energy. It was all positive, and the music was really great.*

Young had been working on an acoustic album called *Silver & Gold*, but he told his partners they could mine any of the songs they liked for the CSNY album. They picked four: "Slowpoke," "Out of Control," "Queen of Them All," and the eventual title track, "Looking Forward." Stills took three writing credits on the album, and Crosby and Nash took two apiece.

Past CSNY endeavors had ended in acrimony, tears, fistfights, and name-calling. This time things were different because, as Crosby noted, "There's no chemical baggage." Crosby had cleaned up in prison and was the recipient in 1994 of a liver transplant. He also had a reputation to uphold as a celebrity sperm donor (to Melissa Etheridge and Julie Cypher); the term "sperm whale" was tossed around during the sessions and subsequent tour rehearsals. Even Stills had beaten his primary demon, cocaine. But despite all the love in the room, *Looking Forward* was largely a critical and commercial disappointment. Still,

CSNY2K Tour, Staples Center, Los Angeles, February 12, 2000. *AP Photo/E. J. Flynn*

Promo cigar box, *Silver & Gold*, 2000. *Courtesy Robert Ferreira*

**He's only one of the great, historically correct artists of all time. Him and Tom Petty and Bob Dylan and Emmylou Harris, these kinds of artists are the foundation of our culture. These people have created the grid that we all can follow, and that's what's beautiful, because he never followed the herd. He's completely original.**

**—Nancy Wilson, Heart**

Music in Head Tour, 2000.

the quartet could point to a sold-out arena tour—its first tour of any kind since 1974—as evidence of its continued appeal. Kicking off as it did just after the turn of the millennium, the tour was dubbed CSNY2K.

Young, having given what he called "the cream of the crop" of his songs to CSNY, still managed to salvage *Silver & Gold*, pulling together songs from a variety of sources. "Some of them are pretty old, some of them are brand new," he said. "They're written in the same state of mind, I think, over the years."

It's still an acoustic album as originally envisioned but with the addition of some sidemen, including Ben Keith, Spooner Oldham, drummer Jim Keltner, bassist Duck Dunn, and vocalists Emmylou Harris and Linda Ronstadt. The picture that emerges from songs such as the title track, "Daddy Went Walkin'," and "Razor Love" is one of family values, middle age, and contented domesticity. "Love and a razor may not be an easy analogy to draw," Young said of the latter song, "but they're really quite similar because your love is inside something, and a razor or a blade, it cuts right to the point. But there's no hate in there. It's not about violence. It's about cutting to the quick, about getting through all the things that get in the way of love."

The song "Buffalo Springfield Again," meanwhile, heads in another direction, giving a shout-out to his old band and offering hope for a reunion. "Maybe now we can show the world what we got," Young sings. The reunion never happened (except, according to Young, in private), but the box set—named, perhaps a tad too matter-of-factly, *Box Set*—did.

Young kept the *Silver & Gold* band together, substituting wife Pegi and half-sister Astrid for Harris and Ronstadt, and hit the road. The series of shows resulted in a live album, his third and least impressive such effort of the decade. *Road Rock V1: Friends and Relatives* features just one new song—"Fool for Your Love," a remnant from the Bluenotes era—plus a cover of Dylan's "All Along the Watchtower" with a guest appearance by the Pretenders' Chrissie Hynde.

*(continued on page 176)*

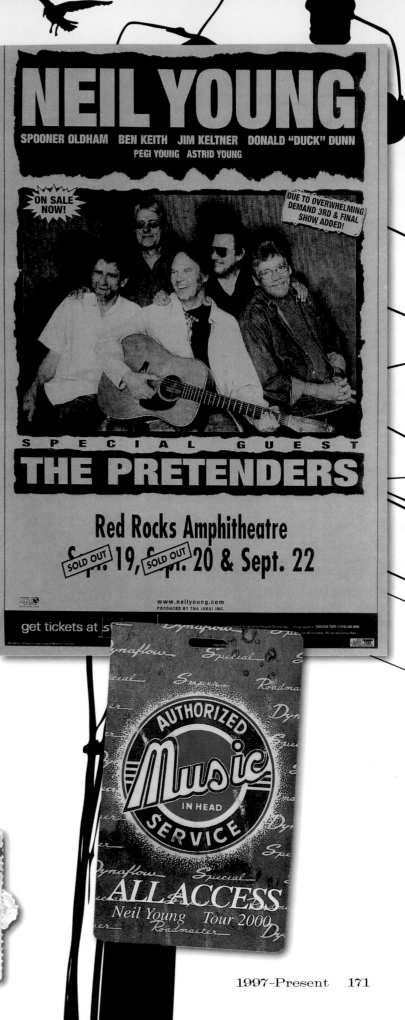

# Heart of Gold
## The Bridge School

Bridge School Benefit, Shoreline Amphitheatre, Mountain View, California, October 23, 2004. *Photo by Tim Mosenfelder/Getty Images*

**AFTER THEIR SON, BEN,** was diagnosed with severe cerebral palsy, Neil Young and his wife, Pegi, were afforded an intensive and sometimes dispiriting look at the state of treatment for children with severe physical and speech impairments. It inspired some of the songs on Neil's albums *re·ac·tor* and *Trans*, but, more importantly, it inspired Pegi to action.

A team composed of Pegi, fellow parent Jim Forderer, and speech and language pathologist

Dr. Marilyn Buzolich laid the groundwork for the Bridge School. It was conceived as a local non-profit program designed, according to its mission statement,

> *to ensure that individuals with severe speech and physical impairments achieve full participation in their communities through the use of augmentative and alternative means of communication (AAC) and assistive technology*

*(AT) applications and through the development, implementation and dissemination of innovative life-long educational strategies.*

It was certainly a cause Neil could get behind. On October 13, 1986, he hosted the first Bridge School Benefit Concert at the Shoreline Amphitheatre in Mountain View, California. Assisted by concert promoter Bill Graham and joined by Bruce Springsteen, Tom Petty, the Eagles' Don Henley, Nils Lofgren, comedian Robin Williams, and a reunited CSNY, he raised a reported $250,000 that allowed Pegi and her cohorts to open a school the following year in Hillsborough, California.

The Bridge School, which opened a permanent facility in 1995, has since grown into an international leader in its field and has implemented a series of worldwide outreach and research programs. Its profile, of course, is ensured by the concerts, which have taken place every year except for 1987, but Neil has always maintained the school's success "is all Pegi. I'm just the public relations man."

He's done a fine job. Expanding to two-night affairs, the concerts have featured special and often "unplugged" performances by a who's-who of popular musicians for one of the most anxiously anticipated music events of each year. Springsteen, Petty, Henley, Pearl Jam, R.E.M., and Sammy Hagar are among

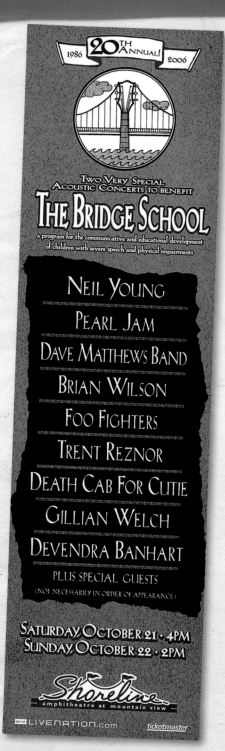

Mountain View, California, 2006.

those who have performed at multiple shows, and Young himself has performed every year—on his own and with CSNY, Crazy Horse, the Stray Gators, and some of his other bands. In 1997, an album—*Bridge School Concerts, Vol. 1*, kicked off by a Young solo performance of "I Am a Child"—was released with proceeds going to the school.

Pegi Young explained:
*One of the things that makes me happiest about having the artists come and play the Bridge Show is that they really get an understanding that they probably didn't have before about people like our students at Bridge. You don't really understand them as human beings, but when they spend a weekend together and they interact, the artists begin to understand what's going on inside. That to me is the best thing. It's much more than a musical moment. It's like a life-altering moment.*

Among those most moved by the experience has been Eddie Vedder, who has performed at several Bridge shows both with Pearl Jam and on his own. "Eddie's one of the dearest friends the Bridge School has outside of my husband," Pegi Young said. "He really has honest and true relationships with the kids."

In 2006, to celebrate the initiative's twentieth anniversary, the Bridge School also hosted its first Heart of Gold Gala, another fundraiser held a week after the concerts, with Elton John providing entertainment.

Information about the Bridge School and its programs can be found at www.bridgeschool.org.

BALLYGOWAN PRESENTS
LONDON FLEADH

SATURDAY
16TH JUNE 2001
11.30AM -10.45PM

FINSBURY PARK
LONDON N4
AN OPEN AIR FESTIVAL

# NEIL YOUNG
## & CRAZY HORSE
## THE WATERBOYS
## GARY MOORE
### AIMEE MANN • STARSAILOR
### THE GIPSY KINGS
### AFRO CELT SOUND SYSTEM • BARE JR
**MOJO STAGE**

## BILLY BRAGG & THE BLOKES
## EVAN DANDO • TEENAGE FANCLUB
### GLENN TILBROOK & THE PARTY
### VICTORIA WILLIAMS, MARK OLSON &
### THE ORIGINAL HARMONY RIDGE CREEKDIPPERS
### ALISHA'S ATTIC • COUSTEAU • ANDY WHITE • CLEM SNID
### PLUS MANY MORE ACTS TO BE ANNOUNCED OVER 2 STAGES

Tickets £35.00 adv
(each ticket subject to a booking fee and conditions)
Available from all Ticketmaster outlets, selected HMV stores and usual agents nationwide & @ www.meanfiddler.com & www.ticketmaster.co.uk

**London Credit Card Hotline 020 7344 0044 (24hrs)**
**National Credit Card Hotline 08701 500 044 (24hrs)**
Stargreen 020 7734 8932, Way Ahead 0115 912 9000. Mean Fiddler Info Line 020 8963 0940 (Mon - Fri 10am - 6pm)
Recorded information line: 09003 404 909 - calls cost 60p per min. Tickets available at face value for cash from
Camden Ticket Shop, Astoria, all other Mean Fiddler Box Offices and Bread & Roses in Clapham.
Subject to licence • Artists not in order of appearance • Bill subject to change.
A MEAN FIDDLER AND WORKERS BEER COMPANY PRESENTATION
www.meanfiddler.com

MOJO

Crazy Horse Eurotour, Berlin, Germany, 2001.

MAREK LIEBERBERG PRESENTS

# NEIL YOUNG CRAZY HORSE
## EUROTOUR 01

SPECIAL GUEST
**the Black Crowes**

Dienstag, 18.30 Uhr
**26.6.`01**
## BERLIN WALDBÜHNE

Berlin Ticket  Telefonischer Kartenservice: 230 88 230,
Fax Kartenservice: 230 88 299 und an allen bekannten Vorverkaufsstellen.
Tickets Online: www.shownet.de - Infos Online: www.deag.de - Örtlicher
Veranstalter: concert concept Veranstaltungs GmbH - Tourneeleitung: Marek
Lieberberg Konzertagentur GmbH - Alle Menschen sind Ausländer - fast überall

radio EINS 95,8 FM

MAREK LIEBERBERG

I love the guy, and sometimes he makes my head turn a little bit because I feel like he releases everything, and I love that about him. "Here's the next album I'm putting out *right now*," and he releases his *Archives* of everything. He really wants you to be part of his entire journey, his entire process, without caring about the criticism or anything that could come with it. I find myself in a position where people are always saying, "Don't put that out right now. You gotta wait," or "You don't want to put that out right now 'cause people might think this or that." And when I look at Neil Young and the career retrospective that he offers, he's doing all kinds of crazy stuff, constantly, and he never stopped. He just kept releasing, kept releasing, kept releasing, and to me that's what we should be doing. And he really is a rocker; I saw him at Glastonbury, and that guy's still playing like he was *in* "Cortez the Killer," just really shredding and doing lengthy jams and taking people on journeys. I have nothing but the utmost respect for the guy. I kinda want to understand his secret to longevity.

—Jason Mraz

*(continued from page 171)*

The album's real flaw, though, is that the band, built for the subtle acoustic stylings of *Silver & Gold*, is ill-suited for the long guitar freakouts of "Cowgirl in the Sand" (clocking in at eighteen minutes), "Words" (eleven minutes), and "Tonight's the Night" (ten and a half minutes).

Following the terrorist attacks of September 11, 2001, Young lent his voice to the chorus of support given to victims' families by artists including Bruce Springsteen, U2, Billy Joel, Dave Matthews, and Alicia Keys. He sang a plaintive rendition of John Lennon's "Imagine," a performance that can be found on *America: A Tribute to Heroes.*

Conjuring the spirit and immediacy of "Ohio" three decades prior, Young also wrote "Let's Roll," which he released just weeks after the attacks. The song takes its title from words spoken by United Airlines Flight 93 passenger Todd Beamer, one of the doomed travelers believed to have overpowered the hijackers before the plane crashed in a Pennsylvania field. "You got to turn on evil when it's coming after you," Young sings grimly. "It struck me as heroic in a legendary way," he said. "These guys weren't doing this to be martyrs or because they thought they would get a payback." He figured, though, that someone else would tell the story in a song before he would:

> I said to myself, "There's gonna be ten people that come out with songs called 'Let's Roll' next week—there'll be two country 'Let's Rolls' and a rock and roll 'Let's roll' and an R&B 'Let's Roll.' They'll be everywhere." So I sat back and waited for six weeks or so, and nothing happened. And then [President George W.] Bush goes on TV and says, "Let's roll," and for me that was the last straw. I said, "I just gotta do this. I don't care if it's the most obvious thing that ever happened."

He performed the song with CSNY when the band went on tour again in 2002. Young thought the quartet's presence in the wake of 9/11 would offer fans "some kind of feeling of comfort . . . seeing that we're still here, and everybody's still here, and we're still doing what we do."

## I just gotta do this. I don't care if it's the most obvious thing that ever happened.

"Let's Roll" eventually found its way onto Young's album *Are You Passionate?* Except for one Crazy Horse track, the album was recorded with Booker T. and the MGs, who Young had first played with at Bobfest. As for favoring the seasoned Stax band over his traditional

*Greendale Tour, Saratoga Springs, New York, 2003. Artist: Bob Masse (bmasse.com)*

backing unit, Young said, "It's just that the groove and the feeling and the vibe of the music was more uplifting." True, the album opened him up to criticism of returning to his old days of genre exercises, positing himself this time as a Southern soul man. But the combination of Young and the MGs turned out to be no more audacious than his signing to Motown Records as a member of the Mynah Birds in the '60s. Though it's surfaced in many different ways over the years, Neil Young has always had soul.

Bonnaroo, Manchester, Tennessee, 2003. *Artist: Pasty Poster Co.*

His next project would take on a variety of dimensions. *Greendale* was a concept album–cum–rock opera that Young fleshed out more fully than almost anything he'd ever done. Beyond the album, there was a companion film—another low-budget flick in the spirit of *Journey through the Past* and *Human Highway*—plus a book and website. All of it was designed to tell the story of the Greens, a fictional small-town American family struggling with issues of corruption, violence, environmental destruction, and media overload. It's a postmillennial rock 'n' roll version of Thornton Wilder's *Our Town*. Young is backed by the Crazy Horse rhythm section of Molina and Talbot (with Sampedro hopping back on board for the tour).

When Young took the album on the road, his high-concept/low-budget show featured cardboard sets of the fictional town and a company of actors who lip-synched his lyrics while he and Crazy Horse played live onstage. Young told *Rolling Stone*:

> *These characters are all part of me, part of my family and my life—and part of the greater family, the American family. The beautiful thing about the* Greendale *show is that I'm standing there for an hour and a half, singing these new songs, and people are not looking at me. They're looking all over. And in the film, I play the music. I sing everything. I see images I want to see, because I filmed a lot of them myself. But I'm not lip syncing, I'm not faking. I really hate that shit.*

He was prepared for—and received—a drubbing from critics and fans alike, though, noting, "I've heard people saying, 'This is worse than *Trans*.'"

Neil's kind of an enigma to me. I'm very aware of Neil and what he does, old and new. I can't figure the guy out—and I don't really need to. Neil's just awesome. He keeps doing his thing. I saw him when I was on tour with Bob [Dylan] and we were in Italy. We were playing a piazza and had a day off in this town, and Neil and Crazy Horse were playing and it was just unbelievable, particularly his solo part of the show. Neil is just part of that awesome handful of people, him or Joni or Bob or Neil Diamond or whoever; they do their thing, and they're obviously lifers.

—Charlie Sexton, Arc Angels

*Greendale* was a surreal experience but nothing like what real life handed Young next. During the sessions for his album *Prairie Wind*, Young was shaving one morning and noticed an object, somewhat like a piece of broken glass, in his field of vision. No matter what he did, it wouldn't go away. "So I went to my doctor," Young told *Time* magazine, "had an MRI and the next morning I went to the neurologist, Dr. Sun—a Chinese guy, very funny guy. He says, 'The good news is, you're here, you're looking good. The bad news is, you've got an aneurysm in your brain. You've had it for a hundred years, so it's nothing to worry about—but it's very serious, so we'll have to get rid of it right away.'"

Young handled the situation with superhuman cool. Drummer Chad Cromwell said in the film *Heart of Gold*:

> *He said, "I got this brain aneurysm." And I mean, the world stopped. It was just like, "You what?" He said, "Yeah, I got this brain aneurysm. I'm going to go to New York next Tuesday and they're gonna do this thing." He goes, "And it's really wild what they're gonna do. . . . They're gonna go in there and they're gonna put these little bitty springs in there. And they're biodegradable and what that does, that makes the body produce this scar tissue which then negates the aneurysm." I'm sitting there going, "Why are you sitting here? How is that?*

# Don't Be Denied
## The Troubled Tale of Young's Official Biography

**WHEN IT COMES TO TALKING** about himself, Neil Young has always been something of a reluctant witness. Interviews are hard to come by. "I just don't like them," he told *Rolling Stone*, though he dutifully does a few to promote most of his major projects.

He did, however, enjoy talking to Jimmy McDonough in 1989 for a *Village Voice* profile. Young subsequently asked McDonough to write the liner notes for a retrospective he was working on, then known as *Decade II*, and the project soon grew into a full-fledged authorized biography.

But in Neil Young's world, little is easy—especially when it cuts as close to the bone as a book.

McDonough certainly did the work, spending eight years accumulating three hundred interviews, including fifty hours spent with Young himself, for *Shakey: Neil Young's Biography*. By the terms of the agreement, McDonough had full creative control save for matters about Young's immediate family, over which the artist retained veto power. It was intimate and comprehensive and had all the makings of a blockbuster—a revealing look inside one of pop culture's most fascinating and ambitious, but guarded, characters.

And it almost didn't come out.

When McDonough finished the manuscript for *Shakey* in 1998, Young decided to pull his support. No specific objections were raised about the content, but Young

contended that McDonough had delivered the manuscript three years after it was originally due and also violated the agreement by delivering it to the publisher, Random House, rather than directly to Young. McDonough responded with a $1.8 million lawsuit in 2000, noting that the delay was mostly due to having to track down Young for interviews— "This guy kept me in a cat-and-mouse game for another three years," McDonough told NPR's Scott Simon—and that Young had waived the contractual deadlines anyway.

Random House sympathized with McDonough. "I am sure that any writer would feel devastated, after spending a decade working on a biography, to have the subject of that biography sabotage its publication," editor-in-chief Ann Godoff wrote in a letter to the author. But the publisher was not willing to go forward with *Shakey* without Young's consent.

The case was settled out of court in 2001, with *Shakey* finally hitting stores in May 2002. McDonough told Reuters that despite the legal punch-up, "This is the book I originally wrote. He didn't screw with it. He let me write it the way I wanted to write it." And he continued to voice admiration for Young as an artist.

"Too much of today's rock 'n' roll is about producing atmosphere for a Wal-Mart store," McDonough said. "There is something about Neil that conveys a real feeling. And he's got it in spades."

He says, 'The good news is, you're here, you're looking good. The bad news is, you've got an aneurysm in your brain. You've had it for a hundred years, so it's nothing to worry about—but it's very serious, so we'll have to get rid of it right away.

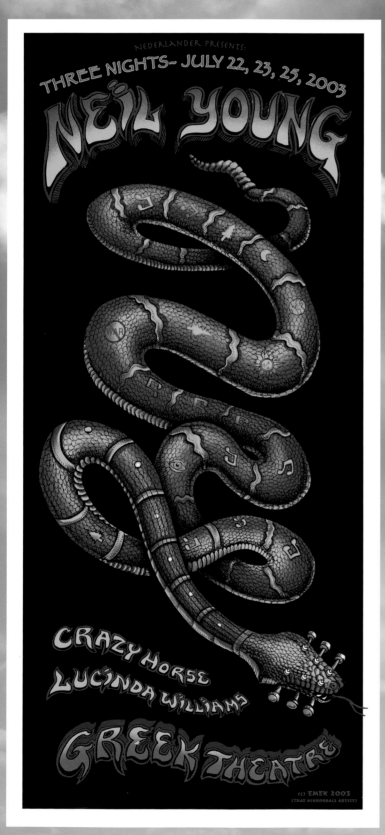

Greendale Tour, Los Angeles, 2003. *Artist: Emek (www.emek.net)*

Duncan, British Columbia, September 17, 2004. *Artist: Bob Masse (bmasse.com)*

*How can it be that you're going there next Tuesday and we're sitting here recording?"*

The operation was a success, the surgeons having accessed Young's brain through his femoral artery. But a couple of days later, the artery burst, and he was rushed back to the hospital. He canceled a scheduled appearance at the Juno awards, forcing him to explain publicly what had happened—which he wouldn't have done otherwise. "I came very close to no one ever knowing," Young said. "I would have had an aneurysm, got rid of it, and no one would know the difference. It would have been so cool."

Cut in Nashville, *Prairie Wind*—as well as *Heart of Gold*, the sumptuous Jonathan Demme concert film that accompanied it—bears the marks of Young's near-death experience. Both are deeply nostalgic and even a little sad as he says goodbye to some of his fellow travelers, including his father, who suffered from dementia before his death. "I had a great relationship with my dad, and I felt like everything was O.K. when he died, that I was at peace with him and everything was cool," Young told *Time*. "Then I went to the service and completely broke down out of nowhere."

On the *Heart of Gold* set with director Jonathan Demme, Ryman Auditorium, Nashville, Tennessee, August 18–19, 2005. © Paramount/Everett Collection/Rex USA

*Prairie Wind*'s closing song, "When God Made Me," is a hymn questioning the creator's motives—not in an angry fashion but a prayerful one. Young told PBS's Charlie Rose the most significant way that his aneurysm had changed him:

> *It gave me more faith. . . . I know there are a lot of stories. There is the Bible. There is the Koran. There are all of these things. Everybody's got one. Everybody has a faith. And there are stories that have gone through the ages, and I respect all of them. But I don't know where I fit in. I just have faith.*

God didn't disappoint Young, but men still did. As the war in Iraq continued to rage, Young suddenly found that he'd had enough. He told *Rolling Stone*:

> *I went down to the coffee machine and there was* USA Today. *The cover showed a large military craft converted into a flying hospital. The caption said something about how we are making great strides in medicine as a result of the Iraq conflict. That just caught me off guard, and I went upstairs and wrote "Families" for one of those soldiers who didn't get to come home. Then I cried in my wife's arms. That was the turning point for me.*

And there was no turning back. The songs for *Living with War*, which he called his "metal folk protest album," poured out of Young, culminating in "Let's Impeach the President," a no-holds-barred attack on George W. Bush.

"You know, it is a sad thing," Young acknowledged to Rose. "It is terrible to be involved in . . . criticizing the president and doing this and that, and talking about things in the first person and getting right in there."

Young created an elaborate section on his website, neilyoung.com, called Living with War Today, a mock news site with stories about the war and its aftermath for soldiers and their families. There are also links to hundreds of protest songs and videos posted by musicians from all over the world. Young also took the album on the road, turning it into a CSNY tour dominated by the album. "We tried sprinkling my songs throughout the show and that didn't work," Young told *Rolling Stone*, "because they disturbed everything. We put them all together, basically, and isolated the other ones."

The tour, captured by Young (under his *nom de film*, Bernard Shakey) in the documentary *CSNY/Déjà Vu*, reveals just how contentious the shows became. Some audience members booed Young's polemics or even walked out, while others sang along or cried while the band sang "Find the Cost of Freedom," an anthem for another war made relevant once again. "It's the real deal," Young said. "I make a whole album about this war, and some people are still stupid enough to say that I just did it for the money because I'm an old fart. They're out of

touch. It's not about the entertainment business, it's about a fucking war that people are getting killed in."

Having said his piece, Young slowly began rolling out samples of his massive *Archives* project. The first piece of the puzzle, *Live at the Fillmore East: March 6 & 7, 1970*, surfaced in 2006. It captures a raging concert performance by Crazy Horse, including the version of "Come On Baby Let's Go Downtown," with vocals by

> I think it was Peter Buck from R.E.M. and Neil Young, and they were doing an interview, and they were talking about music and talking about their love of vinyl and the analog sound compared to the digital sound and what a shame it was the industry kind of pushed it aside.
>
> —Eddie Vedder,
> Neil Young's Rock and Roll Hall of Fame induction speech

With Pegi, Fifth Annual Benefit for the Elton John AIDS Foundation, Waldorf-Astoria Hotel, New York, October 3, 2006. *Photo by Timothy A. Clary/AFP/Getty Images*

Chrome Dreams Tour, Northrup Auditorium, Minneapolis, Minnesota, November 8, 2007. © *Tony Nelson (tonynelsonphoto.com)*

Danny Whitten, that had been culled for *Tonight's the Night*. *Live at Massey Hall 1971* arrived in 2007, offering an especially compelling solo show. Another solo concert, *Live at Canterbury House 1968*, was released in 2008. It contains the version of "Sugar Mountain" that was a long-ago B-side for Young and had made its album debut on *Decade*.

Young continued recording new material even as he mined his past. *Chrome Dreams II*, in typical Youngian fashion, is a sequel to an album that was never released (the legendary *Chrome Dreams* that was raided for songs that eventually wound up on *American Stars 'n Bars*). Some of the *Chrome II* songs date back to the 1980s, notably the extended jam "Ordinary People," which features the Bluenotes. Other tracks range from the gentle *Harvest*-style folk rock of "Beautiful Bluebird" to the meditative "The Way" to the slapdash garage rock of "Dirty Old Man." Its specific connection to the original *Chrome Dreams* is unclear.

Hastily written and recorded, Young's 2009 album *Fork in the Road* seems less like a cohesive album and more like a series of blog entries—which, in a way, it was. Inspired by his efforts to turn a vintage Lincoln Continental into a vehicle running entirely on alternative energy, Young had been posting his thoughts on the automobile industry—as well as some songs—on the news and opinion website *Huffington Post*. Songs like "Johnny Magic" (about his Linc/Volt partner Jonathan Goodwin), "Fuel Line," and "Get Behind the Wheel" continue along the same themes. It's not one of his most musically inventive albums—perhaps the innovation went into the car instead—but it's one of his most immediate.

Soon after *Fork*, Young unloaded the massive *Archives Vol. 1* box set, the first of four or five projected anthologies. He'd been working on the set so long, *Wired* magazine tittered "that the big news in the tech world when it was first announced was Windows 3.0."

*(continued on page 189)*

European Summer Tour, Firenze, Italy, 2008. *Artist: Steuso (www.steuso.com)*

Chrome Dreams Tour, Upper Darby, Pennsylvania, 2007. *Artist: Todd Slater (www.ToddSlater.net)*

I always liked Neil from day one. He's got a real honest, direct delivery. He never seemed to draw too much from anybody else but himself, his own observations. He's not afraid to go out there and work with different people . . . and then he's still rockin', which is great.

—Taj Mahal

He's a brilliant artist, I think. I'm a big admirer of his singing and his music. He's always made really good records. He's always been a stickler for great recorded sounds. He's a studio hound and a microphone hound and uses old equipment that sounds great. But yet he's not so traditionally stumped in it that he can't find something brand new.

—Ricky Skaggs

*Artist: Jake Early (jakeearly.com)*

# Hit the Road
## The Linc/Volt Story

With the Linc/Volt at Salesforce.com's Dreamforce conference in San Francisco, November 3, 2008. *Reuters/Robert Galbraith*

**"JUST SINGIN' A SONG** won't change the world," Neil Young sang in 2009. That's a startling sentiment coming from a man whose music has had an indelible impact on countless listeners. And if Young's music has not changed the world—many would argue that it has—at the very least it's altered our perception of it.

But when Young sang those words on his album *Fork in the Road*, he had something more in mind than simply changing hearts and minds. This time he was more interested in the place where the rubber meets the road. Literally.

Partnering with companies from around the world—most notably Jonathan Goodwin's H-Line Conversions in Wichita, Kansas, and Uli Kruger of Australia's Alternative Energy Technologies (AET)—Young began working on the Linc/Volt, the prototype of a new fuel-efficient car but with a typically Youngian twist. Instead of a tiny vehicle with a futuristic design, the Linc/Volt's body was that of a 1959 Lincoln Continental convertible: a 19.5-foot, two-and-a-half-ton behemoth that looked more like the kind of car Americans want as opposed to what automotive designers and conservationists think they need.

Young explained:

*People love their cars, especially here in America, and have a spirit that they associate with their car. They love their big cars. They love their big roads, and they're big people. So you can't sell a tiny electric car to Americans. You can sell it to some of them, but it's not an easy sell.*

*So there are ways to eliminate roadside refueling, and what we need to do is make these ways attractive to people so they don't lose the spirit of the car.*

The Linc/Volt team's goal was to blend electronic and fuel technologies to create a self-charging, emissions-free vehicle that will achieve 100 miles per gallon or more. It was good for the environment, of course, but Young and his partners had a global political impact in mind, too. As their mission statement read: "By creating this new power technology we hope to reduce the demand for petro-fuels enough to eliminate the need for war over energy supplies, thereby enhancing the security of the USA and other nations throughout the world."

Young, who also owns a 1982 Mercedes coupe diesel that runs on vegetable oil, said:

*The gas station is the tentacle of big oil, which reaches out and touches all of us daily. If you can eliminate roadside refueling, then whatever technology can do that will also change the way we generate power—the heat in our houses and the power that turns on the lights and all those things— and the way the world works. I really think it's time for us to try to do that. No goal was ever met by not setting it.*

Young and company gave the Linc/Volt a big roll-out, taking the car around the country, including to events such as the South by Southwest conference in Austin, Texas, and to Sun Microsystems in California. The project's website detailed its performance. Filmmaker Larry Johnson also chronicled the car's adventures and travels for a documentary film.

And the Linc/Volt was entered in the 2009 Progressive Automotive X Prize contest, competing with 110 other teams for a $10 million prize awarded to the first practical automobile capable of reaching the 100 mpg standards. "We don't really care if we win the $10 million," said Young (although the scientists and craftsmen involved may have felt differently). "We think the race is bigger than that. We think we're in a race against time, basically, for the planet."

"And if [Linc/Volt] isn't the answer," Young added, "maybe it can give someone else some ideas to come up with the answer."

I like the way he is uncompromising and constantly reinvents himself. He's like a musical brother to me in a way. And of course I got more respect for him when he played on my album than I had before. He was just amazing and played brilliantly and with so much heart, and he did it so quickly. I always knew he was a good musician, but I didn't know he had that much fast musical acumen, which was a surprise. His own stuff might be a little more introspective and maybe take a little more time, but he worked very quickly on my album. He allowed me to cop his sound, which is very generous to let somebody do that.

—Booker T. Jones

# Journey through the Past
## The Road to *Archives*

**NEIL YOUNG ASSERTED HIS AMBITIONS** for documenting his own career in 1978 when he issued *Decade*, a then-whopping three-LP set loaded with hits, new and unreleased material, and insightful song-by-song commentary. In the pre–CD box set age, it was the first time a rock 'n' roll artist had surveyed his work with the kind of serious storytelling ambition that was more familiar to jazz and classical retrospectives.

But his next idea made *Decade* look like a 45 rpm single in comparison.

After nearly two decades in development, *Neil Young Archives Volume 1, 1963–1972* surfaced in June 2008 in three formats—Blu-ray, DVD, and CD—and with 128 tracks, nearly half of which were previously unreleased or alternate versions of studio releases. The Blu-ray and DVD packages also included a 238-page book and the long out-of-print 1972 feature film, *Journey through the Past*.

But it was the Blu-ray set that offered the true mother lode: a state-of-the-art interactive experience that allowed users to listen to a particular song while surfing through a variety of images and information—and also, via the Internet and BD Live technology, to be able to update that content with other material as it becomes available.

The wealth of material is exhaustive and exhausting. "I am kind of a pack rat," Young confessed to reporters during a demonstration of *Archives* at JavaOne in San Francisco. "I only give the record company what I want people to hear at the time. So I have a lot of unreleased material. Putting it all together tells a much different story than just what has been produced [for public consumption]."

During the development of the Shakey Platform—named after his *nom de film*, Bernard Shakey—Young explained that his vision of the Blu-ray version of *Archives* is

*a living thing. It never stops. . . . The navigating system is the best. You can drop in at different times of [my] history and see what was going on in the world at that time, the reviews, the photographs, the back story to the music, the outtakes, other takes that were done on the same day . . . everything, just a day-by-day trip.*

*It's a whole new thing. I've made a lot of CDs, and we've made a lot of DVDs, and Blu-ray technology is*

*so far superior to anything else. It's the future, and I would rather focus on what's next.*

Young began talking about *Archives* as *Decade II* during the late '80s, and even at that time, he envisioned an extensive, multivolume set with some degree of interactivity. Release dates were intermittently reported and canceled, and it became something of a music industry Godot. At one point, there was even an online betting pool to guess whether *Archives* would beat Guns N' Roses' equally tardy *Chinese Democracy* to the stores (it didn't). Crazy Horse guitarist Frank "Poncho" Sampedro told *Undercover* in 2003 that he suspected Young was having second thoughts about the project: "I think Neil (and he would never say it) just has a feeling that putting out a boxed set like that is kind of like marking the end of your career."

The true reason for the delay, of course, was waiting for the right technology, which Young's team worked hand-in-hand with software developers to create. "On a broader scale," he told *Guitar World* after *Archives* came out, "we're trying to create a new flow of information. In my case, the music is the glue that holds it all together. But it could be anything; it could be art, it could be film, it could be history."

Young said he envisions four or five volumes of *Archives* over time, though he cautioned that while the second set would come "quicker," it might not show up until "about two or three years" after Volume 1. He also remains interested in putting out single-volume additions to the *Archives* universe. And while he's taken an active role in journeying through the past, he was not necessarily looking to glean new perspective on his work. He noted:

*Strangely enough, I'm pretty detached from it because it's more like a collection of things. It happens to be my life, but it could be anything. I obviously absorbed some of the things I'd seen by doing it and some of the changes that my music and music in general have gone through since '63. But there's a level at which I have to treat it like a product and make sure it's something that's really good and easy to use and has value.*

# Neil Young: A Hero to Working America

IATSE Local 33 Los Angeles Stagehands thank America's "Union Man" Neil Young for refusing to cross the picket line at The Forum in L.A.

35% Pay Cut Is Too Much

www.JusticeAtTheForum.org

## NEIL YOUNG

PERFORMING WITH
BEN KEITH, RICK ROSAS, CHAD CROMWELL, ANTHONY CRAWFORD AND PEGI YOUNG

WITH SPECIAL GUESTS

### WILCO

AND

### EVEREST

DECEMBER 15TH
By Overwhelming Demand 2nd & Final Show Added
ON SALE THIS FRIDAY at 10AM
**DECEMBER 16TH**
MADISON SQUARE GARDEN
The World's Most Famous Arena

WWW.NEILYOUNG.COM

(continued from page 183)

Released on CD, DVD, and Blu-ray, *Vol. 1* spans the years 1963 to 1972 and tells his history the way Young wants it told: warts and all. "You hear the good and the bad," Young told *Rolling Stone*. "A lot of people will say, 'Well, there's a lot of trash on this thing.' But if you take it as a whole, it tells a story. And that's what I like to do."

Telling stories has always been Neil Young's specialty. And despite having entered his sixties, he is still attitudinally true to his family name. No one, not even his hero Bob Dylan, has kept pace with him in terms of keeping his music young, fresh, vital, and forward looking. Young has, at times, faltered and even failed, but he has always remained a thoughtful songwriter, an ever-curious multimedia artist, and a live performer of the highest magnitude.

His wife, Pegi, remains his rock. Young told Charlie Rose:

> Look what I have done in thirty years of marriage. How creative have I been? I have been able to do all kinds of different things, take on different characters, take on different personalities, do wacky things, get totally out of my mind, you know, drinking tequila to get into one thing, doing this and doing that, doing all of these things for all of these characters that I had to live my way through. And yet, she was sticking with me all the way through that. She deserves a medal for being open and free enough to allow me to be myself. Do you know how many people when they get married, they change, they adjust. I have not had to make an adjustment. She has allowed me to be free and taught me the beauty of the family—so I am very fortunate. Behind everyone who, you know, is doing something, there is a partner, somebody like that, a partner.

With family keeping him grounded and a little help from the great beyond, Neil Young is unafraid to fly. "We're gonna get in there and let the muse have us," he says as he prepares to take the stage in *Heart of Gold*. "Take a shot. Send it out."

# Acknowledgments

For the better part of the last four decades—and indeed the better part of our lives—we've been Neil Young fans and followers. We've had our minds blown by favorites like *Everybody Knows This Is Nowhere*, *Zuma*, and *Rust Never Sleeps* and had our ears blown out by too many Crazy Horse shows to count. We've puzzled over odd, outré albums like *Time Fades Away* and *Tonight's the Night*, which repeated listenings eventually turned into favorites. And we've sat through experiments like *Trans*, *Everybody's Rockin'*, and the films *Journey through the Past* and *Human Highway*, figuring we owed the guy one now and then. Submerging ourselves in all of it once again during the intense period of this book's creation was both a joy and a revelation. But it was also a challenge: Taken as a whole, Young's body of work is about staying in the moment and fighting to stay relevant—refusing to either burn out or fade away—regardless of the consequences. In that sense, he asks more of his audience than almost any other artist. But he doesn't do it without demanding it of himself first, which is why he's deserved our continued attention for so long.

We'd like to thank Dennis Pernu at Voyageur Press for signing us on for this book and Danielle Ibister for her wise, patient, and occasionally indulgent management of the project. We're also grateful for the work that Krystyna Borgen, design manager Katie Sonmor, and designer John Barnett put into this. Thanks are due to Doug Allsop, AP Images, Corbis, Jake Early (jakeearly.com), John Einarson, Emek (emek.net), Robert Ferreira, Gijsbert Hanekroot (gijsberthanekroot.nl), Getty Images, Cyril Kieldsen, Bob Leafe (bobleafe.com), The Library and Archives Canada, Bob Masse (bmasse.com), Robert Matheu, Tony Nelson (tonynelsonphoto.com), The Mad Peck, Peter Pontiac (peterpontiac.com), Retna, Reuters Pictures, Rex USA, Joel Schnell at Creative Publishing international, Chester Simpson (Rock-N-RollPhotos.com), Steuso (Stefano Manzi) (steuso.com), Todd Slater (toddslater.com), Nick Warburton (nickwarburton.com), Nurit Wilde (wildeimages.com), and Zuma for their contributions. And thanks, too, to Stephen Scapelliti for his legal stewardship.

Gary sends a fist bump to Dan, a brother from another mother whose friendship is treasured, even after the ardors of working in such close quarters. Great thanks also go to those I work with, and for, on a regular basis, who gave me the leeway and latitude to work on *Neil Young: Long May You Run*—even when they didn't know they were doing it: Jacquelyn Gutc, Julie Jacobson, Nicole Robertson, Steve Frye, and Glenn Gilbert at the *Oakland Press*; David J. Prince, Jessica Letkemann, Bill Werde, and Rob Levin at *Billboard*; Judy Rosen and the gang at the Pulse of Radio; Gayden Wren at the New York Times Syndicate; Brandon Geist, Kory Grow, and Tom Beaujour at *Revolver*; Marcella S. Kreiter and John Hendel at UPI; Bob Kernen and Tom Sharrard at Grokmusic.com; Doug Podell, Jon Ray, and all at WCSX Detroit; Bob Madden, Brian Nelson, Eric Jensen, and Keith Hastings at WHQG (The HOG!) in Milwaukee; Laura Lee and Dave "Redman" Redelberger at Radio 106.7 in Columbus; and a partridge in a pear tree. My gratitude also to the too many friends and relatives to name without missing somebody important, but especially to my beloved Hannah, my dear Shari, and Liebe and Annie the wonder dogs, all of whom never minded when rust, and I, never slept.

Dan returns the fist bump and adds a bro-hug to Gary, without whom none of this would be possible, or nearly as much fun. Thanks to Jody Mitori, Kevin C. Johnson, Barry Gilbert, and Evan Benn at the *St. Louis Post-Dispatch*; Donna Korando at the *St. Louis Beacon*; John Carney, Jon Grayson, Steve Moore, and Kevin Ahern at KMOX; technical advisor and sounding board Jerome Peirick; and Neal Thompson, usurper of bandwidth extraordinaire. Also to Jesse Raya, Chris Peimann, Sarah Samples, Amy Moorehouse, and Angela Brown for service above and beyond the call of duty; the peanut gallery of the Carosello Connection for cheering me on; friends and family members too numerous to mention; and Thomasita Homan, O.S.B., whom I forgot to acknowledge last time. Last, but never least, thanks to the home team—my parents, Eric and Annie Durchholz; my wonderful wife, Mary; my great kids, Wolfgang, Eva, Stefan, and Hans; and the latest addition to our family, Ute—good dog!

# Discography

Since the release of his first commercial recording—the Squires' "The Sultan"/"Aurora" single on a tiny Canadian label—Neil Young has amassed a lengthy discography as a solo artist, a band member, and a guest, as well as the subject of numerous tribute albums. What follows is as comprehensive a list as possible of his "official" recordings in those categories. Although we may know of a few, ahem, "unauthorized" gems that have been passed between fans over the years, and which Young is largely undermining with his ongoing *Archives* collections, we've stuck to the legal stuff in the following pages. The chart positions are from the Billboard 200. Release dates are as specific as possible; there was a time in the music industry when albums hit stores on more of a rolling basis rather than on a specific date, as became the practice later on. And, finally, we know as we write this that the prolific Mr. Young is capable of releasing another album or two—or more—between now and when you're holding the book in your hands. So if there's something you don't see here, blame him.

# Discography I:
# As Band Member or Solo Artist

### Buffalo Springfield
#### *Buffalo Springfield*
Atco 33-200
Recorded June–September 1966 at Gold Star
  Recording Studios and Columbia Recording
  Studio, Hollywood
Produced by Charles Greene and Brian Stone
Released in mono and stereo January 1967
Peak chart position: 80

"Go and Say Goodbye"/"Sit Down I Think I Love You"/"Leave"/"Nowadays Clancy Can't Even Sing"/"Hot Dusty Roads"/"Everybody's Wrong"/"Flying on the Ground Is Wrong"/ "Burned"/"Do I Have to Come Right Out and Say It"/"Baby Don't Scold Me"/"Out of My Mind"/"Pay the Price"

Re-released in mono and stereo, April 1967
  as Atco 33-200A with "For What It's Worth"
  added and "Baby Don't Scold Me" deleted.

### Buffalo Springfield
#### *Buffalo Springfield Again*
Atco 33-226
Recorded January–September 1967 at Gold
  Star Recording Studios, Columbia Recording
  Studio, and Sunset Sound, Hollywood; and
  Atlantic Studios, New York
Produced by Ahmet Ertegun, Richie Furay,
  Charles Greene, Dewey Martin, Jack
  Nitzsche, Stephen Stills, Brian Stone, and
  Neil Young
Released in mono and stereo, November 1967
Peak chart position: 44

"Mr. Soul"/"A Child's Claim to Fame"/ "Everydays"/"Expecting to Fly"/ "Bluebird"/"Hung Upside Down"/"Sad Memory"/"Good Time Boy"/"Rock & Roll Woman"/"Broken Arrow"

## Buffalo Springfield
### *Last Time Around*

Atco SD 33-256
Recorded February 1967–May 1968 at Sunset
Sound, Hollywood, and Atlantic Studios,
New York
Produced by Jim Messina
Released August 1968
Peak chart position: 42

"On the Way Home"/"It's So Hard to
Wait"/"Pretty Girl Why"/"Four Days
Gone"/"Carefree Country Day"/"Special
Care"/"The Hour of Not Quite Rain"/
"Questions"/"I Am a Child"/"Merry-Go-
Round"/"Uno Mundo"/"Kind Woman"

## Neil Young & Crazy Horse
### *Everybody Knows This Is Nowhere*

Reprise 6349
Recorded January–March 1969 at Wally Heider
Recording, Hollywood
Produced by David Briggs and Neil Young
Released May 1969
Peak chart position: 34

"Cinnamon Girl"/"Everybody Knows This Is
Nowhere"/"Round & Round (It Won't Be
Long)"/"Down by the River"/"The Losing End
(When You're On)"/"Running Dry (Requiem
for the Rockets)"/"Cowgirl in the Sand"

## Neil Young
### *Neil Young*

Reprise 6317
Recorded August–October 1968 at Wally
Heider Recording, Sunset Sound, Sunwest
Recording and TTG Recording, Hollywood
Produced by David Briggs, Neil Young, Ryland
Cooder, and Jack Nitzsche
Released November 1968
Peak chart position: —

"The Emperor of Wyoming"/"The Loner"/"If I
Could Have Her Tonight"/"I've Been Waiting
for You"/"The Old Laughing Lady"/"String
Quartet from Whiskey Boot Hill"/"Here We
Are in the Years"/"What Did You Do to My
Life?"/"I've Loved Her So Long"/"The Last
Trip to Tulsa"

## Crosby, Stills, Nash & Young
### *Déjà Vu*

Atlantic SD 7200
Recorded October–December 1969 at Wally
Heider's Studio C, San Francisco, and Wally
Heider's Studio III, Los Angeles
Produced by Crosby, Stills, Nash & Young
Released March 1970
Peak chart position: 1

"Carry On"/"Teach Your Children"/"Almost
Cut My Hair"/"Helpless"/"Woodstock"/
"Déjà Vu"/"Our House"/"4+20"/"Country
Girl" a) "Whiskey Boot Hill" b) "Down,
Down, Down" c) "Country Girl (I Think
You're Pretty)"/"Everybody I Love You"

## Buffalo Springfield
### *Retrospective*

Atco SD 33-283
Recorded 1966–1968
Producers: Charles Greene, Brian Stone,
Stephen Stills, Neil Young, Jack Nitzsche,
Ahmet Ertegun, and Jim Messina
Released February 1969
Peak chart position: 42

"For What It's Worth"/"Mr. Soul"/"Sit
Down, I Think I Love You"/"Kind
Woman"/"Bluebird"/"On the Way
Home"/"Nowadays Clancy Can't Even
Sing"/"Broken Arrow"/"Rock & Roll
Woman"/"I Am a Child"/"Go and Say
Goodbye"/"Expecting to Fly"

## Neil Young
### *After the Gold Rush*

Reprise 6383
Recorded August 1969–June 1970 at Sunset
Sound and Sound City, Hollywood, and Neil
Young's home in Topanga, CA
Produced by Neil Young and David Briggs
with Kendall Pacios
Released June 1970
Peak chart position: 8

"Tell Me Why"/"After the Gold Rush"/"Only
Love Can Break Your Heart"/"Southern
Man"/"Till the Morning Comes"/"Oh,
Lonesome Me"/"Don't Let It Bring You Down"/
"Birds"/"When You Dance I Can Really
Love"/"I Believe in You"/"Cripple Creek Ferry"

## Crosby, Stills, Nash & Young
### 4 Way Street

Atlantic SD 2-902
Recorded June–July 1970 at the Fillmore East,
   New York; Auditorium Theatre, Chicago; and
   the L.A. Forum, Inglewood, CA
Produced by Crosby, Stills, Nash & Young
Released April 1971
Peak chart position: 1

"Suite: Judy Blue Eyes"/"On the Way
Home"/"Teach Your Children"/"Triad"/"The
Lee Shore"/"Chicago"/"Right Between the
Eyes"/"Cowgirl in the Sand"/"Don't Let It
Bring You Down"/"49 Bye Byes"–"America's
Children"/"Love the One You're With"/"Pre-
Road Downs"/"Long Time Gone"/"Southern
Man"/"Ohio"/"Carry On"/"Find the Cost of
Freedom"

The compact disc version of the album,
   Atlantic 82408, released June 1992, also
   includes the songs "King Midas in Reverse,"
   "Laughing," "Black Queen," and "Medley:
   The Loner-Cinnamon Girl-Down by the
   River"

## Neil Young
### Harvest

Reprise 2032
Recorded January–September 1971 at
   Quadraphonic Studios, Nashville; Barking
   Town Hall, London; Broken Arrow Studio
   No. 2, Woodside, CA; and January 1971 at
   UCLA's Royce Hall, Los Angeles
Produced by Elliot Mazer, Neil Young, Jack
   Nitzsche, and Henry Lewy
Released February 1972
Peak chart position: 1

"Out on the Weekend"/"Harvest"/"A Man
Needs a Maid"/"Heart of Gold"/"Are You
Ready for the Country?"/"Old Man"/"There's
a World"/"Alabama"/"The Needle and the
Damage Done"/"Words (Between the Lines of
Age)"

## Neil Young
### Journey through the Past

Reprise 2XS 6480
Recorded 1967–1972
Produced by Neil Young and L. A. Johnson
Released November 1972
Peak chart position: 45

"For What It's Worth"/"Mr. Soul"/"Rock &
Roll Woman"/"Find the Cost of Freedom"/
"Ohio"/"Southern Man"/"Are You Ready for
the Country?"/"Let Me Call You Sweetheart"/
"Alabama"/"Words"/"Relativity Invitation"/
"Handel's Messiah"/"King of Kings"/
"Soldier"/"Let's Go Away for Awhile"

## Neil Young
### Time Fades Away

Reprise 2151
Recorded January 1971 at UCLA's Royce Hall,
   Los Angeles, and on 1973 North American
   tour
Produced by Elliot Mazer and Neil Young
Released October 1973
Peak chart position: 22

"Time Fades Away"/"Journey through the
Past"/"Yonder Stands the Sinner"/"L.A."/
"Love in Mind"/"Don't Be Denied"/
"The Bridge"/"Last Dance"

## Buffalo Springfield
### Buffalo Springfield

Atco SD 2-806
Recorded 1966–1968
Produced by Ahmet Ertegun, Richie Furay,
   Charles Greene, Jim Messina, Stephen Stills,
   Neil Young, Jack Nitzsche, and Brian Stone
Released November 1973
Peak chart position: —

"For What It's Worth"/"Sit Down, I Think
I Love You"/"Nowadays Clancy Can't Even
Sing"/"Go and Say Goodbye"/"Pay the
Price"/"Burned"/"Out of My Mind"/"Mr.
Soul"/"Bluebird"/"Broken Arrow"/"Rock
& Roll Woman"/"Expecting to Fly"/"Hung
Upside Down"/"A Child's Claim to
Fame"/"Kind Woman"/"On the Way Home"/"I
Am a Child"/"Pretty Girl Why"/"Special
Care"/"Uno Mundo"/"In the Hour of Not
Quite Rain"/"Four Days Gone"/"Questions"

### Neil Young
#### *On the Beach*

Reprise 2180
Recorded November 1973–April 1974 at
  Broken Arrow Ranch, Redwood City, CA,
  and Sunset Sound Recorders, Hollywood
Produced by Neil Young, David Briggs, Mark
  Harman, and Al Schmitt
Released July 1974
Peak chart position: 16

"Walk On"/"See the Sky About to
Rain"/"Revolution Blues"/"For the
Turnstiles"/"Vampire Blues"/"On the
Beach"/"Motion Pictures"/"Ambulance Blues"

### Neil Young & Crazy Horse
#### *Zuma*

Reprise 2242
Recorded June 1974–August 1975 at Broken
  Arrow Ranch, Redwood City, CA, and
  Pt. Dume, CA
Produced by Neil Young, David Briggs, and
  Tim Mulligan
Released November 1975
Peak chart position: 25

"Don't Cry No Tears"/"Danger Bird"/"Pardon
My Heart"/"Lookin' for a Love"/"Barstool
Blues"/"Stupid Girl"/"Drive Back"/"Cortez
the Killer"/"Through My Sails"

### Crosby, Stills, Nash & Young
#### *So Far*

Atlantic 18100
Recorded 1969–1970
Produced by Crosby, Stills, Nash & Young and
  Bill Halverson
Released August, 1974
Peak chart position: 1

"Déjà Vu"/"Helplessly Hoping"/"Wooden
Ships"/"Teach Your Children"/"Ohio"/"Find
the Cost of Freedom"/"Woodstock"/
"Our House"/"Helpless"/"Guinnevere"/
"Suite: Judy Blue Eyes"

### The Stills-Young Band
#### *Long May You Run*

Reprise 2253
Recorded February–June 1976 at Criteria
  Studios, Miami
Produced by Stephen Stills, Neil Young, and
  Don Gehman
Released September 1976
Peak chart position: 26

"Long May You Run"/"Make Love to
You"/"Midnight on the Bay"/"Black
Coral"/"Ocean Girl"/"Let It Shine"/"12/8
Blues (All the Same)"/"Fontainebleau"/
"Guardian Angel"

### Neil Young
#### *Tonight's the Night*

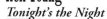

Reprise 2221
Recorded March 1970 at the Fillmore East,
  New York; December 1972 and December
  1973 at Broken Arrow Ranch, Redwood City,
  CA; and August–September 1973 at Studio
  Instrument Rentals, Hollywood
Produced by David Briggs, Neil Young, Tim
  Mulligan, and Elliot Mazer
Released June 1975
Peak chart position: 25

"Tonight's the Night"/"Speakin' Out"/"World
on a String"/"Borrowed Tune"/"Come On Baby
Let's Go Downtown"/"Mellow My Mind"/
"Roll Another Number (For the Road)"/
"Albuquerque"/"New Mama"/"Lookout Joe"/
"Tired Eyes"/"Tonight's the Night–Part II"

### Neil Young
#### *American Stars 'n Bars*

Reprise 2261
Recorded December 1974–April 1977 at
  Quadrafonic Sound Studio, Nashville; Wally
  Heider Studios, Hollywood; Broken Arrow
  Ranch, Redwood City, CA; and Indigo
  Recording Studio, Malibu, CA
Produced by Neil Young, David Briggs, Tim
  Mulligan, and Elliot Mazer
Released May 1977
Peak chart position: 21

"The Old Country Waltz"/"Saddle Up
the Palomino"/"Hey Babe"/"Hold Back
the Tears"/"Bite the Bullet"/"Star of
Bethlehem"/"Will to Love"/"Like a
Hurricane"/"Homegrown"

## Neil Young & Crazy Horse
### *Rust Never Sleeps*

Reprise 2295
Recorded on 1978 North American tour and
    at Broken Arrow Studio, Redwood City, CA;
    and August 1976 and September 1977 at
    Indigo Recording Studio, Malibu, CA; Triad
    Recording, Ft. Lauderdale, FL; and Woodland
    Sound Studios, Nashville
Produced by Neil Young, David Briggs, and
    Tim Mulligan
Released June 1979
Peak chart position: 8

"MY MY, HEY HEY (OUT OF THE BLUE)"/
"THRASHER"/"RIDE MY LLAMA"/
"POCAHONTAS"/"SAIL AWAY"/
"POWDERFINGER"/"WELFARE MOTHERS"/
"SEDAN DELIVERY"/"HEY HEY, MY MY
(INTO THE BLACK)"

## Neil Young
### *Decade*

Reprise 2257
Recorded 1966-1976
Compiled by Neil Young, Tim Mulligan, and
    David Briggs
Released October 1977
Peak chart position: 43

"DOWN TO THE WIRE"/"BURNED"/"MR. SOUL"/
"BROKEN ARROW"/"EXPECTING TO FLY"/"SUGAR
MOUNTAIN"/"I AM A CHILD"/"THE LONER"/"THE
OLD LAUGHING LADY"/"CINNAMON GIRL"/"DOWN BY
THE RIVER"/"COWGIRL IN THE SAND"/"I BELIEVE IN
YOU"/"AFTER THE GOLD RUSH"/"SOUTHERN MAN"/
"HELPLESS"/"OHIO"/"SOLDIER"/"OLD MAN"/
"A MAN NEEDS A MAID"/"HARVEST"/"HEART
OF GOLD"/"STAR OF BETHLEHEM"/"THE NEEDLE
AND THE DAMAGE DONE"/"TONIGHT'S THE NIGHT
(PART 1)"/"TIRED EYES"/"WALK ON"/"FOR THE
TURNSTILES"/"WINTERLONG"/"DEEP FORBIDDEN
LAKE"/"LIKE A HURRICANE"/"LOVE IS A ROSE"/
"CORTEZ THE KILLER"/"CAMPAIGNER"/
"LONG MAY YOU RUN"

## Neil Young & Crazy Horse
### *Live Rust*

Reprise 2296
Recorded on 1978 North American tour
Produced by David Briggs, Tim Mulligan, and
    Bernard Shakey
Released November 1979
Peak chart position: 15

"SUGAR MOUNTAIN"/"I AM A CHILD"/"COMES A
TIME"/"AFTER THE GOLD RUSH"/"MY MY, HEY
HEY (OUT OF THE BLUE)"/"WHEN YOU DANCE I
CAN REALLY LOVE"/"THE LONER"/"THE NEEDLE
AND THE DAMAGE DONE"/"LOTTA LOVE"/"SEDAN D
ELIVERY"/"POWDERFINGER"/"CORTEZ THE KILLER"/
"CINNAMON GIRL"/"LIKE A HURRICANE"/
"HEY HEY, MY MY (INTO THE BLACK)"/
"TONIGHT'S THE NIGHT"

## Neil Young
### *Comes a Time*

Reprise 2266
Recorded November 1975-November 1977
    at Triad Recording, Ft. Lauderdale, FL;
    Columbia Recording Studio, London; Wally
    Heider Recording Studio, Hollywood;
    Woodland Sound Studios, Nashville; Sound
    Shop, Nashville; and Broken Arrow Studio,
    Redwood City, CA
Produced by Neil Young, Ben Keith, Tim
    Mulligan, and David Briggs
Released October 1978
Peak chart position: 7

"GOIN' BACK"/"COMES A TIME"/"LOOK OUT FOR
MY LOVE"/"PEACE OF MIND"/"LOTTA LOVE"/
"HUMAN HIGHWAY"/"ALREADY ONE"/"FIELD OF
OPPORTUNITY"/"MOTORCYCLE MAMA"/"FOUR
STRONG WINDS"

## Neil Young
### *Hawks & Doves*

Reprise 2297
Recorded December 1974-July 1980 at
    Quadrafonic Sound Studio, Nashville; Village
    Recorders, Los Angeles; Indigo Recording
    Studio, Malibu, CA; Triad Recording Studio,
    Ft. Lauderdale, FL; and Gold Star Recording
    Studio, Hollywood
Produced by David Briggs, Tim Mulligan, and
    Neil Young
Released October 1980
Peak chart position: 30

"LITTLE WING"/"THE OLD HOMESTEAD"/"LOST
IN SPACE"/"CAPTAIN KENNEDY"/"STAYIN'
POWER"/"COASTLINE"/"UNION MAN"/"COMIN'
APART AT EVERY NAIL"/"HAWKS & DOVES"

### Neil Young & Crazy Horse
#### re·ac·tor

Reprise 2304

Recorded October 1980–July 1981 at Modern
Recorders, Redwood City, CA

Produced by David Briggs, Tim Mulligan, and
Neil Young with Jerry Napier

Released October 1981

Peak chart position: 27

"Opera Star"/"Surfer Joe and Moe the Sleaze"/
"T-Bone"/"Get Back on It"/"Southern Pacific"/
"Motor City"/"Rapid Transit"/"Shots"

### Neil Young
#### Trans

Geffen 2018

Recorded September 1981–May 1982 at
Modern Recorders, Redwood City, CA, and
Commercial Recorders, Honolulu

Produced by Neil Young, David Briggs, and
Tim Mulligan

Released December 1982

Peak chart position: 19

"Little Thing Called Love"/"Computer Age"/
"We R in Control"/"Transformer Man"/
"Computer Cowboy (a.k.a. Syscrusher)"/
"Hold On to Your Love"/"Sample and Hold"/
"Mr. Soul"/"Like an Inca"

### Neil Young & the Shocking Pinks
#### Everybody's Rockin'

Geffen 4013

Recorded April–May 1983 at Modern
Recorders, Redwood City, CA

Produced by Elliot Mazer and Neil Young

Released July 1983

Peak chart position: 46

"Betty Lou's Got a New Pair of Shoes"/
"Rainin' in My Heart"/"Payola Blues"/
"Wonderin'"/"Kinda Fonda Wanda"/
"Jellyroll Man"/"Bright Lights, Big City"/
"Cry, Cry, Cry"/"Mystery Train"/
"Everybody's Rockin'"

### Neil Young
#### Old Ways

Geffen 24068

Recorded January 1983 at House of David,
Nashville; April 1985 at the Castle,
Franklin, TN; Pedernales Recording Studio,
Spicewood, TX; and June 1984 at the Opry,
Austin, TX

Produced by Neil Young, Ben Keith, David
Briggs, and Elliot Mazer

Released August 1985

Peak chart position: 75

"The Wayward Wind"/"Get Back to the
Country"/"Are There Any More Real
Cowboys?"/"Once an Angel"/"Misfits"/
"California Sunset"/"Old Ways"/
"My Boy"/"Bound for Glory"/"Where Is the
Highway Tonight?"

### Neil Young
#### Landing on Water

Geffen 24109

Recorded August 1983–March 1986 at Broken
Arrow Ranch, Redwood City, CA, and Record
One, Los Angeles

Produced by Neil Young and Danny
Kortchmar

Released July 1986

Peak chart position: 58

"Weight of the World"/"Violent Side"/
"Hippie Dream"/"Bad News Beat"/
"Touch the Night"/"People on the Street"/
"Hard Luck Stories"/"I Got a Problem"/
"Pressure"/"Drifter"

### Neil Young & Crazy Horse
#### Life

Geffen 24154

Recorded November 1986 at Universal
Amphitheatre, Universal City, CA, and
Record One, Los Angeles

Produced by David Briggs, Neil Young, and
Jack Nitzsche

Released June 1987

Peak chart position: 75

"Mideast Vacation"/"Long Walk Home"/
"Around the World"/"Inca Queen"/"Too
Lonely"/"Prisoners of Rock 'n' Roll"/"Cryin'
Eyes"/"When Your Lonely Heart Breaks"/
"We Never Danced"

### Neil Young & the Bluenotes
#### *This Note's for You*

Reprise 25719

Recorded December 1987–January 1988 at Studio Instrument Rentals Stage 6, Hollywood, CA; the Omni, Oakland, CA; and Redwood Digital, San Francisco

Produced by "The Volume Dealers" (Neil Young & Niko Bolas)

Released April 1988

Peak chart position: 61

"Ten Men Workin'"/"This Note's for You"/ "Coupe de Ville"/"Life in the City"/ "Twilight"/"Married Man"/"Sunny Inside"/ "Can't Believe Your Lyin'"/"Hey Hey" / "One Thing"

### Crosby, Stills, Nash & Young
#### *American Dream*

Atlantic 81888

Recorded April 1987 at Graham Nash's home studio, Los Angeles, and February–July 1988 at Redwood Digital, Woodside, CA

Produced by Niko Bolas and Crosby, Stills, Nash & Young

Released November 1988

Peak chart position: 16

"American Dream"/"Got It Made"/"Name of Love"/"Don't Say Good-bye"/"This Old House"/"Nighttime for Generals"/ "Shadowland"/"Drivin' Thunder"/"Clear Blue Skies"/"That Girl"/"Compass"/"Soldiers of Peace"/"Feel Your Love"/"Night Song"

### Neil Young & the Restless
#### *Eldorado*

Reprise 20P2-2651

Recorded December 1988 at the Hit Factory, New York

Produced by "The Volume Dealers" (Neil Young & Niko Bolas)

Released April 1989 (Japan)

Peak chart position: —

"Cocaine Eyes"/"Don't Cry"/"Heavy Love"/"On Broadway"/"Eldorado"

### Neil Young
#### *Freedom*

Reprise 25899

Recorded July 1988–July 1989 at Redwood Digital, Woodside, CA, and the Hit Factory, NY; and June 1989 at Jones Beach, Wantagh, NY

Produced by "The Volume Dealers" (Neil Young & Niko Bolas)

Released October 1989

Peak chart position: 35

"Rockin' in the Free World"/"Crime in the City (Sixty to Zero Part 1)"/"Don't Cry"/"Hangin' on a Limb"/"Eldorado"/"The Ways of Love"/"Someday"/"On Broadway"/ "Wrecking Ball"/"No More"/"Too Far Gone"/"Rockin' in the Free World"

### Neil Young & Crazy Horse
#### *Ragged Glory*

Reprise 26315

Recorded April 1990 at Plywood Digital, Woodside, CA, and April 1990 at the Hoosier Dome, Indianapolis, IN

Produced by David Briggs and Neil Young

Released September 1990

Peak chart position: 31

"Country Home"/"White Line"/"F*!#in' Up"/ "Over and Over"/"Love to Burn"/"Farmer John"/"Mansion on the Hill"/"Days That Used to Be"/"Love and Only Love"/"Mother Earth (Natural Anthem)"

### Neil Young & Crazy Horse
#### *Weld*

Reprise 26671

Recorded on 1991 North American Tour

Produced by Neil Young and David Briggs with Billy Talbot

Released October 1991

Peak chart position: 154

"Hey Hey, My My (Into the Black)"/"Crime in the City"/"Blowin' in the Wind"/"Welfare Mothers"/"Love to Burn"/"Cinnamon Girl"/ "Mansion on the Hill"/"F*!#in' Up"/"Cortez the Killer"/"Powderfinger"/"Love and Only Love"/"Rockin' in the Free World"/"Like a Hurricane"/"Farmer John"/"Tonight's the Night"/"Roll Another Number"

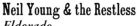

### Neil Young & Crazy Horse
*Arc*

Reprise 26769
Recorded on 1991 North American tour
Produced by Neil Young
Released October 1991
Peak chart position: —

"Arc"

### Neil Young
*Harvest Moon*

Reprise 45057
Recorded September 1991–February 1992 at
  Redwood Digital, Woodside, CA, and Sunset
  Sound, Hollywood, and January 1992 at
  Portland Auditorium, Portland, OR
Produced by Neil Young and Ben Keith
Released October 1992
Peak chart position: 16

"Unknown Legend"/"From Hank to Hendrix"/
"You and Me"/"Harvest Moon"/"War of
Man"/"One of These Days"/"Such a Woman"/
"Old King"/"Dreamin' Man"/"Natural
Beauty"

### Neil Young
*Lucky Thirteen*

Geffen 24452
Recorded 1982–1988
Produced by Neil Young et al.
Released January 1993
Peak chart position: —

"Sample and Hold"/"Transformer Man"/
"Depression Blues"/"Get Gone"/"Don't
Take Your Love Away"/"From Me"/"Once an
Angel"/"Where Is the Highway Tonight?"/
"Hippie Dream"/"Pressure"/"Around the
World"/"Mideast Vacation"/"Ain't It the
Truth"/"This Note's for You"

### Neil Young
*Unplugged*

Recorded February 1993 at Universal Studios,
  Universal City, CA
Produced by David Briggs
Released June 1993
Peak chart position: 23

"The Old Laughing Lady"/"Mr. Soul"/"World
on a String"/"Pocahontas"/"Stringman"/
"Like a Hurricane"/"The Needle and the
Damage Done"/"Helpless"/"Harvest Moon"/
"Transformer Man"/"Unknown Legend"/
"Look Out for My Love"/"Long May You
Run"/"From Hank to Hendrix"

### Neil Young
*Sleeps with Angels*

Reprise 45749
Recorded November 1993–April 1994 at the
  Complex Studios, West Los Angeles
Produced by David Briggs and Neil Young
Released August 1994
Peak chart position: 9

"My Heart"/"Prime of Life"/"Driveby"/"Sleeps
with Angels"/"Western Hero"/"Change Your
Mind"/"Blue Eden"/"Safeway Cart"/"Train of
Love"/"Trans Am"/"Piece of Crap"/"A Dream
That Can Last"

### Neil Young
*Mirror Ball*

Label: Reprise 45934
Recorded January–February 1995 at Bad
  Animals Studio, Seattle
Produced by Brendan O'Brien
Released June 1995
Peak chart position: 5

"Song X"/"Act of Love"/"I'm the
Ocean"/"Big Green Country"/"Truth Be
Known"/"Downtown"/"What Happened
Yesterday"/"Peace and Love"/"Throw Your
Hatred Down"/"Scenery"/"Fallen Angel"

### Neil Young
*Dead Man—Original Soundtrack Recording*

Vapor 46171
Recorded March 1995 at Mason St. Studios, San Francisco
Produced by Neil Young and John Hanlon
Released February 1996
Peak chart position: —

"Guitar Solo, No. 1"/"The Round Stones Beneath the Earth . . . "/"Guitar Solo, No. 2"/"Why Does Thou Hide Thyself, Clouds . . . "/"Organ Solo"/"Do You Know How to Use This Weapon?"/"Guitar Solo, No. 3"/"Nobody's Story"/"Guitar Solo, No. 4"/"Stupid White Men"/"Guitar Solo, No. 5"/"Time for You to Leave, William Blake . . . "/"Guitar Solo, No. 6"

### Crosby, Stills, Nash & Young
*Looking Forward*

Reprise 47436
Recorded November 1996–July 1999 at Ocean Studios, Burbank, CA; Redwood Digital, Woodside, CA; and Ga Ga's Room, Stray Gator Sound, and Conway Studio A, Los Angeles
Produced by Crosby, Stills, Nash & Young, Joe Vitale, Ben Keith, and J. Stanley Johnston
Released October 1999
Peak chart position: 26

"Faith in Me"/"Looking Forward"/"Stand and Be Counted"/"Heartland"/"Seen Enough"/"Slowpoke"/"Dream for Him"/"No Tears Left"/"Out of Control"/"Someday Soon"/"Queen of Them All"/"Sanibel"

### Neil Young with Crazy Horse
*Broken Arrow*

Reprise 46291
Recorded May 1990 and March–April 1996 at Plywood Digital, Woodside, CA, and March 1996 at Old Princeton Landing, Princeton-by-the-Sea, CA
Produced by Neil Young
Released July 1996
Peak chart position: 31

"Big Time"/"Loose Change"/"Slip Away"/"Changing Highways"/"Scattered (Let's Think about Livin')"/"This Town"/"Music Arcade"/"Baby What You Want Me to Do"/"Interstate" (LP only)

### Neil Young
*Silver & Gold*

Reprise 47305
Recorded August 1997–November 1998 at Redwood Digital, Woodside, CA, and May 1999 at Arlyn Studios, Austin, TX
Produced by Neil Young and Ben Keith
Released April 2000
Peak chart position: 22

"Good to See You"/"Silver & Gold"/"Daddy Went Walkin'"/"Buffalo Springfield Again"/"The Great Divide"/"Horseshoe Man"/"Red Sun"/"Distant Camera"/"Razor Love"/"Without Rings"

### Neil Young & Crazy Horse
*Year of the Horse*

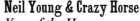

Reprise 46652
Recorded on 1996 tour
Produced by "Horse"
Released June 1997
Peak chart position: 57

"When You Dance, I Can Really Love"/"Barstool Blues"/"When Your Lonely Heart Breaks"/"Mr. Soul"/"Big Time"/"Pocahontas"/"Human Highway"/"Slip Away"/"Scattered"/"Danger Bird"/"Prisoners"/"Sedan Delivery"

### Neil Young Friends & Relatives
*Road Rock V1*

Reprise 48036
Recorded on 2000 North American tour
Produced by Neil Young and Ben Keith
Released November 2000
Peak chart position: 169

"Cowgirl in the Sand"/"Walk On"/"Fool for Your Love"/"Peace of Mind"/"Words"/"Motorcycle Mama"/"Tonight's the Night"/"All Along the Watchtower"

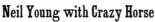

## Buffalo Springfield
### Box Set

Atco/Elektra/Rhino 74324
Recorded 1966–1968
Produced by Buffalo Springfield
Released July 2001
Peak chart position: 194

"There Goes My Babe" (demo)/"Come On" (demo)/"Hello, I've Returned" (demo)/"Out of My Mind" (demo)/"Flying on the Ground Is Wrong" (demo)/"I'm Your Kind of Guy" (demo)/"Baby Don't Scold Me" (demo)/"Neighbor Don't You Worry" (demo)/"We'll See" (demo)/"Sad Memory" (demo)/"Can't Keep Me Down" (demo)/"Nowadays Clancy Can't Even Sing"/"Go and Say Goodbye"/"Sit Down I Think I Love You"/"Leave"/"Hot Dusty Roads"/"Everybody's Wrong"/"Burned"/"Do I Have to Come Right Out and Say It"/"Out of My Mind"/"Pay the Price"/"Down, Down, Down" (demo)/"Flying on the Ground Is Wrong"/"Neighbor Don't You Worry" (remix)/"Down, Down, Down" (remix)/"Kahuna Sunset"/"Buffalo Stomp" (Raga)/"Baby Don't Scold Me"/"For What It's Worth"/"Mr. Soul"/"We'll See"/"My Kind of Love"/"Pretty Girl Why"/"Words I Must Say" (demo)/"Nobody's Fool" (demo)/"So You've Got a Lover" (demo)/"My Angel" (demo)/"No Sun Today"/"Everydays"/"Down to the Wire"/"Bluebird"/"Expecting to Fly"/"Hung Upside Down" (demo)/"A Child's Claim to Fame"/"Rock & Roll Woman"/"Hung Upside Down"/"Good Time Boy"/"One More Sign" (demo)/"The Rent Is Always Due" (demo)/"Round & Round" (demo)/"Old Laughing Lady" (demo)/"Broken Arrow"/"Sad Memory"/"On the Way Home" (previously unreleased mix)/"Whatever Happened to Saturday Night?" (remix)/"Special Care"/"Falcon Lake (Ash on the Floor)" (remix)/"What a Day"/"I Am a Child"/"Questions"/"Merry-Go-Round"/"Uno Mundo"/"Kind Woman"/"It's So Hard to Wait"/"Four Days Gone" (demo)/"For What It's Worth"/"Go and Say Goodbye"/"Sit Down I Think I Love You"/"Nowadays Clancy Can't Even Sing"/"Hot Dusty Roads"/"Everybody's Wrong"/"Flying on the Ground Is Wrong"/"Burned"/"Do I Have to Come Right Out and Say It"/"Leave"/"Out of My Mind"/"Pay the Price"/"Baby Don't Scold Me"/"Mr. Soul"/"A Child's Claim to Fame"/"Everydays"/"Expecting to Fly"/"Bluebird"/"Hung Upside Down"/"Sad Memory"/"Good Time Boy"/"Rock & Roll Woman"/"Broken Arrow"

## Neil Young
### Are You Passionate?

Reprise 48111
Recorded February 2001 at Toast, San Francisco and May–December 2001 at the Site, Marin County, CA
Produced by Neil Young and Booker T. Jones with Duck Dunn and Poncho Sampedro
Released April 2002
Peak chart position: 10

"You're My Girl"/"Mr. Disappointment"/"Differently"/"Quit (Don't Say You Love Me)"/"Let's Roll"/"Are You Passionate?"/"When I Hold You in My Arms"/"She's a Healer"/"Be with You"/"Two Old Friends"/"Goin' Home"

## Neil Young & Crazy Horse
### Greendale

Reprise 48533
Recorded July–September 2002 at Plywood Analog, Woodside, CA
Produced by Neil Young and L. A. Johnson
Released August 2003
Peak chart position: 22

"Falling from Above"/"Double E"/"Devil's Sidewalk"/"Leave the Driving"/"Carmichael"/"Bandit"/"Grandpa's Interview"/"Bringin' Down Dinner"/"Sun Green"/"Be the Rain"

## Neil Young
### Greatest Hits

Reprise 48924
Recorded 1969–1991
Produced by Neil Young et al.
Released November 2004
Peak chart position: 27

"Down by the River"/"Cowgirl in the Sand"/"Cinnamon Girl"/"Helpless"/"After the Gold Rush"/"Only Love Can Break Your Heart"/"Southern Man"/"Ohio"/"The Needle and the Damage Done"/"Old Man"/"Heart of Gold"/"Like a Hurricane"/"Comes a Time"/"Hey Hey, My My (Into the Black)"/"Rockin' in the Free World"/"Harvest Moon"

### Neil Young
*Prairie Wind*

Reprise 49494
Recorded March 2005 at Master-Link, Nashville
Produced by Ben Keith and Neil Young
Released September 2005
Peak chart position: 11

"The Painter"/"No Wonder"/"Fallin' off the Face of the Earth"/"Far from Home"/"It's a Dream"/"Prairie Wind"/"Here for You"/"This Old Guitar"/"He Was the King"/"When God Made Me"

### Neil Young
*Living with War*

Reprise 44335
Recorded March–April 2006 at Redwood Digital Studios, Redwood City, CA, and Capitol Recording Studios, Hollywood
Produced by "The Volume Dealers" (Neil Young & Niko Bolas) with L. A. Johnson
Released May 2006
Peak chart position: 15

"After the Garden"/"Living with War"/"The Restless Consumer"/"Shock and Awe"/"Families"/"Flags of Freedom"/"Let's Impeach the President"/"Lookin' for a Leader"/"Roger and Out"/"America the Beautiful"

### Neil Young & Crazy Horse
*Live at the Fillmore East March 6 & 7, 1970*

Reprise 44429
Recorded March 6 and 7, 1970, at the Fillmore East, New York
Produced by Paul Rothchild
Released November 2006
Peak chart position: 55

"Everybody Knows This Is Nowhere"/"Winterlong"/"Down by the River"/"Wonderin'"/"Come On Baby Let's Go Downtown"/"Cowgirl in the Sand"

### Neil Young
*Living with War: In the Beginning*

Reprise 43265
Recorded 2006 at Redwood Digital Studios
Produced by "The Volume Dealers" (Neil Young & Niko Bolas) with L. A. Johnson
Released as CD/DVD December 2006
Peak chart position: —

"After the Garden"/"Living with War"/"The Restless Consumer"/"Shock and Awe"/"Families"/"Flags of Freedom"/"Let's Impeach the President"/"Lookin' for a Leader"/"Roger and Out"

### Neil Young
*Live at Massey Hall 1971*

Reprise 43328
Recorded January 19, 1971, at Massey Hall, Toronto
Produced by David Briggs and Neil Young
Released March 2007
Peak chart position: 6

"On the Way Home"/"Tell Me Why"/"Old Man"/"Journey through the Past"/"Helpless"/"Love in Mind"/"A Man Needs a Maid"/"Heart of Gold (Suite)"/"Cowgirl in the Sand"/"Don't Let It Bring You Down"/"There's a World"/"Bad Fog of Loneliness"/"The Needle and the Damage Done"/"Ohio"/"See the Sky About to Rain"/"Down by the River"/"Dance Dance Dance"/"I Am a Child"

### Neil Young
*Chrome Dreams II*

Reprise 311932
Recorded late 1980s, 2007
Produced by "The Volume Dealers" (Neil Young & Niko Bolas)
Released October 2007
Peak chart position: 11

"Beautiful Bluebird"/"Boxcar"/"Ordinary People"/"Shining Light"/"The Believer"/"Spirit Road"/"Dirty Old Man"/"Ever After"/"No Hidden Path"/"The Way"

## Crosby, Stills, Nash & Young
### *Déjà Vu Live*

Reprise 512606

Recorded on the 2006 Freedom of Speech Tour

Produced by Neil Young and L. A. Johnson

Released July 2008

Peak chart position: 153

"What Are Their Names?"/"Living With War—Theme"/"After the Garden"/"Military Madness"/"Let's Impeach the President"/"Déjà Vu"/"Shock and Awe"/"Families"/"Wooden Ships"/"Looking for a Leader"/"For What It's Worth"/"Living with War"/"Roger and Out"/"Find the Cost of Freedom"/"Teach Your Children"/"Living with War—Theme"

## Neil Young
### *Sugar Mountain:*
### *Live at Canterbury House, 1968*

Reprise 516758

Recorded November 9-10, 1968, at Canterbury House, Ann Arbor, MI

Produced by Neil Young

Released December 2008

Peak chart position: 40

"(Emcee Intro)"/"On the Way Home"/"Songwriting Rap"/"Mr. Soul"/"Recording Rap"/"Expecting to Fly"/"The Last Trip to Tulsa"/"Bookstore Rap"/"The Loner"/"'I Used to . . .' Rap"/"Birds"/"Winterlong (Excerpt)" & "Out of My Mind—Intro"/"Out of My Mind"/"If I Could Have Her Tonight"/"Classical Gas Rap"/"Sugar Mountain—Intro"/"Sugar Mountain"/"I've Been Waiting for You"/"Songs Rap"/"Nowadays Clancy Can't Even Sing"/"Tuning Rap" & "The Old Laughing Lady—Intro"/"The Old Laughing Lady"/"Broken Arrow"

## Neil Young
### *Fork in the Road*

Reprise 518040

Recorded 2008-2009 at Legacy Studios, New York, and RAK Studios, London

Produced by "The Volume Dealers" (Neil Young & Niko Bolas)

Released April 2009

Peak chart position: 19

"When Worlds Collide"/"Fuel Line"/"Just Singing a Song"/"Johnny Magic"/"Cough Up the Bucks"/"Get Behind the Wheel"/"Off the Road"/"Hit the Road"/"Light a Candle"/"Fork in the Road"

## Neil Young
### *Archives Vol. 1*

Reprise 175292

Recorded July 1963–May 1972

Produced by Neil Young et al.

Released June 2009

Peak chart position: 102

"Aurora" (The Squires)/"The Sultan" (The Squires)/"I Wonder" (The Squires)/"Mustang" (The Squires)/"I'll Love You Forever" (The Squires)/"(I'm a Man and) I Can't Cry" (The Squires)/"Hello Lonely Woman" (Neil Young & Comrie Smith)/"Casting Me Away from You" (Neil Young & Comrie Smith)/"There Goes My Babe" (Neil Young & Comrie Smith)/"Sugar Mountain" (Neil Young)/"Nowadays Clancy Can't Even Sing" (Neil Young)/"Runaround Babe" (Neil Young)/"The Ballad of Peggy Grover" (Neil Young)/"The Rent Is Always Due" (Neil Young)/"Extra, Extra" (Neil Young)/"Flying on the Ground Is Wrong" (Neil Young)/"Burned" (Buffalo Springfield)/"Out of My Mind" (Buffalo Springfield)/"Down, Down, Down" (Neil Young)/"Kahuna Sunset" (Buffalo Springfield)/"Mr. Soul" (Buffalo Springfield)/"Sell Out" (Buffalo Springfield)/"Down to the Wire" (Neil Young)/"Expecting to Fly" (Buffalo Springfield)/"Slowly Burning" (Neil Young)/"One More Sign" (Neil Young)/"Broken Arrow" (Buffalo Springfield)/"I Am a Child" (Buffalo Springfield)/"Everybody Knows This Is Nowhere" (Neil Young)/"The Loner" (Neil Young)/"Birds" (Neil Young)/"What Did You Do to My Life?" (Neil Young)/"The Last Trip to Tulsa" (Neil Young)/"Here We Are in the Years" (Neil Young)/"I've Been Waiting for You" (Neil Young)/"The Old Laughing Lady" (Neil Young)/"I've Loved Her So Long" (Neil Young)/"Sugar Mountain" (Neil Young)/"Nowadays Clancy Can't Even Sing" (Neil Young)/"Down by the River" (Neil Young with Crazy Horse)/"Cowgirl in the

SAND" (NEIL YOUNG WITH CRAZY HORSE)/"EVERYBODY KNOWS THIS IS NOWHERE" (NEIL YOUNG WITH CRAZY HORSE)/"SUGAR MOUNTAIN" (NEIL YOUNG)/"THE OLD LAUGHING LADY" (NEIL YOUNG)/"FLYING ON THE GROUND IS WRONG" (NEIL YOUNG)/"ON THE WAY HOME" (NEIL YOUNG)/"I'VE LOVED HER SO LONG" (NEIL YOUNG)/"I AM A CHILD" (NEIL YOUNG)/"1956 BUBBLEGUM DISASTER" (NEIL YOUNG)/"THE LAST TRIP TO TULSA" (NEIL YOUNG)/"BROKEN ARROW" (NEIL YOUNG)/"WHISKEY BOOT HILL" (NEIL YOUNG)/"EXPECTING TO FLY" (NEIL YOUNG)/"CINNAMON GIRL" (NEIL YOUNG WITH CRAZY HORSE)/"RUNNING DRY" (REQUIEM FOR THE ROCKETS)" (NEIL YOUNG WITH CRAZY HORSE)/"ROUND & ROUND (IT WON'T BE LONG)" (NEIL YOUNG WITH CRAZY HORSE)/"OH LONESOME ME" (NEIL YOUNG WITH CRAZY HORSE)/"BIRDS" (NEIL YOUNG WITH CRAZY HORSE)/"EVERYBODY'S ALONE" (NEIL YOUNG WITH CRAZY HORSE)/"I BELIEVE IN YOU" (NEIL YOUNG WITH CRAZY HORSE)/"SEA OF MADNESS" (CROSBY, STILLS, NASH & YOUNG)/"DANCE DANCE DANCE" (NEIL YOUNG WITH CRAZY HORSE)/"COUNTRY GIRL" (CROSBY, STILLS, NASH & YOUNG)/"HELPLESS" (CROSBY, STILLS, NASH & YOUNG)/"IT MIGHT HAVE BEEN" (NEIL YOUNG WITH CRAZY HORSE)/"EVERYBODY KNOWS THIS IS NOWHERE" (NEIL YOUNG & CRAZY HORSE)/"WINTERLONG" (NEIL YOUNG & CRAZY HORSE)/"DOWN BY THE RIVER" (NEIL YOUNG & CRAZY HORSE)/"WONDERIN'" (NEIL YOUNG & CRAZY HORSE)/"COME ON BABY, LET'S GO DOWNTOWN" (NEIL YOUNG & CRAZY HORSE)/"COWGIRL IN THE SAND" (NEIL YOUNG & CRAZY HORSE)/"TELL ME WHY" (NEIL YOUNG)/"AFTER THE GOLD RUSH" (NEIL YOUNG)/"ONLY LOVE CAN BREAK YOUR HEART" (NEIL YOUNG)/"WONDERIN'" (NEIL YOUNG)/"DON'T LET IT BRING YOU DOWN" (NEIL YOUNG)/"CRIPPLE CREEK FERRY" (NEIL YOUNG)/"SOUTHERN MAN" (NEIL YOUNG)/"TILL THE MORNING COMES" (NEIL YOUNG)/"WHEN YOU DANCE I CAN REALLY LOVE" (NEIL YOUNG WITH CRAZY HORSE)/"OHIO" (CROSBY, STILLS, NASH & YOUNG)/"ONLY LOVE CAN BREAK YOUR HEART" (CROSBY, STILLS, NASH & YOUNG)/"TELL ME WHY" (CROSBY, STILLS, NASH & YOUNG)/"MUSIC IS LOVE" (DAVID CROSBY, GRAHAM NASH & NEIL YOUNG)/"SEE THE SKY ABOUT TO RAIN" (NEIL YOUNG)/"ON THE WAY HOME" (NEIL YOUNG)/"TELL ME WHY (NEIL YOUNG)/"OLD MAN" (NEIL YOUNG)/"JOURNEY THROUGH THE PAST" (NEIL YOUNG)/"HELPLESS (NEIL YOUNG)/"LOVE IN MIND" (NEIL YOUNG)/"A MAN NEEDS A MAID" (NEIL YOUNG)/"HEART OF GOLD (SUITE)" (NEIL YOUNG)/"COWGIRL IN THE SAND" (NEIL YOUNG)/"DON'T LET IT BRING YOU DOWN" (NEIL YOUNG)/"THERE'S A WORLD" (NEIL YOUNG)/"BAD FOG OF LONELINESS" (NEIL YOUNG)/"THE NEEDLE AND THE DAMAGE DONE" (NEIL YOUNG)/"OHIO" (NEIL YOUNG)/"SEE THE SKY ABOUT TO RAIN" (NEIL YOUNG)/"DOWN BY THE RIVER" (NEIL YOUNG)/"DANCE DANCE DANCE" (NEIL YOUNG)/"I AM A CHILD (NEIL YOUNG)/"HEART OF GOLD" (NEIL YOUNG)/"THE NEEDLE AND THE DAMAGE DONE" (NEIL YOUNG)/"BAD FOG OF LONELINESS" (NEIL YOUNG WITH THE STRAY GATORS)/"OLD MAN" (NEIL YOUNG WITH THE STRAY GATORS)/"HEART OF GOLD" (NEIL YOUNG WITH THE STRAY GATORS)/"DANCE DANCE DANCE" (NEIL YOUNG)/"A MAN NEEDS A MAID" (NEIL YOUNG WITH THE LONDON SYMPHONY ORCHESTRA)/"HARVEST" (NEIL YOUNG WITH THE STRAY GATORS)/"JOURNEY THROUGH THE PAST" (NEIL YOUNG WITH THE STRAY GATORS)/"ARE YOU READY FOR THE COUNTRY?" (NEIL YOUNG WITH THE STRAY GATORS)/"ALABAMA" (NEIL YOUNG WITH THE STRAY GATORS)/"WORDS" (BETWEEN THE LINES OF AGE)" (NEIL YOUNG WITH THE STRAY GATORS)/"SOLDIER" (NEIL YOUNG)/"WAR SONG" (NEIL YOUNG & GRAHAM NASH WITH THE STRAY GATORS)

ALSO RELEASED ON DVD AND BLU-RAY.

## Neil Young
### *Dreamin' Man Live '92*

Reprise 511277-2
Recorded 1992
Produced by Neil Young and John Hanlon
Released December 2009

"DREAMIN' MAN"/"SUCH A WOMAN"/"OLD KING RAP"/"OLD KING"/"ONE OF THESE DAYS"/"HARVEST MOON"/"YOU AND ME"/"FROM HANK TO HENDRIX"/"UNKNOWN LEGEND"/"NATURAL BEAUTY"/"WAR OF MAN"

# Discography II: Singles

THE SQUIRES
V Records 109 (Canada)
Released 1963

"THE SULTAN"/"AURORA"

BUFFALO SPRINGFIELD
Atco 6428
Released 1966

"NOWADAYS CLANCY CAN'T EVEN SING"/
"GO AND SAY GOODBYE"

BUFFALO SPRINGFIELD
Atco 6452
Released 1966

"BURNED"/"EVERYBODY'S WRONG"

BUFFALO SPRINGFIELD
Atco 6452
Released 1966

"FOR WHAT IT'S WORTH"/
"DO I HAVE TO COME RIGHT OUT AND SAY IT"

BUFFALO SPRINGFIELD
Atco 6499
Released 1967

"BLUEBIRD"/"MR. SOUL"

BUFFALO SPRINGFIELD
Atco 6519
Released 1967

"ROCK 'N' ROLL WOMAN"/
"A CHILD'S CLAIM TO FAME"

BUFFALO SPRINGFIELD
Atco 6545
Released 1968

"EXPECTING TO FLY"/"EVERYDAYS"

BUFFALO SPRINGFIELD
Atco 6572
Released 1968

"UNO MUNDO"/"MERRY-GO-ROUND"

BUFFALO SPRINGFIELD
Atco 6615
Released 1968

"FOUR DAYS"/"ON THE WAY HOME"

NEIL YOUNG
Reprise 0785
Released 1968

"THE LONER"/"SUGAR MOUNTAIN"

NEIL YOUNG
Reprise 0819
Released 1969

"EVERYBODY KNOWS THIS IS NOWHERE"/
"THE EMPEROR OF WYOMING"

NEIL YOUNG
Reprise 0836
Released 1969

"DOWN BY THE RIVER"/"THE LOSING END"

NEIL YOUNG
Reprise 0861
Released 1969

"OH LONESOME ME"/"SUGAR MOUNTAIN"

CROSBY, STILLS, NASH & YOUNG
Atlantic 2735
Released 1970

"WOODSTOCK"/"HELPLESS"

CROSBY, STILLS, NASH & YOUNG
Atlantic 2735
Released 1970

"TEACH YOUR CHILDREN"/
"COUNTRY GIRL"

NEIL YOUNG
Reprise 0898
Released 1970

"OH LONESOME ME"/
"I'VE BEEN WAITING FOR YOU"

CROSBY, STILLS, NASH & YOUNG
Atlantic 2740
Released 1970

"OHIO"/"FIND THE COST OF FREEDOM"

NEIL YOUNG
Reprise 0911
Released 1970

"CINNAMON GIRL"/"SUGAR MOUNTAIN"

CROSBY, STILLS, NASH & YOUNG
Atlantic 2760
Released 1970

"OUR HOUSE"/"DÉJÀ VU"

NEIL YOUNG
Reprise 0958
Released 1970

"ONLY LOVE CAN BREAK YOUR HEART"/"BIRDS"

NEIL YOUNG
Reprise 0992
Released 1971

"WHEN YOU DANCE I CAN REALLY LOVE"/
"SUGAR MOUNTAIN"

NEIL YOUNG
Reprise 1065
Released 1972

"HEART OF GOLD"/"SUGAR MOUNTAIN"

NEIL YOUNG
Reprise 1084
Released 1972

"OLD MAN"/"THE NEEDLE AND THE DAMAGE DONE"

NEIL YOUNG & GRAHAM NASH
Reprise 1099
Released 1972

"WAR SONG"/
"THE NEEDLE AND THE DAMAGE DONE"

| | |
|---|---|
| NEIL YOUNG<br>Reprise 1184<br>Released 1973 | "TIME FADES AWAY"/"LAST TRIP TO TULSA" |
| NEIL YOUNG<br>Reprise 1209<br>Released 1974 | "WALK ON"/"FOR THE TURNSTILES" |
| NEIL YOUNG<br>Reprise 1344<br>Released 1975 | "LOOKING FOR A LOVE"/"SUGAR MOUNTAIN" |
| NEIL YOUNG<br>Reprise 1350<br>Released 1976 | "DRIVE BACK"/"STUPID GIRL" |
| THE STILLS-YOUNG BAND<br>Reprise 1365<br>Released 1976 | "LONG MAY YOU RUN"/"12-8 BLUES" |
| THE STILLS-YOUNG BAND<br>Reprise 1378<br>Released 1976 | "MIDNIGHT ON THE BAY"/"BLACK CORAL" |
| NEIL YOUNG<br>Reprise 1390<br>Released 1978 | "HEY BABE"/"HOMEGROWN" |
| NEIL YOUNG<br>Reprise 1391<br>Released 1977 | "LIKE A HURRICANE"/"HOLD BACK THE TEARS" |
| NEIL YOUNG<br>Reprise 1395<br>Released 1978 | "COMES A TIME"/"MOTORCYCLE MAMA" |
| NEIL YOUNG<br>Reprise 1396<br>Released 1978 | "FOUR STRONG WINDS"/"HUMAN HIGHWAY" |
| NEIL YOUNG<br>Reprise 49031<br>Released 1979 | "HEY HEY, MY MY (INTO THE BLACK)"/<br>"MY MY, HEY HEY (OUT OF THE BLUE)" |
| NEIL YOUNG<br>Reprise 49189<br>Released 1979 | "CINNAMON GIRL" (LIVE)/"THE LONER" (LIVE) |
| NEIL YOUNG<br>Reprise 49555<br>Released 1980 | "HAWKS AND DOVES"/"UNION MAN" |
| NEIL YOUNG<br>Reprise 49641<br>Released 1981 | "STAYIN' POWER"/"CAPTAIN KENNEDY" |
| NEIL YOUNG<br>Reprise 49870<br>Released 1981 | "SOUTHERN PACIFIC"/"MOTOR CITY" |
| NEIL YOUNG<br>Reprise 50014<br>Released 1982 | "OPERA STAR"/"SURFER JOE AND MOE THE SLEAZE" |
| NEIL YOUNG<br>Geffen 29887<br>Released 1982 | "LITTLE THING CALLED LOVE"/"WE R IN CONTROL" |
| NEIL YOUNG<br>Geffen 20105<br>Released 1983 | "SAMPLE AND HOLD" (REMIX)/"MR. SOUL"/<br>"SAMPLE AND HOLD" (SINGLE VERSION) |
| NEIL YOUNG<br>Geffen 29707<br>Released 1983 | "MR. SOUL" (PART 1)/"MR. SOUL" (PART 2) |
| NEIL YOUNG<br>Geffen 29574<br>Released 1983 | "WONDERIN'"/"PAYOLA BLUES" |
| NEIL YOUNG<br>Geffen 29433<br>Released 1983 | "CRY CRY CRY"/"PAYOLA BLUES" |
| NEIL YOUNG<br>Geffen 28883<br>Released 1985 | "GET BACK TO THE COUNTRY"/"MISFITS" |
| NEIL YOUNG<br>Geffen 28623<br>Released 1986 | "WEIGHT OF THE WORLD"/"PRESSURE" |
| NEIL YOUNG<br>Geffen 28196<br>Released 1987 | "MIDEAST VACATION"/"LONG WALK HOME" |
| NEIL YOUNG<br>Reprise 27908<br>Released 1988 | "TEN MEN WORKIN'"/"I'M GOIN'" |
| NEIL YOUNG<br>Reprise 27848<br>Released 1988 | "THIS NOTE'S FOR YOU" (LIVE)/"THIS NOTE'S FOR YOU" |
| CROSBY, STILLS, NASH & YOUNG<br>Atlantic 88966<br>Released 1989 | "THIS OLD HOUSE"/<br>"GOT IT MADE" |
| NEIL YOUNG<br>Reprise 22776<br>Released 1989 | "ROCKIN' IN THE FREE WORLD" (LIVE)/<br>"ROCKIN' IN THE FREE WORLD" |

NEIL YOUNG
Reprise 7599
Released 1990

"MANSION ON THE HILL" (EDIT)/
"MANSION ON THE HILL"/"DON'T SPOOK THE HORSE"

NEIL YOUNG
Reprise 7599-21759
Released 1991

"OVER AND OVER"/"DON'T SPOOK THE HORSE"

NEIL YOUNG
Reprise
Released 1990

"CRIME IN THE CITY"

NEIL YOUNG
Reprise 9-18685-2
Released 1992

"HARVEST MOON"/"OLD KING"

NEIL YOUNG
Reprise
Released 1994

"CHANGE YOUR MIND"

NEIL YOUNG
Reprise
Released 1994

"LONG MAY YOU RUN" (LIVE)

NEIL YOUNG
Reprise PRO-CD-7646
Released 1995

"DOWNTOWN"/"BIG GREEN COUNTRY"

NEIL YOUNG
Reprise
Released 1996

"PEACE AND LOVE"

NEIL YOUNG
Reprise 43731
Released 1996

"BIG TIME"/"BIG TIME" (EDIT)/"INTERSTATE"

NEIL YOUNG
Reprise
Released 2002

"LET'S ROLL"

NEIL YOUNG
Reprise 371196
Released 2007

"ORDINARY PEOPLE"

# Discography III: As Guest Artist

ELYSE
Tetragrammatron
Released 1968; reissued on Orange Twin (OTR001), 2001
Neil Young: guitar and vocals on "Houses"

*Elyse*

THE MONKEES
Colgems 5008
Released 1968
Neil Young: guitar on "As We Go Along"

*Head*

VARIOUS ARTISTS
Cotillion CT3-500
Released 1970
Crosby, Stills, Nash & Young: "Sea of Madness" and "Wooden Ships"

*Woodstock: Music from the Original Soundtrack and More*

DAVID CROSBY
Atlantic 7203
Released 1971
Neil Young: vocals

*If I Could Only Remember My Name*

BUFFY SAINTE-MARIE
Vanguard 79311
Released 1971
Neil Young: guitar, harmonica

*She Used to Wanna Be a Ballerina*

GRAHAM NASH
Atlantic 7204
Released 1971
Neil Young (as Joe Yankee): piano on "Man in the Mirror"

*Songs for Beginners*

GRIN                                                                    *Grin*
   Epic 64272
   Released 1971
   Neil Young & Crazy Horse: "See What Love Can Do," "Outlaw," and
      "Pioneer Mary"

VARIOUS ARTISTS                                              *Woodstock Two*
   *Cotillion SD 2-400*
   Released 1971
   Crosby, Stills, Nash & Young: "Guinnevere," "4+20," and "Marrakesh
      Express"

JONI MITCHELL                                                         *Hejira*
   Elektra 1087
   Released 1976
   Neil Young: harmonica on "Furry Sings the Blues"

CRAZY HORSE                                                       *Crazy Moon*
   RCA 3054
   Released 1978
   Neil Young: guitar, associate producer

THE BAND                                                       *The Last Waltz*
   Warner Bros. 3146
   Released 1978
   Neil Young: "Helpless"

EMMYLOU HARRIS                                           *Light of the Stable*
   Warner Bros. 3484
   Released 1979
   Neil Young: vocals on "Light of the Stable"

VARIOUS ARTISTS                                      *Sounds of Asbury Park*
   Visa 7014
   Released 1980
   Neil Young: "High School Graduation"

VARIOUS ARTISTS                                     *Where the Buffalo Roam:*
   Backstreet/MCA 5126                                *Original Soundtrack*
   Released 1980
   Neil Young: "Buffalo Stomp," "Ode to Wild Bill #1," "Ode to Wild Bill
      #2," "Home, Home on the Range," "Ode to Wild Bill #3," "Ode to
      Wild Bill #4," and "Buffalo Stomp Refrain"

WILLIE NELSON                                                     *Half Nelson*
   Sony 39990
   Released 1985
   Neil Young: vocals on "Are There Any More Real Cowboys?"

STEALIN' HORSES                                              *Stealin' Horses*
   *Arista 8520*
   Released 1985
   Neil Young: harmonica on "Harriet Tubman"

VARIOUS ARTISTS                            *USA for Africa: We Are the World*
   Polygram 824822
   Released 1985
   Northern Lights (including Neil Young): "Tears Are Not Enough"

WARREN ZEVON                                            *Sentimental Hygiene*
   Virgin 86012
   Released 1987
   Neil Young: guitar on "Sentimental Hygiene"

TRACY CHAPMAN                                                    *Crossroads*
   Elektra/WEA 60888
   Released 1989
   Neil Young: guitar, piano on "All That You Have Is Your Soul"

WARREN ZEVON                                              *Transverse City*
   Atlantic 91068
   Released 1989
   Neil Young: vocals on "Splendid Isolation," guitar on "Gridlock"

CROSBY, STILLS & NASH                             *Crosby, Stills & Nash*
   Atlantic 82319-2
   Released 1991
   Crosby, Stills, Nash & Young: "Almost Cut My Hair," "Teach Your
      Children," "Horses through a Rainstorm," "Déjà Vu," "Helpless," "4 +
      20," "Carry On," "Woodstock," "Ohio," "Our House," "The Lee Shore,"
      "Music Is Love," "See the Changes," "Homeward through the Haze,"
      "Taken at All," "Soldiers of Peace," and "Find the Cost of Freedom"

EMMYLOU HARRIS                                                        *Duets*
   Reprise 25791
   Released 1990
   Neil Young: vocals on "Star of Bethlehem"

ROBBIE ROBERTSON                                                 *Storyville*
   Geffen 24303
   Released 1991
   Neil Young: vocals on "Soap Box Preacher"

NILS LOFGREN                                                    *Crooked Line*
   Rykodisc 238
   Released 1992
   Neil Young: vocals, harmonica on "You"; vocals on "Someday"; guitar
      on "Drunken Driver"

RUSTY KERSHAW                                                 *Now and Then*
   Domino 8002
   Released 1992
   Neil Young: harmonica, vocals

RANDY BACHMAN                                                    *Any Road*
   BMG
   Released 1992
   Neil Young: guitar, vocals on "Prairie Town"

BOB DYLAN — *The 30th Anniversary Concert Celebration*
Columbia 53230
Released 1993
Neil Young: "Just Like Tom Thumb's Blues" and "All Along the Watchtower"

VARIOUS ARTISTS — *Philadelphia*
Epic Soundtrax 57624 *(Music from the Motion Picture)*
Released 1993
Neil Young: "Philadelphia"

ROB WASSERMAN — *Trios*
GRP 4021
Released 1994
Neil Young: guitar, vocals, handclaps on "Easy Answers"

BEN KEITH & FRIENDS — *Seven Gates: A Christmas Album*
Warner Bros 45773
Released 1994
Neil Young: organ, guitar, vocals

EMMYLOU HARRIS — *Wrecking Ball*
Asylum 61854
Released 1995
Neil Young: harmonica, vocals

PEARL JAM — *Merkinball*
Sony 78199
Released 1995
Neil Young: guitar, vocals, pump organ

RANDY BACHMAN — *Merge*
True North 117
Released 1996
Neil Young: guitar, vocals on "Made in Canada"

VARIOUS ARTISTS — *Twang! A Tribute to Hank Marvin & the Shadows*
Capitol 33928
Released 1996
Neil Young and Randy Bachman: "Spring Is Nearly Here"

VARIOUS ARTISTS — *The Bridge School Concerts, Vol. 1*
Reprise 46824
Released 1997
Neil Young: "I Am a Child"

VARIOUS ARTISTS — *No Boundaries: A Benefit for the Kosovar Refugees*
Sony 63653
Released 1999
Neil Young: "War of Man"

LINDA RONSTADT & EMMYLOU HARRIS — *Western Wall: The Tucson Sessions*
Asylum 62408
Released 1999
Neil Young: vocals

VARIOUS ARTISTS — *Saturday Night Live: 25 Years, Vol. 2*
DreamWorks 50206
Released 1999
Neil Young: "No More"

VARIOUS ARTISTS — *Farm Aid: Keep America Growing, Vol. 1*
Redline 75003
Released 2000
Neil Young: "Homegrown" and "Mother Earth (Natural Anthem)"

JOANNE SHENANDOAH — *Eagle Cries*
Red Feather 7005
Released 2001
Neil Young: guitar

VARIOUS ARTISTS — *America: A Tribute to Heroes*
Interscope 93188
Released 2001
Neil Young: "Imagine"

KITTENS FOR CHRISTIAN — *Privilege of Your Company*
Serjical Strike/Red Ink 71128
Released 2003
Neil Young: guitar

BOBBY CHARLES — *Last Train to Memphis*
Proper Pairs 10
Released 2004
Neil Young: guitar, vocals

STEPHEN STILLS — *Man Alive!*
Talking Elephant 077
Released 2005
Neil Young: guitar on "Round the Bend" and "Different Man"

RICHIE FURAY — *The Heartbeat of Love*
Kerygma Records
Released 2006
Neil Young: guitar, vocals on "Kind Woman"

JERRY LEE LEWIS — *Last Man Standing*
Artists First 20001
Released 2006
Neil Young: vocals on "You Don't Have to Go"

DAVID CROSBY — *Voyage*
Atlantic/Rhino 77628
Released 2006
Crosby, Stills, Nash & Young: "Déjà Vu," "Almost Cut My Hair," "Compass," "Homeward through the Haze," "Climber," and "Dream for Him"; Neil Young on "Music Is Love" and "Cowboy Movie"

VARIOUS ARTISTS — *The Complete Motown Singles, Vol. 6*
Motown/Hip-O Select 078720
Released 2006
The Mynah Birds (Neil Young, Bruce Palmer, Rick James): "It's My Time" and "Go On and Cry"

VARIOUS ARTISTS                          *The Bridge School Collection Vol. 1*
iTunes
Released 2006
Crosby, Stills, Nash & Young: "This Old House"; Neil Young: "Comes
  a Time"/"Sugar Mountain"; Neil Young & Dave Matthews: "Cortez
  the Killer"

VARIOUS ARTISTS                          *The Bridge School Collection Vol. 2*
iTunes
Released 2006
Crosby, Stills, Nash & Young: "Change Partners," "American Dream,"
  "Our House," "Déjà Vu"; Neil Young: "This Note's for You," "Crime
  in the City"; Neil Young & Crazy Horse: "Days That Used to Be"

VARIOUS ARTISTS              *Goin' Home: A Tribute to Fats Domino*
Vanguard 79840
Released 2007
Neil Young: "Walking to New Orleans"

PEGI YOUNG                                      *Pegi Young*
Warner Bros. 16230
Released 2007
Neil Young: guitar, electric sitar, harmonica, vocals

GRAHAM NASH                                     *Reflections*
Rhino 446076
Released 2009
Crosby, Stills, Nash & Young: "Our House," "Teach Your Children,"
  "Taken At All," "Soldiers of Peace," and "Heartland"

BOOKER T.                                       *Potato Hole*
Anti 86948
Released 2009
Neil Young: guitar

CROSBY, STILLS & NASH                           *Demos*
Atlantic/Rhino 519624
Released 2009
Neil Young: "Music Is Love"

VARIOUS ARTISTS                          *Woodstock 40 Years On:*
Rhino 519761                             *Back to Yasgur's Farm*
Released 2009
Crosby, Stills, Nash & Young: "Sea of Madness" and "Wooden Ships"

# Discography IV: Tribute Albums

VARIOUS ARTISTS          *The Bridge: A Tribute to Neil Young*
Caroline
Released 1989

SOUL ASYLUM, "BARSTOOL BLUES"/VICTORIA WILLIAMS, "DON'T LET IT
BRING YOU DOWN"/THE FLAMING LIPS, "AFTER THE GOLD RUSH"/NIKKI
SUDDEN, "CAPTAIN KENNEDY"/LOOP, "CINNAMON GIRL"/NICK CAVE,
"HELPLESS"/PIXIES, "WINTERLONG"/SONIC YOUTH, "COMPUTER AGE"/
PSYCHIC TV, "ONLY LOVE CAN BREAK YOUR HEART"/DINOSAUR JR., "LOTTA
LOVE"/HENRY KAISER, "THE NEEDLE AND THE DAMAGE DONE"—"TONIGHT'S
THE NIGHT"/BONGWATER, "MR. SOUL"/B.A.L.L., "MY MY, HEY HEY (OUT
OF THE BLUE)"/HENRY KAISER, "WORDS (BETWEEN THE LINES OF AGE)"

VARIOUS ARTISTS          *Borrowed Tunes: A Tribute to Neil Young*
Sony Music
Released 1994

COLIN LINDEN, "INTRO"/HEMINGWAY CORNER, "TELL ME WHY"/JANN
ARDEN, "BIRDS"/CRASH VEGAS, "POCAHONTAS"/LAWRENCE GOWAN, "HEART
OF GOLD"/JIM WITTER AND CASSANDRA VASIK, "HUMAN HIGHWAY"/
JEFF HEALEY, "HARVEST"/THE BREITS, "NOWADAYS CLANCY CAN'T EVEN
SING"/LORI YATES, "HELPLESS"/THE WALTONS, "ONLY LOVE CAN BREAK
YOUR HEART"/AMANDA MARSHALL, "DON'T LET IT BRING YOU DOWN"/
PRESCOTT-BROWN, "COMES A TIME"/MALCOLM BURN, "PARDON MY
HEART"/ROSE CHRONICLES, "OLD MAN"/COWBOY JUNKIES, "TIRED EYES"/
RHEOSTATICS AND BOURBON TABERNACLE CHOIR, "EVERYBODY KNOWS THIS

Is Nowhere"/David Wilcox, "Transformer Man"/Stephen Fearing, "Thrasher"/Marc Jordan, "Borrowed Tune"/Skydiggers, "Mr. Soul"/Barney Bentall and the Legendary Hearts, "Like a Hurricane"/Our Lady Peace, "The Needle and the Damage Done"/Junkhouse, "F*!#in' Up"/Blue Rodeo, "I've Been Waiting for You"/Big Sugar, "When You Dance I Can Really Love"/Colin Linden, "Tonight's the Night"/Treble Charger, "Albuquerque"/54-40, "Cortez the Killer"/Chocolatey, "Burned"/Philosopher Kings, "Coupe de Ville"/Head, "Look Out for My Love"/Andy Curran, "Cinnamon Girl"/Wild T and the Spirit, "Down by the River"/Randy Bachman, "The Loner"/Mystery Machine, "Southern Man"/Art Bergmann and One Free Fall, "Prisoners of Rock 'n' Roll"

| Various Artists | *Pickin' on Neil Young* |
| CMH | |
| Released 1998 | |

"'Til the Morning Comes (Intro)"/"Needle and the Damage Done"/"Mr. Soul"/"Cowgirl in the Sand"/"Only Love Can Break Your Heart"/"Old Man (Take a Look at My Life)"/"After the Gold Rush (Interlude)"/"Cinnamon Girl"/"Southern Man"/"Ohio"/"Hey Hey, My My (Into the Black)"/"Everybody Knows This Is Nowhere"/"Comes a Time"/"'Til the Morning Comes (Reprise)"

| Various Artists | *This Note's for You Too!:* |
| Inbetweens Records | *A Tribute to Neil Young* |
| Released 1999 | |

Treble Spankers, "Aurora"/Ron & the Splinters, "Burned"/Matt Piucci, "Down to the Wire"/Sonya Hunter, "Expecting to Fly"/Mushroom, "The Emperor of Wyoming"/Tom Stevens, "Everybody Knows This Is Nowhere"/Bevis Frond, "I've Been Waiting for You"/Big in Iowa, "Cinnamon Girl"/Shane Faubert, "Running Dry"/Lee Ranaldo, "Winterlong"/Tom Rapp, "After the Gold Rush"/Hitchin' Post, "Tell Me Why"/Bobby Sutliff, "Don't Let It Bring You Down"/Coal Porters, "Ohio"/Continental Drifters, "When You Dance I Can Really Love"/Steven Roback, "The Needle and the Damage Done"/Russ Tolman & Richard McGrath, "Old Man"/Richard Lloyd, "Heart of Gold"/Steve Wynn, "Time Fades Away"/Map of Wyoming, "Don't Be Denied"/Chris Cacavas, "Tonight's the Night"/Walkabouts, "Albuquerque"/Eric Ambel, "Revolution Blues"/Pat Thomas & the Family Jewels, "Vampire Blues"/Ghosthouse, "Don't Cry No Tears"/Hallo Venray, "Cortez the Killer"/Rich Hopkins & the Luminarios, "Like a Hurricane"/Chris Burroughs, "Powderfinger"/Snares & Kites "Campaigner"/Harvest, "The Old Country Waltz"/Golden Watusis, "Hey Hey, My My"/Empty Set, "Too Lonely"/Van Christian, "This Note's for You"/Absolute Zeros, "Don't Cry"/Ad Vanderveen, "Days That Used to Be"/Lazy Sunday, "Old King"/Slobberbone, "Piece of Crap"

| Various Artists | *Everybody Knows This Is Norway:* |
| Switch Off Records | *A Norwegian Tribute to Neil Young* |
| Released 2001 | |

Behind Barns Bluegrass Boys, "Out on the Weekend"/Ring, "Mellow My Mind"/Kenneth, Kim, Fredrik & Elisabeth, "Here We Are in the Years"/My Rhyme, "Razor Love"/American Suitcase, "Through My Sails"/Oyster, "Needle and the Damage Done"/Home Groan, "Barstool Blues"/Electric Jam Soul Aquarium, "Prisoners of Rock 'n' Roll"/Salvation Circus, "Cinnamon Girl"/Funguson, "War of Man"/Reverend Lovejoy, "Look Out for My Love"/Magnetic Tapes, "Old Laughing Lady"/Wagle, "Little Wing"/Madrugada, "Thrasher"/Safe in Santiago, "Safeway Cart"/Thee Unmist, "A Man Needs a Maid"/Slowburn & the Soft Rebels, "Out on the Weekend"

| Various Artists | *Mirror Ball Songs* |
| Electric Sal | |
| Released 2001 | |

Aya Tanka, "Only Love Can Break Your Heart"/Freebo, "Dreamin' Man"/Noise on Trash, "Out on the Weekend"/Commonbill, "Campaigner"/General, "Harvest"/Ahh! Folly Jet, "I Am a Child"/Sakana, "Buffalo Springfield Again"/Indian Rope, "Helpless"/Labcry, "Like a Hurricane"/Sugar Plant, "Philadelphia"

| Various Artists | *Rusted Moon:* |
| Vitamin Records | *String Quartet Tribute to Neil Young* |
| Released 2002 | |

"Rockin' in the Free World"/"After the Gold Rush"/"Harvest Moon"/"Ohio"/"Lotta Love"/"Heart of Gold"/"Southern Man"/"Harvest"/"Down by the River"/"N.Y.T."

| Various Artists | *Headed for the Ditch:* |
| Lower Peninsula Records | *A Michigan Tribute to Neil Young* |
| Released 2006 | |

Dave Lawson, "Lookin' for a Love"/Gerudo, "When You Dance I Can Really Love"/Saturday Looks Good to Me, "See the Sky About to Rain"/The Casionauts, "Southern Man"/Ian Saylor, "Soldier"/New Granada, "Barstool Blues"/Will Yates, "Tell Me Why"/The Drinking Problem, "Saddle Up the Palomino"/Edward, "Birds"/The Rick Johnson Rock and Roll Machine, "We R in Control"/The Hard Lessons, "Hey Hey, My My"

VARIOUS ARTISTS
Universal
Released 2007

*Borrowed Tunes II:*
*A Tribute to Neil Young*

54-40, "Borrowed Tune"/Jets Overhead, "Mr. Soul"/Dala, "Ohio"/Barenaked Ladies, "Wonderin'"/City and Colour, "Cowgirl in the Sand"/Harpoondodger & Pat Robitaille, "Sugar Mountain"/Great Lake Swimmers, "Don't Cry No Tears"/Danny Michel, "After the Gold Rush"/Finger Eleven, "Walk On"/Andre, "Alabama"/Tom Cochrane, "Old Man"/Tom Wilson, "Expecting to Fly"/Chantal Kreviazuk, "A Man Needs a Maid"/Alana Levandoski, "Don't Be Denied"/Ron Sexsmith, "Philadelphia"/Dave Gunning, "A Dream That Can Last"/Melissa McClelland, "Cinnamon Girl"/Liam Titcomb, "Bandit"/Kyle Riabko, "Helpless"/Neverending White Lights, "Change Your Mind"/Raine Maida, "Don't Let It Bring You Down"/Jeremy Fisher, "Harvest"/The Trews, "Come On Baby Let's Go Downtown"/Jorane, "Needle and the Damage Done"/Grimskunk, "Rockin' in the Free World"/Matt Mays, "Sample and Hold"/Astrid Young, "Sleeps with Angels"/Attack in Black, "A Man Needs a Maid"/Blackie & the Rodeo Kings, "Unknown Legend"/Adrienne Pierce, "Pocahontas"/Joel Kroeker, "When God Made Me"/The Saint Alvia Cartel, "Thrasher"/Justin Nozuka, "Bad Fog of Loneliness"/Cuff the Duke, "Words (Between the Lines of Age)"/Tara MacLean, "Natural Beauty"/George Canyon, "Harvest Moon"/Chris Seldon, "Long May You Run"

VARIOUS ARTISTS
Uncut Magazine
Released 2007

*Like a Hurricane*

Sonic Youth, "Computer Age"/Patty Hurst Shifter, "Mr. Soul"/Paul Weller, "Birds"/The Waco Brothers, "Revolution Blues"/Carrie Rodriguez with Tim Easton, "Cortez the Killer"/Dream Syndicate, "Cinnamon Girl"/The Walkabouts, "On the Beach"/Matthew Sweet & Susanna Hoffs, "Everybody Knows This Is Nowhere"/The Wailin' Jennys, "Old Man"/The Flaming Lips, "After the Gold Rush"/k.d. Lang, "Helpless"/The Be Good Tanyas, "For the Turnstiles"/The Alarm, "Rockin' in the Free World"/Cowboy Junkies, "Tired Eyes"/Low and Dirty Three, "Down by the River"/Jay Farrar, "Like a Hurricane"

NILS LOFGREN
Hypertension UK/Zoom 2008

*The Loner: Nils Sings Neil*

"Birds"/"Long May You Run"/"Flying on the Ground"/"I Am a Child"/"Only Love Can Break Your Heart"/"Harvest Moon"/"Like a Hurricane"/"The Loner"/"Don't Be Denied"/"World on a String"/"Mr. Soul"/"Winterlong"/"On the Way Home"/"Wonderin'"/"Don't Cry No Tears"

VARIOUS ARTISTS
American Laundromat
Released 2008

*Cinnamon Girl: Women Artists*
*Cover Neil Young for Charity*

Tanya Donelly, "Heart of Gold"/Britta Phillips, "I Am a Child"/Kate York, "Comes a Time"/Lori McKenna, "Needle and the Damage Done"/Jill Sobule, "Down by the River"/Veruca Salt, "Burned"/Josie Cotton, "Cowgirl in the Sand"/Dalia, "A Man Needs a Maid"/Darcie Miner, "Ohio"/Carmen Townsend, "Everybody Knows This Is Nowhere"/Euro-Trash Girl, "Cinnamon Girl"/Julie Peel, "I Believe in You"/Luff, "Tell Me Why"/Dalia, "Ohio"/Elk City, "Helpless"/Amilia K. Spicer, "Only Love Can Break Your Heart"/Louise Post, "Sugar Mountain"/The Watson Twins, "Powderfinger"/Kristin Hersh, "Like a Hurricane"/Cindy Wheeler, "Old Man"/Heidi Gluck, "Walk On"

# Selected Filmography

## As Director (Bernard Shakey)
*Journey through the Past*, 1972 (Released as part of *Neil Young Archives Vol. 1 (1963-1972)*, Reprise, 2009)
*Rust Never Sleeps*, 1979 (Warner Reprise Video, 1993)
*Human Highway*, 1982 (Warner Reprise Video, 1993)
*Muddy Track*, 1987 (unreleased)
*Greendale*, 2003 (Sanctuary, 2004)
*CSNY/Déjà Vu*, 2008 (Lions Gate, 2008)

## As Actor
*Human Highway*, 1982 ("Lionel Switch")
*Made in Heaven*, 1987 ("Truck Driver")
*'68*, 1988 ("Westy")
*Love at Large*, 1990 ("Rick")
*Greendale*, 2003 (as Bernard Shakey: "Wayne Newton")

## Composer
*Dead Man*, 1995 (Score)
*Philadelphia*, 1993 ("Philadelphia")
*Where the Buffalo Roam*, 1980 ("Buffalo Stomp," "Ode to Wild Bill #1," "Ode to Wild Bill #2," "Home, Home on the Range," "Ode to Wild Bill #3," "Ode to Wild Bill #4," "Buffalo Stomp Refrain")

## Concert Films / Videos
*Rust Never Sleeps*, 1979 (Warner Reprise Video, 1993)
INTRODUCTION/"STAR SPANGLED BANNER"/"A DAY IN THE LIFE" (UNDERSCORE)/"SUGAR MOUNTAIN"/"I AM A CHILD"/"COMES A TIME"/"AFTER THE GOLD RUSH"/"THRASHER"/"MY MY, HEY HEY (OUT OF THE BLUE"/"STAGE ANNOUNCEMENTS"/"WHEN YOU DANCE I CAN REALLY LOVE"/"THE LONER"/"WELFARE MOTHERS"/"THE NEEDLE AND THE DAMAGE DONE"/"LOTTA LOVE"/"SEDAN DELIVERY"/ "POWDERFINGER"/"CORTEZ THE KILLER"/"CINNAMON GIRL"/"LIKE A HURRICANE"/"HEY HEY, MY MY (INTO THE BLACK)"/"END CREDITS: "SCHOOL DAYS" (UNDERSCORE)/"TONIGHT'S THE NIGHT"

*Neil Young in Berlin*, 1982 (Warner Reprise Video, 1991)
"CINNAMON GIRL"/"COMPUTER AGE"/"A LITTLE THING CALLED LOVE"/ "OLD MAN"/"THE NEEDLE AND THE DAMAGE DONE"/"AFTER THE GOLD RUSH"/"TRANSFORMER MAN"/"SAMPLE AND HOLD"/"HEY HEY, MY MY"/"LIKE A HURRICANE"/"BERLIN"

*SoloTrans* (Shakey Pictures, 1984)
"HEART OF GOLD"/"OLD MAN"/"HELPLESS"/"OHIO"/"DON'T BE DENIED"/"I GOT A PROBLEM"/"MR. SOUL"/"PAYOLA BLUES"/"GET GONE"/"DON'T TAKE YOUR LOVE AWAY FROM ME"/"DO YOU WANNA DANCE?"

*Freedom*, 1989 (Warner Reprise Video, 1991)
"CRIME IN THE CITY"/"THIS NOTE'S FOR YOU"/"NO MORE/"TOO FAR GONE"/"AFTER THE GOLD RUSH"/"OHIO"/"ROCKIN' IN THE FREE WORLD"

*Ragged Glory*, 1990 (Warner Reprise Video, 1991)
"F*!#IN' UP"/"FARMER JOHN"/"OVER AND OVER"/"MANSION ON THE HILL"

*Weld*, 1990 (Warner Reprise Video, 1991)
"STAR SPANGLED BANNER" (JIMI HENDRIX)/"HEY HEY, MY MY"/"CRIME IN THE CITY"/"BLOWIN' IN THE WIND"/"LOVE TO BURN"/"CINNAMON GIRL"/"MANSION ON THE HILL"/"F*!#IN' UP"/"CORTEZ THE KILLER"/ "POWDERFINGER"/"LOVE AND ONLY LOVE"/"ROCKIN' IN THE FREE WORLD"/"WELFARE MOTHERS"/"TONIGHT'S THE NIGHT"/"ROLL ANOTHER NUMBER"

*MTV Unplugged*, 1993 (Warner Reprise Video 1993)
"THE OLD LAUGHING LADY"/"MR. SOUL"/"WORLD ON A STRING"/ "POCAHONTAS"/"STRINGMAN"/"LIKE A HURRICANE"/"THE NEEDLE AND THE DAMAGE DONE"/"HELPLESS"/"HARVEST MOON"/"TRANSFORMER MAN"/"UNKNOWN LEGEND"/"LOOK OUT FOR MY LOVE"/"LONG MAY YOU RUN"/"FROM HANK TO HENDRIX"

*Sleeps with Angels*, 1994 (unreleased)
"MY HEART"/"PRIME OF LIFE"/"SLEEPS WITH ANGELS"/"TRANS AM"/ "SAFEWAY CART"/"PIECE OF CRAP"

*The Complex Sessions*, 1994 (Warner Reprise Video, 1995)
"MY HEART"/"PRIME OF LIFE"/"CHANGE YOUR MIND"/"PIECE OF CRAP"

*Year of the Horse*, 1997 (USA Home Entertainment, 1999)
"F*!#IN' UP"/"SLIP AWAY"/"BARSTOOL BLUES"/"STUPID GIRL"/"BIG TIME"/"TONIGHT'S THE NIGHT"/"SEDAN DELIVERY"/"LIKE A HURRICANE"/"MUSIC ARCADE"

*Silver & Gold*, 2000 (Warner Reprise Video, 2000)
INTRO/"LOOKING FORWARD"/"OUT OF CONTROL"/"BUFFALO
SPRINGFIELD AGAIN"/"PHILADELPHIA"/"DADDY WENT
WALKIN'"/"DISTANT CAMERA"/"RED SUN"/"LONG MAY YOU
RUN"/"HARVEST MOON"/"THE GREAT DIVIDE"/"SLOWPOKE"/"GOOD TO
SEE YOU"/"SILVER & GOLD"

*Red Rocks Live: Neil Young Friends and Relatives*, 2000
(Warner Reprise Video, 2000)
INTRO/"MOTORCYCLE MAMA"/"POWDERFINGER"/"EVERYBODY KNOWS
THIS IS NOWHERE"/"I BELIEVE IN YOU"/"UNKNOWN LEGEND"/"FOOL
FOR YOUR LOVE"/"BUFFALO SPRINGFIELD AGAIN"/"RAZOR
LOVE"/"DADDY WENT WALKIN'"/"PEACE OF MIND"/"WALK
ON"/"WINTERLONG"/"BAD FOG OF LONELINESS"/"WORDS"/"HARVEST
MOON"/"WORLD ON A STRING"/"TONIGHT'S THE NIGHT"/"COWGIRL IN
THE SAND"/CREDITS/"MELLOW MY MIND"

*Neil Young: Heart of Gold*, 2006 (Paramount, 2006)
"THE PAINTER"/"NO WONDER"/"FALLING OFF THE FACE OF THE
EARTH"/"FAR FROM HOME"/"IT'S A DREAM"/"PRAIRIE WIND"/"HERE
FOR YOU"/"THIS OLD GUITAR"/"WHEN GOD MADE ME"/"I AM A
CHILD"/"HARVEST MOON"/"HEART OF GOLD"/"OLD MAN"/"NEEDLE
AND THE DAMAGE DONE"/"OLD KING"/"COMES A TIME"/"FOUR STRONG
WINDS"/"ONE OF THESE DAYS"/"THE OLD LAUGHING LADY"

*Neil Young Trunk Show*, 2009 (Clinica Estetico)
"HARVEST"/"THE SULTAN"/"SPIRIT ROAD"/"MELLOW MY MIND"/
"CINNAMON GIRL"/"SAD MOVIES"/"HARVEST"/"CINNAMON GIRL"/
"OH LONESOME ME"/"KANSAS"/"SPIRIT ROAD"/"NO HIDDEN
PATH"/"AMBULANCE BLUES"/"MELLOW MY MIND"/"THE BELIEVER"/
"LIKE A HURRICANE"/"COWGIRL IN THE SAND"/"THE SULTAN"

# Guest Appearances
*The Johnny Cash Show,* 1971 (Sony Columbia Legacy, 2009)
"THE NEEDLE AND THE DAMAGE DONE"

*The Last Waltz,* 1978 (MGM, 1991)
"HELPLESS"

*Bob Dylan: The 30th Anniversary Birthday Celebration*
(Sony, 1993)
"JUST LIKE TOM THUMB'S BLUES," "ALL ALONG THE WATCHTOWER"

# Sidemen

Everybody's Rockin': A guide to Neil Young's primary sidemen

**John Barbata**
DRUMS
With Neil: Stray Gators; CSNY
  Others: The Turtles, Jefferson Airplane/Starship, Eric Clapton, Leon Russell, Dave Mason

**Jeff Blackburn**
BASS
With Neil: The Ducks

**Tom Bray**
TRUMPET
With Neil: The Bluenotes, Ten Men Working, *This Note's for You*, *Are You Passionate?*, *Living with War*, *Chrome Dreams II*, *Déjà Vu Live* (CSNY)
  Others: Blondie Chaplin, Brian Sacaw

**Oscar Butterworth**
DRUMS
With Neil: *Silver & Gold*
Others: Jewel, Steve Forbert, Jon Lord, Ben Keith

**Kenny Buttrey**
DRUMS, PERCUSSION
With Neil: *Harvest*, Stray Gators, *Tonight's the Night*, *Freedom*, *Harvest Moon*
  Others: Elvis Presley, Bobby Bare, Bob Dylan, Peter, Paul & Mary, Joan Baez, Al Kooper, Eric Andersen, Jerry Jeff Walker, Linda Ronstadt, Dan Fogelberg, Kris Kristofferson, Waylon Jennings, Buffy Sainte-Marie, J. J. Cale, Loudon Wainwright III, Ian Matthews, Gordon Lightfoot, Brewer & Shipley, the Pousette-Dart Band, Jimmy Buffett, the Oak Ridge Boys, Jesse Winchester, Leo Kottke, Chuck Berry, Levon Helm, Roy Orbison, Jerry Lee Lewis, Delbert McClinton, Willie Nelson, Flatt & Scruggs, the Monkees, John Hammond Jr., Donovan, Hank Snow, Sleepy LaBeef, George Jones

**Larry Byrom**
BACKING VOCALS, GUITAR
With Neil: *Everybody's Rockin'*, the Shocking Pinks, the Redwood Boys, *Old Ways*
  Others: The Precious Few, the Hard Times, T.I.M.E., Steppenwolf, Ratchell, Barbara Mandrell, Eddie Rabbit, Reba McEntire, Dolly Parton, Kenny Rogers, Brooks & Dunn, Clint Black, Randy Travis, Tanya Tucker, Lorrie Morgan

**Claude Cailliet**
TROMBONE
With Neil: *This Note's for You*, the Bluenotes, Ten Men Working, *Freedom*, *Chrome Dreams II*
  Others: Bongo-Logic, Seth Marsh, Tom Theabo

**Larry Cragg**
BARITONE SAXOPHONE, BACKING VOCALS, GUITAR, GUITAR TECH
With Neil: *This Note's for You*, the Bluenotes, Ten Men Working, *Freedom*, *Harvest Moon*, *Chrome Dreams II*
  Others: Nils Lofgren, CSNY, Ben Keith & Friends, Dreamachine

**Joe Craviotta**
DRUMS
With Neil: The Ducks

**Anthony Crawford**
BACKING VOCALS, GUITAR, BASS, MANDOLIN, PERCUSSION
With Neil: *Everybody's Rockin'*, *Trans*, International Harvesters, the Shocking Pinks, the Redwood Boys, *Old Ways*, *Are You Passionate?*, *Prairie Wind*, *Fork in the Road*
  Others: Steve Winwood, Vince Gill, Rosanne Cash, Steve Forbert, Eddie Rabbitt, Patty Loveless, Kelly Willis, Pete Anderson, Billy Montana, Danny Tate, Joy Lynn White, Dwight Yoakam, Kate Campbell, Crystal Gayle, Burrito Deluxe, the Bar-Kays, Howard Hewett, Pegi Young, solo albums

**Chad Cromwell**
DRUMS
With Neil: CSNY, *This Note's for You*, the Bluenotes, Ten Men Working, the Lost Dogs, the Restless, *Freedom*, *Are You Passionate?*, *Prairie Wind*, *Living with War*, *Chrome Dreams II*, *Fork in the Road*
  Others: Joe Walsh, John Trudell, Danny Tate, Joan Baez, Ashley Cleveland, Amy Grant, Kim Richey, John Berry, LeAnn Rimes, Mark Knopfler, Michael Bolton, Victoria Shaw, Matraca Berg, Allison Moorer, Chris Knight, Donny Osmond, Randy Scruggs, Gary Allan, Earl Thomas Conley, Jim Lauderdale, Mac McAnally, Jeff Foxworthy, John Michael Montgomery, Kenny Chesney, Lee Ann Womack, Peter Frampton, Bill Engvall, the Sky Kings, Blake Shelton, Rodney Crowell, Jeffrey Steele, John Anderson, Pam Tillis, Jack Ingram, Abra Moore, Willie Nelson, Rick Trevino, Jessica Simpson, T. Graham Brown, Mary Chapin Carpenter, Brooks & Dunn, Keb' Mo', Sugarland, Marty Stuart, Trent Tomlinson, Mitch Ryder, Phil Vassar, Jeffrey Steele, Jeff Bates, Frankie Miller, Raul Malo, Toby Keith, Vince Gill, Trisha Yearwood, Lady Antebellum

## Tim Drummond
BASS

With Neil: *Harvest*, Stray Gators, *On the Beach*, *Zuma*, *American Stars 'n Bars*, *Comes a Time*, *Hawks & Doves*, the Harvesters, the Shocking Pinks, *Everybody's Rockin'*, *Old Ways*, *Harvest Moon*

   Others: Lonnie Mack, James Brown, Rusty Kershaw, Charlie Daniels, J. J. Cale, Ronnie Hawkins, Willis Alan Ramsey, Bob Dylan, Lee Clayton, Graham Nash, Crosby & Nash, Paul Butterfield, CSN, Rick Danko, Hoyt Axton, Michelle Phillips, Ry Cooder, John Mayall, Dave Davies, Bob Dylan, Bette Midler, Don Henley, Joe Henry, Bobby Byrd, Tracy Nelson, Neil Diamond, Jewel, Joe Simon, Captain Beefheart & the Magic Band, Steve Forbert, Stevie Ray Vaughan, A. J. Croce, Was (Not Was)

## Donald "Duck" Dunn
BASS

With Neil: 1992 tour, *Silver & Gold*, *Are You Passionate?*

   Others: Booker T. & the MGs, Otis Redding, Wilson Pickett, the Mar-Keys, Albert King, Eddie Floyd, Isaac Hayes, William Bell, the Staple Singers, Mitch Ryder, Freddie King, Bill Withers, Herbie Mann, Rita Coolidge, Doug Clifford, Elvis Presley, Duane Allman, Muddy Waters, Sam & Dave, Rod Stewart, John Prine, Leon Russell, the Manhattan Transfer, Levon Helm, Roy Buchanan, the Blues Brothers, Rance Allen Group, the Emotions, Billy Swan, Tom Petty & the Heartbreakers, Leo Sayer, Peter Frampton, Stevie Nicks, Bob Dylan, Eric Clapton, Jimmy Buffett, Rufus Thomas, Carla Thomas, Don Covay, Muddy Waters, Willie Dixon, Tony Joe White, John Fogerty, Tinsley Ellis, Ray Charles, Yvonne Elliman, Boz Scaggs, Joan Baez, Jerry Lee Lewis, Natalie Merchant

## Bela Fleck
BANJO

With Neil: *Old Ways*

   Others: Bela Fleck & the Flecktones, Tony Trischka, Ricky Skaggs, David Grisman, Tony Rice, New Grass Revival, the Statler Brothers, Sam Bush, Nanci Griffith, Doc Watson, Jerry Douglas, Kathy Mattea, John Stewart, Jesse Winchester, Leon Redbone, Randy Travis, Mark O'Connor, Maura O'Connell, Jann Browne, Rhonda Vincent, the Chieftains, Danny Tate, Shawn Colvin, Col. Bruce Hampton & the Aquarium Rescue Unit, Trish Hinojosa, Phish, Marty Stuart, Roy Rogers, Travis Tritt, Ginger Baker, Bruce Hornsby, Rodney Crowell, Paul Brady, Asleep at the Wheel, Steve Wariner, Garth Brooks, Victor Wooten, Dave Matthews Band, Del McCoury, Leftover Salmon, Eddie from Ohio, Chris Thile, Jorma Kaukonen, Dar Williams, Natalie MacMaster, Gov't Mule, Nelly Furtado, Mike Gordon, Bernie Williams, Jimmy Sturr, Chick Corea, Tim O'Brien, Rory Gallagher, Edgar Meyer, Mike Stern, Keller Williams, Alison Krauss, Lyle Lovett, John Oates, Doc Watson, McCoy Tyner, J. D. Souther, Little Feat, Charlie Haden Family & Friends, Jeff Coffin, Donna the Buffalo, Assembly of Dust

## John Fumo
TRUMPET

With Neil: CSNY, *This Note's for You*, the Bluenotes, Ten Men Working, *Freedom*, *Chrome Dreams II*

   Others: Bongo-Logic, Monna Bell, Vinny Folia Large Ensemble, Tierra, the Brian Setzer Orchestra, Micky Dolenz, Bob Mamet, Malo, Steuart Liebig, Chaka Khan, John Tesh, G. E. Stinson, k.d. lang, Dianne Reeves, Faith Hill, Caravana Cubana, Dana Glover, Time Lapse Consortium, Deborah Gibson, Lucero, Kashif, Lydia Lunch, Ray Anthony, Cirque du Soleil, Steve Tyrell, Meat Loaf, solo albums

## George Grantham
DRUMS

With Neil: *Neil Young*

   Others: Poco, Richie Furay, Ricky Skaggs, Sylvia, Steve Wariner, Gaither Vocal Band, Ronnie McDowell

## Levon Helm
DRUMS

With Neil: *Hawks & Doves*

   Others: Ronnie Hawkins & the Hawks, Bob Dylan, The Band, John Hammond, Todd Rundgren, Jesse Winchester, John Martyn, Martin Mull, Jackie Lomax, Ringo Starr, the Cate Brothers, Kinky Friedman, Paul Butterfield, Carlene Carter, Los Lobos, Roger Waters, Michelle Shocked, Nils Lofgren, John Sebastian, Bonnie Raitt, Joe Walsh, Martina McBride, Carl Perkins, John Anderson, Emmylou Harris, Mercury Rev, Largo, Charlie Musselwhite, Guy Davis, Crowmatix, Ronnie Earl, the Dixie Hummingbirds, Artie Tatum, Rufus Wainright, the Nitty Gritty Dirt Band, Norah Jones, Ollabelle, Keith Emerson, Frank Black, Crosby & Nash, the Holmes Brothers, Ida, Colin Linden, Graham Nash, Jorma Kaukonen, solo albums

## Karl Himmel
DRUMS

With Neil: *American Stars 'n Bars*, *Comes a Time*, *Hawks & Doves*, *Trans*, *Everybody's Rockin'*, the Shocking Pinks, *Old Ways*, *Prairie Wind*

   Others: Rusty Kershaw, Charlie Daniels, Jimmy Buffett, Mother Earth, Bob Dylan, J. J. Cale, Earl Scruggs, Joe Tex, Leon Russell, the Doobie Brothers, Billy Joe Shaver, Dave Davies, Lefty Frizzell, Roy Buchanan, Sleepy LaBeef, Doc & Merle Watson, Bobby Charles, George Jones, James Talley, Pegi Young, Doug Kershaw

## Booker T. Jones
KEYBOARDS
With Neil: 1992 tour, *Are You Passionate?*
   Others: Booker T. & the MGs, Otis Redding, Albert King, Carla Thomas, William Bell, Wilson Pickett, Eddie Floyd, Johnnie Taylor, Mitch Ryder, Delaney & Bonnie, Stephen Stills, Bill Withers, Rita Coolidge, Bob Dylan, Bob Neuwirth, Richie Havens, the Manhattan Transfer, *A Star Is Born* (1976), Levon Helm, Willie Nelson, Earl Klugh, Rodney Crowell, Rosanne Cash, Carlos Santana, David Lindley & El Rayo-X, Bruce Willis, Soul Asylum, John Lee Hooker, Natalie Cole, Bruce Cockburn, Five Blind Boys of Alabama, Don Covay, Boz Scaggs, Jody Watley, Trish Hinojosa, Natalie Merchant, Was (Not Was), Rancid, solo albums

## Steve Jordan
DRUMS, KEYBOARDS, PRODUCTION
With Neil: *Landing on Water*
   Others: Sonny Rollins, David Sanborn, the Brecker Brothers, Don Cherry, Cissy Houston, Taj Mahal, Cat Stevens, the Blues Brothers, Ashford & Simpson, John Mayall, Herbie Mann, John Scofield, Steely Dan, Donald Fagen, Spyro Gyra, Bonnie Tyler, George Benson, Mark Knopfler, Stevie Nicks, the Rolling Stones, Toto, the Pretenders, Brian Setzer, Mike Stern, Chuck Berry, Bob Dylan, Ivan Neville, Sam Phillips, Keith Richards, Don Henley, Soul Asylum, the Neville Brothers, Southside Johnny & the Asbury Jukes, Bernie Worrell, James Taylor, the Fabulous Thunderbirds, Garland Jeffries, Johnnie Johnson, The Band, Billy Joel, John Sebastian, Patti Austin, Booker T. & the MGs, Roberta Flack, Debbie Gibson, B. B. King, Bee Gees, Robben Ford, Cracker, Stacy Lattisaw, Little Steven, Amanda Marshall, Keb' Mo', Sheryl Crow, Joey Ramone, Jon Spencer Blues Explosion, Cyndi Lauper, Alicia Keys, Ziggy Marley, John Mayer, Lyle Lovett, Patti Scialfa, Daryl Hall & John Oates, Buddy Guy, Bruce Springsteen, Herbie Hancock, the Pretenders, Robert Cray

## Ben Keith
PEDAL STEEL, GUITAR, DOBRO, SAXOPHONE
With Neil: *Harvest*, the Stray Gators, *Time Fade Away*, *On the Beach*, *American Stars 'n Bars*, *Comes a Time*, *Hawks & Doves*, *This Note's for You*, the Bluenotes, Ten Men Working, Grey Riders, the International Harvesters/the Harvesters, the Lost Dogs, the Santa Monica Flyers, *Everybody's Rockin'*, the Shocking Pinks, Transband, *Trans*, *Old Ways*, *Freedom*, *Harvest Moon*, *Unplugged*, *Road Rock V1: Friends and Relatives*, CSNY, *Silver & Gold*, *Are You Passionate?*, *Prairie Wind*, *Chrome Dreams II*, *Fork in the Road*
   Others: Patsy Cline, Ringo Starr, Mother Earth, Charlie Daniels, Chris Smither, Todd Rundgren, Steve Goodman, Ian & Silvia, The Band, Terry Reid, Graham Nash, Bob Neuwirth, Michael d'Abo, Blue, Anne Murray, Emmylou Harris, Crosby & Nash, Eric Andersen, Billy Joe Shaver, Lonnie Mack, Leon and Mary Russell, Bobby Bare, Warren Zevon, Willie Nelson, Bob Dylan, Jimmy Webb, Ian Tyson, Pat McLaughlin, Linda Ronstadt, Jewel, Tracy Nelson, the Crickets, Bobby Charles, Steve Forbert, International Submarine Band, Bobby Charles, Crosby & Nash, Pegi Young, *Seven Gates: A Christmas Album/Christmas at the Ranch*

## Danny Kortchmar
GUITAR, KEYBOARDS, PRODUCTION
With Neil: *Landing on Water*
   Others: Carole King, James Taylor, the Monkees, the Fugs, Jackie DeShannon, Crosby & Nash, the Section, Donovan, Flo & Eddie, Bill Wyman, Nilsson, Linda Ronstadt, Neil Sedaka, Ringo Starr, David Cassidy, J. D. Souther, Sam & Dave, Jennifer Warnes, Jackson Browne, Pointer Sisters, Warren Zevon, Yvonne Elliman, Stephen Stills, Bonnie Raitt, David Sanborn, Karla Bonoff, Cheech & Chong, Graham Nash, Bob Dylan, Bob Seger, Don Henley, Dwight Twilley, CSN, Bette Midler, Stevie Nicks, Dolly Parton, Tracy Chapman, David Crosby, Jon Bon Jovi, Daryl Hall & John Oates, Timothy B. Schmit, Spinal Tap, John Waite, Joe Cocker, the Fabulous Thunderbirds, Spin Doctors, Billy Joel, Eric Carmen, Martin Sexton, Dada, Evan and Jaron, Kim Carnes, Rod Stewart, Hanson, Buddy Guy, Etta James, Marc Cohn, Mick Jagger, Solomon Burke

## Joe Lala
PERCUSSION
With Neil: Stills-Young Band, *Trans*, Transband
   Others: The Blues Image, Pacific Gas & Electric, Stephen Stills, Manassas, Poco, Joe Walsh, Rick Derringer, Bill Wyman, Gene Clark, Souther-Hillman-Furay Band, Dan Fogelberg, Neil Diamond, Bee Gees, Firefall, the Outlaws, Rod Stewart, Rick Danko, Andy Gibb, the Allman Brothers Band, McGuinn Clark & Hillman, Pousette-Dart Band, Graham Nash, Barbra Streisand, Jackson Browne, CSN, Dionne Warwick, Grace Slick, Ringo Starr, Dave Mason, the Hollies, Kenny Rogers, Don Felder, Bill Wyman, Spirit, Whitney Houston, David Crosby, CSN, Harry Chapin, Chicago, Latimore

## Steve Lawrence
TENOR SAXOPHONE
With Neil: *American Dream* (CSNY), *This Note's for You*, the Bluenotes, Ten Men Working, *Freedom*
   Others: Evergreen Blues Band, Buddy Miles, Blondie Chaplin, Crazy Horse, Joe Walsh, Hugh Cornwell

## Nils Lofgren
GUITAR, KEYBOARDS, VOCALS
With Neil: *After the Gold Rush*, *Tonight's the Night*, Crazy Horse, Transband, *Trans*, Santa Monica Flyers, *Unplugged*
   Others: Grin, Crazy Horse, Stephen Stills, Kathi McDonald, Tim Curry, Rod Stewart, John Eddie, Bruce Springsteen & the E Street Band, Ringo Starr & His All-Star Band, Lou Gramm, Steve Forbert, Patti Scialfa, Buckshot LeFonque, Red Henry, Carl Perkins, the Kennedys, Tommy Lepson & the Lazy Boys, Danny Federici, Lincoln, Bob McGrath, George Benson, Martin Sexton, Willie Nelson, solo albums

## Jim Messina
BASS, GUITAR, VOCALS
With Neil: *Neil Young*
  Others: Buffalo Springfield, Poco, Jim Messina & the Jesters, Brewer & Shipley, Loggins & Messina, Casey Kelly, Hoyt Axton, Richie Furay, Earl Scruggs, Brooks & Dunn, solo albums

## Bob Mosley
BASS, GUITAR, VOCALS
With Neil: The Ducks
  Others: Moby Grape, solo albums

## Dewey Lyndon "Spooner" Oldham
KEYBOARDS
ROCK AND ROLL HALL OF FAME INDUCTEE (2009, SIDEMAN)
With Neil: *Comes a Time, Old Ways*, the Harvesters, the International Harvesters, *Unplugged, Looking Forward* (CSNY), *Road Rock V1: Friends and Relatives, Silver & Gold, Prairie Wind, Déjà Vu Live* (CSNY)
  Others: Wilson Pickett, Aretha Franklin, Etta James, Henry Gross, King Curtis, Rita Coolidge, Solomon Burke, Arthur Alexander, Duane Eddy, Duane Allman, Arlo Guthrie, Percy Sledge, Gene Clark, Everly Brothers, Linda Ronstadt, Bob Dylan, Jackson Browne, Dan Penn, Roger McGuinn, Maria Muldaur, Donnie Fritts, Bob Seger, John Hammond, Flying Burrito Brothers, Townes Van Zandt, J. J. Cale, John Prine, Green on Red, Chuck Prophet, Terry Evans, Candi Staton, James Carr, Nick Lowe & the Impossible Birds, Jewel, Jon Tiven's Ego Trip, Kate Campbell, Don Everly, Steve Forbert, Irma Thomas, Delaney Bramlett, Willy DeVille, Drive-By Truckers, Bobby Charles, Hacienda Brothers, Frank Black, Pegi Young, Bettye LaVette, Cat Power, Amos Lee

## Bruce Palmer
BASS, VOCALS
ROCK AND ROLL HALL OF FAME INDUCTEE (WITH BUFFALO SPRINGFIELD, 1997)
With Neil: *Trans*, Transband
  Others: Buffalo Springfield, Douglas Wain, solo album

## Rick Palombi
VOCALS
With Neil: *Trans, Everybody's Rockin'*, the Shocking Pinks/the Redwood Boys, *Old Ways*
  Others: Eddie Rabbitt, Laura Branigan, Julie Brown, Martika, Peter Allen, Asphalt Ballet, Karen Lehner

## Greg Reeves
BASS
With Neil: *After the Gold Rush, Déjà Vu* (CSNY)
  Others: John Sebastian, Crosby & Nash, Dave Mason, the Ruby Rakes, Tom Armstrong, James Hardway, LVX Collective, Nyee Moses

## Rick "the Bass Player" Rosas
BASS
With Neil: *This Note's for You*, the Bluenotes, Ten Men Working, the Lost Dogs, the Restless, *Freedom, Are You Passionate?, Prairie Wind, Living with War, Chrome Dreams II, Déjà Vu Live* (CSNY), *Fork in the Road*
  Others: Joe Walsh, Saison, Johnny Rivers, Terry Reid, Pegi Young, Savana

## James Taylor
VOCALS AND BANJO
ROCK AND ROLL HALL OF FAME INDUCTEE (2000)
With Neil: *Harvest, Harvest Moon*
  Others: Solo career, Carole King, Tom Rush, Joni Mitchell, Kate Taylor, Alex Taylor, Livingston Taylor, Carly Simon, David Sanborn, Linda Ronstadt, Crosby & Nash, Garland Jeffreys, Lucy Simon, John Hall, George Jones, Jimmy Buffett, *Sesame Street*, George Benson, Steve Winwood, Graham Nash, Ricky Skaggs, Milton Nascimento, Art Garfunkel, Tom Scott, Randy Newman, the Manhattan Transfer, Maura O'Connell, Mark O'Connor, CSN, AIDA, Sting, Yo-Yo Ma, Maceo Parker, Shawn Colvin, Kate Markowitz

## Rufus Thibodeaux
FIDDLE
With Neil: *Comes a Time, Hawks & Doves, Old Ways*, the Harvesters, the International Harvesters, the Grey Riders
  Others: Slim Harpo, Sleepy LaBeef, Lightnin' Slim, Jim Reeves, Porter Wagoner, Zachary Richard, Hank Williams Jr., Lazy Lester, Ben Keith and Friends, Nathan Abshire, Bobby Charles

## Joe Vitale
PERCUSSION
With Neil: *Long May You Run* (Stills-Young Band), *American Dream* (CSNY), *Looking Forward* (CSNY)
  Others: Joe Walsh, Michael Stanley, Rick Derringer, Bill Wyman, Jay Ferguson, Stephen Stills, CSN, the Outlaws, Dan Fogelberg, the Eagles, Peter Frampton, Graham Nash, Boz Scaggs, the Henry Paul Band, Mickey Thomas, John Entwistle, Al Kooper, Don Felder, Michael Brewer, David Crosby, Zakk Wylde/Black Label Society, Saison

# Resources

## Books

Doufrenchou, Carole. *Neil Young.* New York: Quick Fox, 1998.

Einarson, John. *Neil Young: Don't Be Denied.* Kingston, Ont.: Quarry Press, 1992.

Hoskyns, Barney. *Hotel California: The True-Life Adventures of Crosby, Stills, Nash, Young, Mitchell, Taylor, Browne, Ronstadt, Geffen, the Eagles, and Their Many Friends.* Hoboken, NJ: John Wiley & Sons, 2006.

McDonough, Jimmy. *Shakey: Neil Young's Biography.* New York: Random House, 2002.

Petridis, Alex. *Neil Young.* New York: Thunder's Mouth Press, 2000.

Robertson, John. *Neil Young: The Visual Documentary.* London: Omnibus Press, 1994.

Simmons, Sylvie. *Neil Young: Reflections in Broken Glass.* Edinburgh: Mojo Books, 2001.

Walker, Michael. *Laurel Canyon: The Inside Story of Rock and Roll's Legendary Neighborhood.* New York: Faber and Faber, 2006.

Williams, Paul. *Neil Young: Love to Burn: Thirty Years of Speaking Out, 1966–1996.* London: Omnibus Press, 1997.

Young, Scott. *Neil and Me.* Toronto: McLelland & Stewart, 1997.

## Magazines

*Billboard*
*Guitar World*
*Guitar World Acoustic*
*Mojo*
*Music Connection*
*Musician*
*Q*
*Rolling Stone*
*Stereophile*
*Total Guitar*
*Uncut*
*Wired*

## Films and Videos

*Neil Young: Heart of Gold.* Paramount Pictures, 2006
*Year of the Horse: Neil Young and Crazy Horse Live.* Seville, 1997

## Liner Notes

Buffalo Springfield, *Box Set* (Rhino, 2001)
Crosby, Stills & Nash, *Crosby, Stills & Nash* (Atlantic, 1991)
David Crosby, *Voyage* (Atlantic/Rhino, 2006)
Graham Nash, *Reflections* (Rhino, 2009)
Neil Young, *Archives Vol. 1* (Reprise, 2009)
Neil Young, *Decade* (Reprise, 1977)

## Newspapers and Wire Services

*Oakland (Mich.) Press*
Reuters
*Riverfront Times*
*St. Louis Post-Dispatch*
*Starbeat* (New York Times Syndication Sales)
United Press International
*Village Voice*

## Television

*Charlie Rose*
*American Masters: Neil Young—Don't Be Denied*

## Radio

*National Public Radio*
*Rockline*

## Websites

billboard.com
bridgeschool.org
cdnow.com
huffingtonpost.com
imdb.com
neilyoung.com
rollingstone.com
thrasherswheat.com
wallofsound.com

# Index

# About the Authors

Daniel Durchholz is co-editor of *MusicHound Rock: The Essential Album Guide* and a former editor at *Request* and *Replay* magazines and at STLtoday.com. His byline has appeared in the *St. Louis Post-Dispatch*, the *Chicago Tribune*, the *Washington Post*, *Rolling Stone*, *Billboard*, *Stereophile*, and many other publications. His weekly music segment can be heard on *The Carney Show* on KMOX-AM (St. Louis) and online at KMOX.com. He lives in Wildwood, Missouri.

Gary Graff is an award-winning music journalist based in Detroit. He is a regular contributor to the *New York Times* Features Syndicate, *Billboard*, UPI, the *Cleveland Plain Dealer*, *Revolver*, and other publications, as well as to radio stations in Detroit and Milwaukee. He is the editor of *The Ties That Bind: Bruce Springsteen A to E to Z* and the series editor of the MusicHound Essential Album Guides. He lives in Beverly Hills, Michigan.

U.S. and Canada Fall Tour, Madison Square Garden, New York, December 15, 2008. *Photo by Joe Kohen/WireImage for* New York Post*/Getty Images*